Landmarks in Rhetoric and Public Address

Three Arabic Treatises on Aristotle's *Rhetoric*

The Commentaries of

al-Fārābī, Avicenna, and Averroes

Translated, with introduction and notes, by
Lahcen Elyazghi Ezzaher

Southern Illinois University Press
Carbondale

Printed in the United States of America

18 17 16 15 4 3 2 1

Library of Congress Cataloging-in-Publication Data
Ezzaher, Lahcen E., [date] author.
Three Arabic Treatises on Aristotle's Rhetoric : the Commentaries of al-Fārābī, Avicenna, and Averroes / Translated, with introduction and notes, by Lahcen Elyazghi Ezzaher.
pages cm. — (Landmarks in rhetoric and public address)
Includes bibliographical references and index.
ISBN 978-0-8093-3413-1 (pbk. : alk. paper)
ISBN 0-8093-3413-5 (pbk. : alk. paper)
ISBN 978-0-8093-3414-8 (ebook)
ISBN 0-8093-3414-3 (ebook)
1. Aristotle. Rhetoric. 2. Rhetoric—Early works to 1800. 3. Farabi. Khatabah. 4. Avicenna, 980–1037. Kitab al-majmu. 5. Averroës, 1126–1198. Talkhis al-khatabah. I. Farabi. Khatabah. English. II. Avicenna, 980–1037. Kitab al-majmu. English. III. Averroës, 1126–1198. Talkhis al-khatabah. Selections. English. IV. Title.
PA3893.R4E99 2015
808.5—dc23 2014037568

The paper used in this publication meets the minimum requirements of American National Standard for Information Sciences—Permanence of Paper for Printed Library Materials, ANSI Z39.48-1992. ♾

Contents

Acknowledgments

The research toward this publication has been supported and facilitated by several academic institutions and individuals. First, I am grateful to the University of Northern Colorado for a generous sabbatical leave and for a substantial Provost Fund grant for faculty scholarship and professional development during the academic year of 2010–11. My thanks go to the editors of *Rhetorica* and *Advances in the History of Rhetoric* for granting me permission to reprint my Arabic-English translation of al-Fārābī's and Avicenna's commentaries on Aristotle's *Rhetoric*.

I am also deeply indebted to a number of colleagues for their help and support throughout the publication process of this work. First and foremost, I wish to thank Professor James J. Murphy for his insightful comments on the translations and annotations. Many of his suggestions led me to further reflect on problems concerning the interpretation of the Arabic texts or called my attention to publications or research questions and contexts that I had not been aware of before. I also thank Professor Rita Copeland, for her faith in this project and her valuable comments, and Professor Chouki El Hamel, who kindly shared with me his profound knowledge of Arabic language and Islamic intellectual history and alerted me to some very important questions and issues when I was revising the manuscript.

My gratitude extends as well to Karl Kageff, editor in chief at Southern Illinois University Press, for having encouraged me to publish this work in this series. Throughout the entire publication of this work, Karl showed an enormous amount of patience, support, and encouragement. I also want to thank Wayne Larsen, project editor, for his help with the final stages of publication of this book.

Many thanks go to Joyce Bond, copy editor, whose queries and suggestions for editing changes were very helpful.

It is my great pleasure to express my gratitude to these institutions and colleagues, without whose support I never would have been able to undertake this project.

Three Arabic Treatises on Aristotle's *Rhetoric*

Introduction

Standard histories of medieval rhetoric and philosophy inform us that the rediscovery of Aristotle's logical works in medieval Europe advanced the development of the scholastic method of learning and teaching, which lay at the heart of university curricula and spread scholastic habits of mind into the public sphere as well. These histories also tell us that Aristotelian logic, along with grammar and rhetoric, constituted what is known as the *trivium*, the three most important liberal arts used in scholasticism in various disciplines, especially philosophy and theology. And finally, we find that Jewish, Christian, and Muslim philosophers in medieval times took up the scholastic method as a tool to bring together faith and reason in their theological and philosophical investigation and argumentation.[1]

Scholars such as Dimitri Gutas, Richard Walzer, Deborah Black, and James Murphy, to name just a few, remind us of the fact that Arabic translations of Aristotle's logical works, directly from the Greek or through Syriac, and commentaries on them played an important part in the medieval revival of European interest in the rhetoric and logic of Aristotle. This in turn influenced the rise of universities and the shaping of Western intellectual life. Arabic translators ranged widely in their Aristotelian interests, including rhetoric as well as numerous other works. It is important, therefore, to understand the Arabic movement toward translating Aristotle's works in a systematic fashion. As Richard Walzer explains, "Islamic

1. For further discussion of this point, see Alex Novikoff, *The Medieval Culture of Disputation: Pedagogy, Practice, and Performance* (Philadelphia: University of Pennsylvania Press, 2013); James J. Murphy, *Medieval Rhetoric: A Select Bibliography* (Toronto: University of Toronto Press, 1989); and Jorge J. E. Gracia and Timothy B. Noone, eds., *A Companion to Philosophy in the Middle Ages* (Malden, MA: Blackwell, 2002).

philosophers, although continuing the Greek tradition, can rightly claim to be understood and appreciated in their own setting and according to their own intentions which may be different from those of their Greek predecessors."[2]

Our earliest records on the Arabic commentary tradition on the *Rhetoric* of Aristotle come from the tenth century. For example, in his bibliographical work *Kitāb al-Fihrist* (*Book of the Index*),[3] Arab bibliographer Abū al-Faraj ibn Isḥāq al-Nadīm (d. 995 or 998) gives a comprehensive index and description of books written in Arabic by Arab and non-Arab scholars. This index is arranged in ten treatises (*maqālāt*) on a wide variety of subjects. The first six treatises deal with books on subjects such as the scriptures of Muslims, Jews, and Christians, with emphasis on the Qur'an and Qur'anic sciences; grammar and philology; history, biography, and genealogy; poetry; scholastic theology (*ᶜilm al-kalām*); and law and tradition. The last four treatises deal with books on subjects such as philosophy and the ancient sciences; legends, fables, and magic; the doctrines of nonmonotheistic creeds; and alchemy.

On the subject of rhetoric, Ibn al-Nadīm gives the following information about the scholarship on Aristotle's *Rhetoric* available in Arabic in his time:

On *Rhetorica*[4]

> And it means "oratory." It is found in an old translation. It was said that Isḥāq [ibn Ḥunayn[5]] translated it into Arabic and that Ibrāhīm ibn ᶜAbd Allāh also did a translation [of the treatise]. Abū Naṣr al-Fārābī wrote a commentary on it. I saw this book in Aḥmad ibn al-Ṭayyib's handwriting. It is an old translation [of the *Rhetoric*] in about one hundred leaves.[6]

---

2. Richard Walzer, *Greek into Arabic: Essays on Islamic Philosophy* (Cambridge, MA: Harvard University Press, 1962), 1.
3. This work has been translated from Arabic into English and edited by Bayard Dodge. See Bayard Dodge, ed., *The Fihrist of al-Nadīm: A Tenth-Century Survey of Muslim Culture*, 2 vols. (New York: Columbia University Press, 1970). The Arabic version is available in an edition prepared by Riḍā Taġaddud and published by Dār al-Masīra in Beirut (1988).
4. Ibn al-Nadīm gives the transcription in Arabic of the term *rhetorica* (*riṭorīqā*), which, he explains, means *al-Khaṭābah*. This is the Arabic word for rhetoric in the sense of public speaking, which is normally rendered in English as *oratory*.
5. For consistency, I use the transcription Ḥunayn throughout this book except where it appears as Ḥunain in the sources I cite.
6. Ibn al-Nadīm, *Kitāb al-Fihrist*, ed. Riḍā Taġaddud (Beirut: Dār al-Masīra, 1988), 310 (my translation). My English translation of al-Nadīm's account on *Rhetorica* differs from the translation suggested by Dodge with respect to the mention of Aḥmad ibn al-Ṭayyib.

The past passive construction "It was said" (*qīla*), which Ibn al-Nadīm uses in this note, aims to convey the meaning of anonymity (*al-majhūl*) and also indicates that the information provided is based on word of mouth.[7] Elsewhere in *al-Fihrist*, in an entry on Alexander of Aphrodisias, Ibn al-Nadīm gives this information concerning the *Rhetoric*:

> Abū Zakariyyā' [Yaḥyā ibn ᶜAdī] said that he had asked Ibrāhīm ibn ᶜAbd Allāh to give him, for fifty dinars, a copy of the *Sophistics*, a copy of the *Rhetoric*, and a copy of the *Poetics*, which were translated by Isḥāq [ibn Ḥunayn], but he would not sell them. [Ibrāhīm ibn ᶜAbd Allāh] burned [the manuscripts] at the time of his death.[8]

In *Ikhbār al-ᶜUlamā' bi-Akhbār al-Ḥukamā'*, usually referred to as *Akhbār al-Ḥukamā'* (*History of Philosophers*),[9] historian of Islamic culture Jamāl al-Dīn al-Qifṭī (1172–1248) devotes an entry to Yaḥyā ibn ᶜAdī, one of the most important Christian Arabic thinkers of the tenth century (896–974). Here al-Qifṭī refers to Yaḥyā ibn ᶜAdī as "the logician" who was a student of Abū Bishr Mattā ibn Yūnus and Abū Naṣr al-Fārābī.[10] In this sense, Ibn al-Nadīm's note should help dispel, to a great degree, any sense of obscurity around the Arabic translation of the *Rhetoric*, and we can safely conclude that the treatise was rendered in Arabic by Isḥāq ibn Ḥunayn and also by Ibrāhīm ibn ᶜAbd Allāh. Modern Arabic scholar ᶜAbd al-Raḥmān Badawī (1917–2002) suggests that an earlier Arabic version of the *Rhetoric* could, in fact, have come down to us from a Syriac translation done by Ḥunayn ibn Isḥāq (809–73) or one of the translators working

---

I have relied on historian al-Qifṭī's reading of the account: "On *Rhetorica*. And it means oratory. It is found in an old translation. It was said that Isḥāq ibn Ḥunayn translated it into Arabic and that Ibrāhīm ibn ᶜAbd Allāh also translated it. Al-Fārābī, Abū Naṣr, wrote a commentary on it. This book was seen in the handwriting of Aḥmad ibn al-Ṭayyib al-Sarakhsī, in about one hundred leaves. It is an old translation." Jamāl al-Dīn Al-Qifṭī, *Ikhbār al-ᶜUlamā' bi-Akhbār al-Ḥukamā'* [History of philosophers], ed. August Müller and Julius Lippert (Leipzig, Germany: Theodor Weicher, 1903), 37–38.

7. For more information on the structure of the Arabic sentence, see Vicente Cantarino, *Syntax of Modern Arabic Prose* (Bloomington: Indiana University Press, 1975). Also see Vit Bubenik's essay "Thematization and Passivization in Arabic," *Lingua* 49 (1979): 295–313.

8. Ibn al-Nadīm, *al-Fihrist*, 313 (my translation).

9. Al-Qifṭī's *Ikhbār al-ᶜUlamā' bi-Akhbār al-Ḥukamā'* [History of philosophers] was edited by Muḥammad Amīn al-Khā'ijī in 1906. Al-Khā'ijī's edition was based on a 1903 edition prepared by August Müller and Julius Lippert, which bears the name Ibn al-Qifṭī and the title *Tā'rīkh al-Ḥukamā'* [History of philosophers].

10. See al-Qifṭī, *Tā'rīkh al-Ḥukamā'*, 361.

with him.[11] Uwe Vagelpohl, in his ground-breaking study, *Aristotle's Rhetoric in the East: The Syriac and Arabic Translation and Commentary Tradition*, quite rightly situates the translation of the *Rhetoric* in what he describes as "a wider process of cultural exchange that led to the adaptation and transformation of large parts of Greek learning to fit the unique religious, intellectual, political and social circumstances of Islamic culture."[12] Students of rhetoric will find the works of modern scholars such as Richard Walzer, Gerhard Endress, Dimitri Gutas, Richard Goulet, Maroun Aouad, Muhsin Mahdi, Nicholas Rescher, and Uwe Vagelpohl very useful sources of information, for they give broader and yet valuable accounts of the history of the Greek-Arabic translation movement.

In *al-Fihrist*, Ibn al-Nadīm tells an attractive story, though not necessarily founded on verifiable historical facts, about a possible beginning of the history of the Greek-Arabic translation. The story is about a dream the Abbasid caliph al-Ma'mūn, who reigned from 813 until his death in 833, once had, and I quote it at length because of its significance:

> Al-Ma'mūn dreamed of a man of a fair complexion, imbued with life, with a broad brow and joined eyebrows [. . .], a man of good qualities sitting by him on his bed. Al-Ma'mūn said: I felt awe in his presence and asked: "Who are you?" He said: "I am Aristotle." I was overjoyed to see him and said: "Oh, wise man, can I ask you a question?" He said: "Do." I asked: "What is beauty?" He replied: "What reason judges to be beautiful." I asked: "What else?" He said: "What the law judges to be beautiful." I asked: "What else?" He said: "What the general public judges to be beautiful." I asked: "What else?" He said: "There is nothing else."[13]

Al-Ma'mūn evidently was elated by Aristotle's visit, especially as the Greek philosopher brought with him a sophisticated system of logic, which would help the caliph prevent the collapse of a young Islamic state that was torn in those times by internal conflict among various theological schools, such as Ashᶜarism

11. For information about the life and works of Ḥunayn ibn Isḥāq, see Giuseppe Gabrieli's biographical essay, "Ḥunayn ibn Isḥāq," *Isis* 6 (1924): 282–92. Also see Max Meyerhof, "New Light on Ḥunain ibn Isḥaq and His Period." *Isis* 8, no. 4 (1926): 685–724. The Arabic sources on Ḥunayn ibn Isḥāq include Ibn al-Nadīm's *Kitāb al-Fihrist*; al-Qifṭī's *Ta'rīkh al-Ḥukamā'* [History of philosophers]; and Ibn Abī Uṣaibiᶜa's *ᶜUyūn al-Anbā' fī Ṭabaqāt al-Aṭibbā'*, ed. A. Müller, 5 vols. (Cairo and Konigsberg, Germany, 1882–84).

12. Uwe Vagelpohl, *Aristotle's Rhetoric in the East: The Syriac and Arabic Translation and Commentary Tradition* (Leiden, Netherlands: Brill, 2008), 10.

13. Ibn al-Nadīm, *Kitāb al-Fihrist*, 303–4 (my translation).

and Manichaeism.[14] Al-Ma'mūn is known in the history of Arabic culture as the founder of *Bayt al-Ḥikma* (House of Wisdom), for he was a zealous lover of Greek philosophical thought and Aristotelian logic. During his reign, the House of Wisdom was an important center for translation of ancient Greek scientific and philosophical works into Arabic. The age of al-Ma'mūn, known as an age of Islamic renaissance, spurred the rediscovery of Hellenic culture and guaranteed the survival and transmission of ancient Greek philosophy into medieval European centers of learning. For example, the development and organization of Aristotle's logical corpus, which was transmitted through Arabic-Latin translations to the West, included *Isagoge* (*al-isāghūjī*), *Categoriae* (*al-maqūlāt*), *De Interpretatione* (*al-ᶜibārah*), *Analytica Priora* (*al-qiyās*), *Analytica Posteriora* (*al-burhān*), *Topica* (*al-jadal*), *De Sophisticis Elenchis* (*al-mughālaṭah* or *al-safsaṭah*), *Rhetorica* (*al-khaṭābah*), and *Poetica* (*al-shiᶜr*).[15]

With respect to rhetoric, the ancient Arabic translation we have available is *Al-Khaṭābah: Al-Tarjama al-ᶜarabiyya al-Qadīma* (*Rhetoric: The Ancient Arabic Translation*), edited by ᶜAbd al-Raḥmān Badawī in 1959 and also made accessible in a later edition prepared in 1979.[16] An improved version of the Arabic text is available in Malcolm C. Lyons's *Aristotle's Ars Rhetorica: The Arabic Version*.[17] The Bibliothèque Nationale in Paris has a manuscript (ar. 2346) containing the unique extant Arabic translation of Aristotle's *Rhetoric*. In his 1948 work *Les Catégories d'Aristote dans leurs versions syro-arabes* (*Aristotle's "Categories" in Their Syro-Arabic Versions*), Khalil Georr dates the translation of the *Rhetoric* back to the beginning of the ninth century. This translation is available in a copy prepared by Abū ᶜAlī ibn al-Samḥ (d. 1027), who was a student of the Christian Aristotelian Yaḥyā ibn ᶜAdī.

Al-Fārābī marks a significant starting point in the history of the commentary tradition on Aristotle's *Rhetoric* in Arabic. After al-Fārābī, this tradition will be

14. The Ashᶜarītes were the followers of Imām Abū al-Ḥasan al-Ashᶜarī (d. 936). See Richard Frank, *Classical Islamic Theology: The Ashᶜarītes. Texts and Studies on the Development and History of Kalam*, vol. 3, ed. Dimitri Gutas, Variorum Collected Studies Series (Burlington, VT: Ashgate, 2008).

15. See Nicholas Rescher, *The Development of Arabic Logic* (Pittsburgh: University of Pittsburgh Press, 1964).

16. It is worth mentioning that the work of Badawī has vastly enriched our knowledge of Arabic sources, for Badawī studied with dedication and effectiveness important aspects of the reception of ancient Greek philosophy into Arabic.

17. Malcolm C. Lyons, *Aristotle's Ars Rhetorica: The Arabic Version. A New Edition, with Commentary and Glossary* (Cambridge, UK: Pembroke Arabic Texts, 1982).

taken up by two other major figures in the history of Arabic-Islamic thought, Avicenna (980–1037) and Averroes (1126–98). As Nicholas Rescher explains in his discussion of the transmission of Aristotle's logical works into Arabic, al-Fārābī, Avicenna, and Averroes constitute "links in a chain whose earlier members include such Greek-language scholars as Alexander of Aphrodisias, Porphyry, Themistius, and Ammonius."[18] Scholar Harry Wolfson suggests that the translation movement from the Greek into Arabic began with the works of al-Kindī and ended with those of Averroes.[19] However, the influence of the Muslim philosophical tradition continued well beyond the death of Averroes, especially with the emergence of Jewish Averroists, such as Maimonides, Isaac Albalag, and Moses Narboni, and also of Christian Averroists, such as the French philosopher, theologian, and political writer John of Jandun (1285/9–1328), who was considered one of the most influential thinkers in the Latin Averroist tradition, for his work carried this tradition from Paris to Bologna, Padua, and Erfurt in the fourteenth century.[20]

The Western Adoptions of Arabic Translations

In his discussion of the scholarship done on Aristotle's *Rhetoric* in the Middle Ages, historian of rhetoric James Murphy explains that "[the] *Rhetorica* first reached the Latin West in the form of thirteenth-century translations from Arabic commentators."[21] In effect, Hermannus Alemannus (d. 1272) was an active member in the Arabic-Latin translation movement in Toledo from 1240 to 1256. G. Luquet, Hermannus Alemannus's biographer, informs us that Hermannus was a contemporary of Roger Bacon and was principally recognized for having translated into Latin Averroes's *Middle Commentary on Aristotle's Nicomachean Ethics* in 1240, al-Fārābī's glosses on the *Rhetoric* in 1250, and Averroes's *Middle Commentary on the Poetics* in 1256.[22] As William Boggess

18. Rescher, *Development of Arabic Logic*, 22.
19. See Harry Wolfson, "The Twice-Revealed Averroes," *Speculum* 36, no. 3 (1961): 373–92.
20. See James South's essay "John of Jandun" in *A Companion to Philosophy in the Middle Ages*, ed. J. J. E. Gracia and T. B. Noone (Oxford: Blackwell, 2002), 372–73. For a good introduction on Averroism in the Jewish tradition, see O. Leaman, "Jewish Averroism," in *History of Islamic Philosophy*, ed. S. H. Nasr and O. Leaman (London: Routledge, 1996), 768–80.
21. James Murphy, *Rhetoric in the Middle Ages: A History of Rhetorical Theory from Saint Augustine to the Renaissance* (Berkeley: University of California Press, 1974), 90.
22. G. Luquet, "Hermann l'Allemand," *Revue de l'histoire des religions* [Review of the history of religions] 44 (1901): 407–22.

puts it, Hermannus's Latin translation of Averroes's *Middle Commentary on the Poetics* constituted, for more than two hundred years, "the major source of Aristotelian poetic doctrine in the West."[23]

In their comprehensive work, *Medieval Grammar and Rhetoric: Language Arts and Literary Theory, A.D. 300–1475*, Rita Copeland and Ineke Sluiter make available an annotated English translation of a substantial selection from Hermannus Alemannus's Latin *Didascalia in Rhetoricam Aristotelis ex glosa Alpharabi*, which, as the editors explain, was thought until recently to be the only extant version of al-Fārābī's "Great Commentary" on Aristotle's *Rhetoric*. The *Didascalia* is the introductory section to al-Fārābī's *Sharḥ Kitāb al-Khaṭābah li-Arisṭūṭālīs*. Copeland and Sluiter inform us that Giles of Rome (d. 1316) consulted Hermannus's Arabic-Latin translation of Aristotle's *Rhetoric* and the *Didascalia* when he produced, around 1272, his commentary on William of Moerbeke's translation of the *Rhetoric* from the Greek text.[24] In sum, the body of scholarship done in the West on the works of al-Fārābī, Avicenna, and Averroes indicates that these commentators came to the Latins, to put it in F. E. Peters's words, as "fully accredited interpreters of Aristotle."[25] Therefore, given the enormous importance of Aristotelian thought in Western society, this must surely be one of the most significant cultural exchanges of the period.

However, Greek logic was met with fierce resistance by conservative Muslim jurists (*fuqahā'*), such as Ibn Taymiyya (1263–1328), and literary critics, such as Abū Ḥayyān al-Tawḥīdī (930–1023), who viewed this science as part of "invasive sciences" (*ᶜulūm dakhīlah*)—that is, sciences that were not indigenous and did not belong to the language and thought of the Arabs. For example, in Jalāl al-Dīn al-Suyūṭī's (ca. 1445–1505) abridgment of Ibn Taymiyya's *Al-Radd ᶜalā al-Manṭiqiyyīn* (*Against the Greek Logicians*), which al-Suyūṭī titled *Jahd al-qarīḥah* fī *tajrīd al-Naṣīḥah*, Ibn Taymiyya summarizes his resistance to Greek logic and attack on Greek logicians, as well as their Muslim followers, in this statement, which I quote at length because of its significance:

> It is astonishing that these people claim to want to protect the true Religion with their defective minds and false syllogisms. What they have done instead

23. William F. Boggess, "Hermannus Alemannus' Latin Anthology of Arabic Poetry," *Journal of the American Oriental Society* 88, no. 4 (1968): 657.

24. Rita Copeland and Ineke Sluiter, eds., *Medieval Grammar and Rhetoric: Language Arts and Literary Theory, A.D. 300–1475* (Oxford, UK: Oxford University Press, 2010), 735–36.

25. F. E. Peters, *Aristotle and the Arabs: The Aristotelian Tradition in Islam* (New York: State University of New York Press, 1968), 222.

> is that which only the heretics, the enemies of religion, have dared to do. They have neither protected Islam nor defeated the enemy. What is also astonishing is that they avoid following and imitating the infallible prophets who speak noting but the truth. Instead, they imitate, associate with, those whom they know to be fallible, who are at times wrong and at others right. It is only God who ensures the truth.[26]

By "these people," Ibn Taymiyya refers to Avicenna (ca. 980–1037) and Muḥammad ibn Zakaryā' al-Rāzī (865–925), whose minds have been rendered, according to him, "defective" because "they imitate" and "associate with" the Greeks, whose minds are "fallible" and produce "false syllogisms." Ibn Taymiyya makes his position against the Greeks and their Muslim followers clear when he calls them "heretics" and "the enemies of religion." For Ibn Taymiyya, the way to the truth is the way of God and his prophets.

Abū Ḥayyān al-Tawḥīdī, an influential tenth-century representative of Arabic belles-lettres (*al-adab*), disparages Greek logic in his work *Al-Imtā^c wa al-Mu'ānasa* (*Enjoyment and Conviviality*). A series of salon discussions took place in the presence of Ibn Sa^{c}dān, a famous vizier of the Buyid ruler Samsam al-Dawla during the time of the Abbasid caliph al-Ṭā'i^c (974–91), and these are recorded in his work. In the chapter titled "Night Eight," al-Tawḥīdī describes a debate on the merits of logic and grammar between Abū Bishr Mattā ibn Yūnus, a Nestorian master under whom al-Fārābī studied logic, and Arabic grammarian Abū Sa^{c}īd al-Sīrāfī. Mattā ibn Yūnus states his position in the debate when he explains that logic is "a language instrument by means of which we tell what is sound and correct from what is unsound and incorrect." He also emphasizes the universal character of logic, indicating that "with regard to rational things, people are the same, [for] four and four are eight among all nations." Al-Sīrāfī situates logic in a purely linguistic context and asks, "If logic was laid down by a man from the Greeks and was based upon the language of the Greeks, [. . .] where does it become necessary for the Turks, the Hindus, the Persians, and the Arabs to study it and take it as a judge who will rule in their favor or against them so that they accept what he says to them and reject the thing of which he disapproves?"[27] Al-Sīrāfī clearly comes out

26. Jalāl al-Dīn al-Suyūṭī, *Jahd al-qarīḥah fī tajrīd al-Naṣīḥah* [Against the Greek logicians], ed. ^{c}Ali Sāmī al-Nashshār (Cairo: Maṭb^{c}at al-Sa^{c}āda, 1947), 173–74. The abridgment was also edited in 1970 by Su^{c}ād ^{c}Abd al-Rāziq and ^{c}Ali Sāmī al-Nashshār (Cairo: Dār al-Naṣr lil-Ṭibā^{c}a).

27. Abū Ḥayyān al-Tawḥīdī, *Al-Imtā^c wa al-Mu'ānasa*, ed. A. Amin and A. Al-Zayn (Cairo,

the winner in this debate in the eyes of the vizier and the other participants at the salon discussion that night.

However, the assimilation of Greek logic into the Arabic philosophical tradition survived such fierce attacks from the part of conservative Arabic jurists and men of letters. Following the program of instruction in the Syrian academies, Arabic logicians (*al-manṭiqiyyūn*) produced commentaries on Aristotle's logical works in three forms: the short commentary (*al-majmūᶜ*), the purpose of which is to give the gist of argument in Aristotle's work at the elementary level; the middle commentary (*talkhīṣ*), which is a paraphrase that offers additional explanation of the work at the secondary level; and the large commentary (*tafsīr* or *sharḥ*), which begins with a quotation from the Greek text and gives a detailed exposition of the quotation at the advanced level. This program of instruction corresponds to an educational system that, as Rescher suggests, "did not proceed by continuous acquisition of new materials, but by iterative deepening of material already familiar."[28]

The Structure of This Work

This book consists of Arabic-English translations of the commentaries of al-Fārābī, Avicenna, and Averroes on Aristotle's *Rhetoric*, known in Arabic scholarship as *Kitāb al-Khaṭābah*. Al-Fārābī's commentary, *Kitāb al-Khaṭābah* (*Book of Rhetoric*), essentially follows Aristotle's discussion of general principles of persuasion in Book I, chapter 2, of the *Rhetoric*. Avicenna's *Kitāb al-Majmūᶜ aw al-Ḥikmah al-ᶜArūḍiyya fī Maᶜānī Kitāb Rīṭōrīqā* (*Compendium; or, Al-ᶜArūḍī's Philosophical Treatise on the Meanings of the Book of Rhetoric*) is a compendium of Book I of the *Rhetoric*. Averroes's *Middle Commentary, Talkhīṣ Kitāb al-Khaṭābah* (*Exposition of the Book of Rhetoric*), gives an extended exposition of Books I, II, and III of the *Rhetoric*.[29] Because al-Fārābī's and Avicenna's commentaries focus only on Book I of the *Rhetoric*, I have selected from Averroes's *Middle Commentary* only the part that deals with Book I (*al-maqāla al-'ūlā*); however, I also include a summary of the main points in the commentary on Book II (*al-maqāla al-thāniya*) and Book III (*al-maqāla al-thālita*). This focus on Book I is motivated by the desire to give

1953), 80 (my translations). "A man from the Greeks" is a reference to Aristotle, whom al-Fārābī, Avicenna, and Averroes consider the founder of logic.

28. Rescher, *Development of Arabic Logic*, 36.

29. The term *kitāb* (book) is commonly used to refer to a philosophical treatise in the Arabic scholarly tradition.

the reader a consistent and coherent picture of the manner in which the three commentators read the first book of Aristotle's treatise.[30]

Moreover, the translation of the commentaries aims to give the English-speaking student and scholar of rhetoric not only access to these significant treatises but also the opportunity to situate these works in the context of confluence of cultures, specifically the Western culture and the Arabic-Muslim culture. Therefore, when examined against Aristotle's *Rhetoric*, the Arabic commentaries offer the student and scholar of rhetoric ample opportunities to observe and reflect on the ways in which they stay close to Aristotle's treatise and seek to act as its double, on the one hand, or depart from the treatise and place themselves in the realm of difference, on the other. Equally important, when read in conjunction with the existing tradition of Greek and Latin commentaries, the Arabic commentaries offer a promising field of research, for they broaden our view of a treatise that has, for nearly twenty-five hundred years, exerted enormous influence in the making of rhetorical history and theory in both the East and West. For example, seen from the perspective of resemblance, the commentaries show that they primarily aim to draw from Aristotle's treatise universal principles of persuasion shared by all nations. But when viewed in the context of differences, the commentaries call on us to examine and appreciate the historical, linguistic, and cultural spheres in which they were produced and ultimately will help us understand the distance between the commentaries' authors and the treatise that they sought to bring closer to the minds of an Arabic-speaking audience.

In the process of rendering these Arabic commentaries in English and, more important, in my attempt to make these texts more accessible to an English-speaking audience, I have been constantly aware of the challenge posed by the desire to reproduce the Arabic texts as faithfully as possible while keeping in mind the necessity to stay within the syntactic and semantic boundaries of the English language. Thus I have tried to achieve a balance by combining the use of a controlled word-for-word translation, but with a keen sense of focus on the rules of English syntax and semantics, with a translation allowing for more freedom of grammatical structure without losing track of the intended meaning in the source-language text. As the Arabic alphabet is different from the Latin alphabet used in the English language, I have adopted in transcribing Arabic

30. Readers fluent in French can see Maroun Aouad's excellent Arabic-French translation of Averroes (Ibn Rushd)'s *Commentaire moyen à la Rhétorique d'Aristote* [Middle commentary on Aristotle's *Rhetoric*], 3 vols. (Paris: Vrin, 2002).

names and technical terms the *International Journal of Middle East Studies* system to render Arabic words and sounds in English writing.

This book is concerned with the art of commentary, an important Arabic intellectual tradition that spans a period of more than three hundred years. Although this period is by no means uniform, given the stretch of space from Baghdad to Cordoba, it can be broken into smaller units, and thus we can speak of the age of al-Fārābī (870–950), the age of Avicenna (980–1037), and the age of Averroes (1126–98). Chapter 1 is devoted to al-Fārābī's *Book of Rhetoric*; chapter 2 is about Avicenna's *Compendium; or, Al-ᶜArūdī's Philosophical Treatise on the Meanings of the Book of Rhetoric*; and chapter 3 focuses on Averroes's *Middle Commentary on the Book of Rhetoric (Book I).*

The field of research that this work opens for the student and scholar of rhetoric can be described briefly by asking the following questions:

1. How did al-Fārābī, Avicenna, and Averroes read the *Rhetoric* of Aristotle?
2. What are the lines of continuity and discontinuity within this Arabic commentary tradition left by these three philosophers?
3. How does the Arabic commentary tradition on the *Rhetoric* situate itself in relation to the Greek and Latin commentary tradition on Aristotle's treatise? What are the similarities between the two traditions? What are the differences?

Addressing these questions may seem difficult in some respects, given the complex nature of each commentary tradition. However, it is well worth embarking on this task, especially given the fact that the Greek cultural and philosophical tradition was never completely interrupted, and that while it declined for a few centuries in the West, it gained a new life and a new dimension in the Muslim world.

1. Al-Fārābī's *Book of Rhetoric*

Al-Fārābī (870–950)

Chronicler Jamāl al-Dīn al-Qifṭī informs us that Muḥammad ibn Muḥammad ibn Ṭarkhān Abū Naṣr al-Fārābī was of Turkish descent.[1] He was born in Fārāb, in what is now Uzbekistan, in 870. His father was a Persian officer in the Turkish military, and his mother was Turkish. In the Aristotelian School of Baghdad, al-Fārābī studied the Arabic language and Islamic theology. He also studied philosophy and logic under two well-known Nestorian teachers of logic, Abū Bishr Mattā ibn Yūnus (ca. 870–940) and Yuḥannā ibn Ḥailān (ca. 850–920). Abū Bishr Mattā ibn Yūnus translated Aristotle's *Posterior Analytics* into Arabic from a Syriac translation made available by Isḥāq ibn Ḥunayn (ca. 830–911) and also rendered in Syriac the *Poetics* and the *Sophistics*. Yuḥannā ibn Ḥailān was versed in philosophy, Christian theology, and logic. Al-Fārābī was also a contemporary of Yaḥyā ibn ᶜAdī (893–974), who produced newer translations of Aristotle's logical works from Syriac into Arabic. These Nestorian masters, who knew Greek, Syriac, and Arabic, had inherited the Christian Neoplatonist tradition handed down by the last representatives of the Alexandrian school.

Not much is known about al-Fārābī before he was fifty. Al-Qifṭī informs us that he traveled extensively around the Muslim world, for he visited academic circles of linguists, dialecticians, literary critics, and commentators on Greek philosophical works in Baghdad, Aleppo, Damascus, and Cairo. He received benefits under the patronage of Prince Saif al-Dawla al-Ḥamadānī in Iraq, where he lived

1. For this biographical note on al-Fārābī, I have drawn on Jamāl al-Dīn al-Qifṭī's work *Tā'rīkh al-Ḥukamā'* [History of philosophers], ed. August Müller and Julius Lippert (Leipzig, Germany: Theodor Weicher, 1903), 277–78.

for about thirty years, writing and teaching before he died in the year 950. In addition to Arabic, al-Fārābī knew Turkish, Persian, and Kurdish. He did not know Syriac or Greek, but still he is considered in Islamic philosophy the first to have rendered Greek logic in Arabic, for he brought Aristotle's logical scheme close to the Arabic-Islamic mind.[2] He was largely influential among Muslim philosophers, especially Avicenna and Averroes, who followed in his steps in commenting on Aristotle's philosophical works and expanding the scope of Aristotelian logic.

In his monumental work, al-Fārābī attempts to show the unity of philosophy, despite differences of time, place, and culture. For al-Fārābī, just as with scientific truth, the ends of philosophy do not change. This explains his interest in reconciling Plato's philosophical ideas with Aristotle's philosophy and ultimately philosophy with religion. Al-Fārābī must have been inspired by the work of Neoplatonist philosophers, such as Simplicius, in thinking of such reconciliation. He put his thoughts down in a treatise titled *Al-Jam*ᶜ *Bayna Ra'yaiy al-Ḥakīmayn Aflāṭūn al-Ilāhī wa Arisṭū*. In *Iḥṣā' al-*ᶜ*Ulūm* (*Book of the Enumeration of Sciences*), al-Fārābī classifies Aristotle's works into two categories. In the first one, he puts *Categoriae*, *De Interpretatione*, *Analytica Priora*, *Analytica Posteriora*, *Topica*, *Sophistica*, *Rhetorica*, and *Poetica*. Following the late Alexandrian commentators on Aristotle, al-Fārābī treats the *Rhetoric* and the *Poetics* as part of Aristotle's *Organon*. That al-Fārābī includes the *Rhetoric* and the *Poetics* in this first category is quite significant because, as Deborah Black explains, "Aristotle's *Organon* represented the main source of logical speculation for the philosophers of the Middle Ages, and was a major inspiration for their epistemological doctrine as well."[3] In the second category, al-Fārābī puts Aristotle's eight books on physical matters and also includes *Metaphysics*, *Ethics*, and *Politics*. He also devotes a whole series of commentaries to the *Organon*. With regard to the art of rhetoric, al-Fārābī gives us this brief statement about Aristotle's treatise in *Kitāb Falsafat Aflāṭūn wa Arisṭū* (*The Philosophy of Plato and Aristotle*):

> [Aristotle] gave an account of the art [that is, rhetoric] that enables man to persuade the multitude regarding (*a*) all theoretical things and (*b*) those practical things in which it is customary to confine oneself to using persuasive arguments based on particular examples drawn from men's activities when

2. Nicholas Rescher's *Studies in the History of Arabic Logic* (Pittsburgh: University of Pittsburgh Press, 1963) traces the history of logic from the Hellenistic and Alexandrian Greeks through the Syrian Nestorians to Arabic-speaking Muslim philosophers.
3. Deborah L. Black, *Logic and Aristotle's "Rhetoric" and "Poetics" in Medieval Arabic Philosophy* (Leiden, Netherlands: E. J. Brill, 1990), 1.

> conducting their public business—that is, the activities through which they labor together toward the end for which man is made.[4]

In sum, al-Fārābī's work on Greek philosophical texts, particularly those of Aristotle and Plato, gave him a reputable position in Islamic philosophy from which he earned the title "the second teacher," after Aristotle.

Al-Fārābī's *Kitāb al-Khaṭābah* (*Book of Rhetoric*) is available in two editions, one edited by Muḥammad Salīm Sālim and the other by J. Langhade and M. Grignaschi.[5] The work essentially follows Aristotle's discussion of general principles of persuasion in Book I, chapter 2, of the *Rhetoric*. The English translation that I provide in this book is based on the two Arabic editions available; however, I have closely followed the excellent critical edition prepared by Langhade and Grignaschi, in which they include punctuation and paragraph division to make the text clear to read. In my effort to render the Arabic text in English, I frequently compared my translation against their French translation and also against W. Rhys Roberts's English translation of the Greek text of Aristotle's *Rhetoric*, especially when I encountered some passages in which al-Fārābī's style was not easily comprehended. Al-Fārābī's commentary may be divided into sections as follows.

Introduction: Definition of Rhetoric (248b–251b)

Al-Fārābī defines rhetoric as a syllogistic art the purpose of which is persuasion. He also compares persuasion with teaching in the demonstrative arts. Persuasion is a sort of opinion that has an object of opposition, either more or less apparent or hidden.

On Belief and Certitude (252a–253b)

In this section, al-Fārābī engages in a discussion of the views of the ancients on the notion of certitude and draws the conclusion that it is not possible that we have two opposite beliefs about the same thing simultaneously.

On Opinion, Doubt, and Immediate Point of View (254a–256a)

Al-Fārābī identifies two types of opinion. One type does not present a person with an opposite. He gives a number of examples to illustrate this case. With the

4. Muhsin Mahdi, trans., *Alfarabi's Philosophy of Plato and Aristotle* (New York: Free Press of Glencoe, 1962), 92.

5. Abū Naṣr Al-Fārābī, *Kitāb Fī al-Manṭiq: Al-Khaṭābah*, ed. Muḥammad Salīm Sālim (Cairo: Dār al-Kitāb, 1976); J. Langhade and M. Grignaschi, eds., *Al-Fārābī: Deux ouvrages inédits sur la rhétorique* [Al-Fārābī: Two unpublished works on rhetoric] (Beirut: Dar el-Mashreq, 1971). Langhade and Grignaschi inform us that they used two manuscripts that had been recently discovered: manuscript no. 812 of Ḥamidiye Collection in Istanbul and manuscript no. 231, TE 41, of the University of Bratislava Library.

other type of opinion, the person knows the opposite. Al-Fārābī also explains that strong opinion in every person is one to which there is no opposite. He defines doubt as a moment when the soul stops between two opposite opinions, resulting from two things that are equal in clarity and strength. He also mentions the ancients (probably the Sophists), who relied on rhetorical means until Aristotle came along and was the first to possess the means by which he framed universal laws, arranged in a technical manner and firmly put in logic.

On the Enthymeme and the Example (256b)

Al-Fārābī defines an *enthymeme* as a statement composed of two joined premises that we use by omitting one premise. He explains that the example has the force of a syllogism and can be used for persuasive purposes.

On the Types of Listeners (257a–257b)

Al-Fārābī breaks the audience into three types: those we want to persuade, the opponent, and the judge. The opponent may be real or apparent. The usefulness of the opponent is to make the arguments that the speaker advances more persuasive. Al-Fārābī discusses some conditions that allow for fairness in judging a case, the most important of which is the ability to clearly distinguish which one of the two opposing arguments is more persuasive.

On the Moral Character of the Speaker and the Enthymeme (258a–268a)

Al-Fārābī recognizes the importance of the moral excellence of the speaker, but he also argues that if moral excellence is not well established, the speaker will need arguments to show his superior moral character by means of which he aims to persuade his audience. The speaker can achieve that goal only by means of the enthymeme.

On the Sign and the Proof (268b–270a)

Al-Fārābī identifies two types of signs. In one type, the common term is more general than the predicate and the subject altogether. In the other type, the common term is more particular than the predicate and the subject altogether. For al-Fārābī, the most authentic proof is one by whose existence something must necessarily exist. The types of proofs vary according to the types of causes.

On Comparison (270b–271b)

In this section, al-Fārābī discusses the composition of comparison and shows that comparison is nearly close to an enthymeme or a syllogism.

Conclusion

Al-Fārābī closes his commentary with words of praise to Allah.

248 **Kitāb al-Khaṭābah**

(The Book of Rhetoric)

In the Name of Allah, the Merciful, the Compassionate

Rhetoric is a syllogistic art, the purpose of which is persuasion in all ten genera.[6] What happens in the mind of the hearer as a result of persuasion is the ultimate goal of the acts of rhetoric.

Persuasion is a sort of opinion, and opinion, in general, is the belief that the thing is such or is not such; what we believe of the thing may be
249a different from the mode of existence of that thing in itself. When a person is not certain of the truth of one of two things related to one another, each one of them is then an object of inquiry. The truth of everything that is an object of inquiry is then unknown. If it is said that opinion is not the belief in the truth of what can be proved untrue, but rather the belief in what cannot be proved untrue, then that is not an opinion, but certitude, and there was an error in naming it. Also in belief, there must be either truth or untruth, whether the proposition is affirmative or negative. Assent may concern what cannot be other than itself. And that is knowledge.[7]

Persuasion, in the art of rhetoric, is similar to teaching in the demonstrative arts.[8] It is akin to the knowledge that a learner acquires through

6. We find the meaning of the term *genera* in al-Fārābī's *Philosophy of Plato and Aristotle*, in which he states, "There [Aristotle] began first to investigate and enumerate the instances of being from which the first premises are compounded, that contain the questions to be investigated, and that are the primary significations of the expressions generally accepted by all. These are the [*summa genera*] whose being is attested by sense-perception and of which every intelligible is based on some sensible thing. He confined all of them to ten genera, called them categories, and set them down in a book called in Greek *Katègorías* and in Arabic *al-Maqūlāt* (*categories*). See Muhsin Mahdi's English translation, *Alfarabi's Philosophy of Plato and Aristotle* (New York: Free Press of Glencoe, 1962), 4:82–83.

7. For a thorough discussion of the concepts of *ᶜilm* (knowledge) and *yaqīn* (certitude) in al-Fārābī's terminology, see Deborah Black's excellent essay "Knowledge (ᶜilm) and Certitude (yaqīn) in al-Fārābī's Epistemology," *Arabic Sciences and Philosophy* 16 (2006): 11–45. As Black suggests, ᶜilm is equivalent to the Greek term *epistēmē*.

8. Following the tradition of Alexander of Aphrodisias, the three Muslim commentators seem to take the term ἀντίστροφος, translated into Arabic as *mithlu*

learning. The attention a listener pays to a speaker, his willingness to persevere and his reflection on what is said, all these are similar to learning. The meaning of the word *al-qanāᶜa* has been transferred, to render this meaning [of persuasion], from "being content with something" that is like a portion of it, even if it is possible to obtain more of it.[9] In fact, when people meet in their transactions and livelihood, they are content to believe each other in what they are discoursing about and to refer to one another's sayings, to the point that they call this knowledge.

Opinion and certitude have this in common, that they are both a point of view. To have a point of view is to believe that something is such or is not such. It is as a genus to them both and they are as its species. The propositions in which points of view are expressed and by which discourses are made are either necessary or possible. Of things necessary, some are absolutely necessary; others are necessary at certain times, and before those times, it was possible for them to exist or not to exist. To these the word "contingent" is attributed. Certitude exists in necessary propositions **249b**
only. It seems there are various types of certitude according to various types of necessary propositions. Thus there is what is absolutely certain and what is certain at a given moment of time and ceases to be certain. As to possible propositions, there is absolutely no certitude in them. I do not mean that our knowledge of the possible is a possible that is not certitude; I only mean that if something can possibly exist or not exist in the future, it will not be possible for us to have certain knowledge that it exists or that it does not exist. Thus our belief that something can possibly exist is absolutely not certitude.

In general, persuasion and opinion may be about the different types of what is necessary and about what is possible. The term "possible" has in the first place two meanings. The first one refers to the unknown, the meaning of which necessarily implies the existence of an object of inquiry that is proper to study. The second one refers to one of the aspects of the

(al-Fārābī), *tushriku* (Avicenna), and *tunāsibu* (Averroes), to imply the sense of similarity between rhetoric and dialectic. For an informed survey of the rendering of Aristotle's term ἀντίστροφος in the European commentary traditions on the *Rhetoric* from classical times to the modern period, see Lawrence D. Green, "Aristotelian Rhetoric, Dialectic, and the Traditions of ἀντίστροφος," *Rhetorica* 8, no. 1 (1990): 5–27.

9. The terms *al-qanāᶜa* and *al-iqnāᶜ* belong to the same semantic field and both point to the meaning of persuasion.

existence of several future matters. Our ignorance of what does not yet pertain to which of the two opposites of the object of inquiry is the appropriate and the true is what is possible from our part only and does not constitute a notion existing in the matter outside of us. The possible that is requisite in opinion is not the possible that signifies something existing for the matter itself outside of the soul; it is the possible that signifies what is possible from our part only. This means that we do not know if that which we believe corresponds or does not correspond to the thing that exists. Because the matter is inseparable from something coming to the soul from outside, opinion becomes as if there were ignorance in it
250a tied to a science; our belief is such because it depends on what happens to the soul from outside; in that case, it is like a science; and our belief that we are not certain that what is in our souls corresponds to the matter outside of the soul is like ignorance of the correspondence between our belief and the existing matter. This is concerning the existence of that which is necessary, but which is possible from our part.

There is also what consists, in a certain manner, of possibility, as when we say, "Zayd is standing." As long as [Zayd] is standing, this is, during this time, necessary; whereas before, it was possible that this could be or could not be [the case].

As to pure necessity, which is not tainted by any possibility, it is not possible for the same person, at the same time, to have both opinion and certitude about it. But as to necessity, which is tainted by possibility, it is possible that the same person at the same time will have both opinion and certitude about it. In effect, this person may have certitude about its existence in the present and opinion about its existence in the future. The cause of our ignorance is that we have formed an opinion about pure necessity from our part; as to necessity that is tainted by something, this opinion is from our part while it exists in the present, and from its part while it exists in the future, because it can or cannot exist according to our opinion and belief.

Opinion can be strong, and it can be weak. It can be of the type in which a person does not perceive opposition, and it can also be of the type in which a person perceives opposition and is able to represent it either separately on his own or when he is discoursing with other people. Opinion is strong when there is less opposition, and it is weak when there is more opposition. As to persuasion, it does not diminish when a person perceives opposition.

Every person reinforces persuasion in dealing with others or annuls it by thorough examination or by allowing what he thinks is more useful. If he benefits from the lowest degrees of persuasion, he does not go any higher. If he finds that the lowest degree of persuasion does not help him **250b**
achieve what he wants, he will examine it thoroughly and reinforce it. If he finds that it will be more useful for him to nullify something from it, he will oppose it, bearing in mind its force.

Persuasion, even when we reach a more assertive state in it, has to have an object of opposition, either more or less apparent or hidden. That which opposes opinion may be hidden from the part of the person who believes and argues, and it may be hidden from the part of the matter being discussed.

This is due to the fact that a point of view may encounter numerous oppositions whose role is to guide a person and draw his attention to the error of his point of view, either in part or entirely, and to what is appropriate and should be believed. He is not aware of these oppositions, either because he is negligent and prefers to be mentally idle, or because he is too preoccupied with the necessities of life to examine thoroughly those oppositions, or because he is preoccupied with the exclusive study of a type of matter other than the type of matter in which he is not aware of opposition, or because of a mental deficiency, which is due either to his young age and which ceases to exist, or to a natural disposition which does not cease to exist. The strength of his natural disposition to understand things that are normally understood by syllogisms may be limited to a degree, or it may be limited to a certain type of things only. If he were to aim past that limit, either in everything or in a certain type of matter, his strength will weaken. Strength is weakened through fatigue and exhaustion caused by the study of previous matters.

If he had started considering this [matter] and had examined it with all his power, he would have pulled out its opposites, the way things happen with physical strength. When a person examines something and **251a**
has a point of view about it, and pursues that point of view to the limit of his strength, and no opposition to that point of view appears to him, nor the truth of its opposite, because of the fact that what is opposed to his point of view is hidden from his perspective, then he has proved the truth of that point of view according to his ability.

The opposite can also be hidden with respect to the matter itself, for reasons and states in the matter, as when the opposites are taken from things that are meant to be observed and tested, and the person encounters an obstacle that prevents him from observing and testing them, either because they are distant in time and space, or because of another obstacle—for example, when, in the study of animal anatomy, we need to observe several internal organs but cannot possibly do that, either because of a lack of equipment or because the Law does not permit us to do that.[10]

Sometimes oppositions are vague, and to detect them, the person needs additional strength borrowed from another art that he does not possess, or the error in the universal proposition is so subtle and the oppositions to it are so few. When a person does not perceive an opposite to a point of view and knows that this opposite is hidden to him only from his perspective, he must hold that point of view suspect and not rely upon it, and he must not trust it completely.

It is difficult for a person to know from which side a vague opposite comes, whether from his side or from the side of the matter itself. Also, a person is far from suspecting himself in his beliefs, for he trusts his point of view, especially when the opposite does not appear to him, after he has desired for long what he believes.

The soundest opinion is determined in relation to each person, not in relation to itself. The surest opinion is one that a person has put all his effort into studying, and has not encountered any opposition to it, or
251b has dismantled any opposition to it. His belief becomes absolutely free of any opposition, especially if he does not have any doubt about the truth of his belief.

It was in this manner that the ancients justified their points of view in speculative matters. They would look for the syllogism appropriate to an object of inquiry, and when they found it, they would make of it a point of view. Then they would pursue that point of view and seek out its oppositions and contrast it to its opposite. When they did not find any opposite, or found opposites that they were able to dismantle and refute, they would then adopt that point of view and believe it was true. This was regarding the point of view of each particular person.

As to solid opinions, inquiry about them is achieved through dialectical means more than through rhetorical means; however, this does not guarantee that it corresponds to the truth of the matter.

10. The term referred to here is *al-Sharīʿa*, or Islamic law based on the Qur'an and the Tradition of the Prophet Muḥammad, known as *al-Ḥadīth*.

There are various things that cause the end of belief: death of the person who believes; or deterioration of the mind; or forgetfulness; or forgetfulness of proof; or the end of the matter about which there was belief, through destruction, or transformation into the opposite of what it had been, or a fallacy that gets into it and that the person who believes does not detect, or a true opposite that shows him the error of his belief. In the same way, certitude ends with the death of the person who believes, or the deterioration of his mind, or his forgetfulness. But it does not cease with the end of the matter or with the end of opposites, as it has been shown in *Kitāb al-Burhān* (*Book on Demonstration*).[11] Considered in an absolute manner, of the properties of certitude, when it occurs, there is the fact that it never ends as long as the person who believes is sane and his mind is sane. However, temporary certitude ceases with the destruction of the matter or when the matter changes into its opposite, despite
the fact that the person who believes is sane and his mind is sound. Of **252a**
the properties of opinion, there is the fact that it can cease in the future, without its being forgotten, and that is despite the sanity of the person who believes, the soundness of his mind, and the integrity of the matter.

In sum, every belief that is acquired at a certain time and that can cease in the future by opposition is an opinion. And every belief that stood for a while and then ceased by opposition was an opinion before it ended. And the person who held that belief did not sense that it was opinion.

Some ancients raised the question about the subject of point of view that is particular to each individual person and said, "Are you confident that you are not going to turn away from the points of view in which you believe today and embrace their opposites?" In the same way, one asks, "Did you not have a point of view in the past that you believed was sound and true and then you turned away from it so that its opposite today has become what its opposite was yesterday? What guarantee do you have that you will not turn away from this point of view in favor of its first opposite?" There are other, similar questions regarding these ancient issues. The purpose of all these [questions] was simply to show that such points of view were opinions and insufficient in speculative matters, by means of which points of view were at the level of certitude, and that they should not be considered of the level of certitude.

11. Aristotle's *Posterior Analytics* is known in the Islamic philosophical tradition as *Kitāb al-Burhān* (*Book on Demonstration*).

Insufficient answers to these questions have been given because of [some of the ancients'] poor knowledge of the ways of certitude. Thus some of them said, "I do not turn away from this specific point of view as long as I am in this state of mind." This is not an answer that will include one's points of view in the definition of certitude, because there is no difference between this statement and the following one: "I do not turn away from these points of view as long as I do not know of an opposite that will destroy them, or as long as the proofs that make them appear
252b true in my mind are not proved wrong." Such is the state of opinions. For an opinion, when an opposite against it does not appear, is similar to certitude for the person who believes it.

Others among the ancients thought that there should not be an answer to this question and that it should be dropped because it was a false question. In effect, they had claimed that these questions and other, similar ones were limited to the destruction of the point of view of every person asking questions with the aim of obliterating the point of view of another person, and that they obliterated all points of view and did not allow a person to believe in any point of view. Not to allow [a person to believe in any point of view] is impossible, since every person has a point of view, to the extent that when someone says, "There is absolutely no point of view," his statement itself is a point of view.

These ancients' claim that such questions must be dropped and are not worth answering, for the reasons that they suggested, and also their claim that the questions are invalid because they are related to the points of view of the person who raises questions about them are erroneous and absurd, because if the points of view of the questioner were all opinions, and if he felt or admitted they were opinions, they would not turn against him and invalidate his points of view. The questioner will have simply committed to the implications of his questions before he asks those questions. His aim is to show that to the person who does not feel or acknowledge that his points of view, as they are, are indeed opinions, but thinks that they are certitude or makes people believe that they are certitude. Moreover, if there was certitude or an element of certitude in the questioner's points of view, that certitude would not turn against him and invalidate his points of view—because certitude can never be removed by an opposite—or invalidate each particular point of view, or all the points of view, or the points of view of everyone. Points of view are invalidated only for the person who does not see or acknowledge, regarding points of view in this state, that they are opinion and should remain opinion. As to the person whose point of view is certitude, or an opinion that he acknowledges is an opinion, these questions do not invalidate his point of view.

Why do such questions not deserve an answer? Does this not resemble the case in which a statement widely known authenticates a proposition, and a syllogistic statement authenticates its opposite, to the degree that the widely known statement and the syllogistic statement oppose each other? Does this not resemble the case in which there are two syllogistic statements, one of which implies the opposite of what the other implies? Do we reject one of the two statements? Do we not listen to it or to the person using it in his discourse? Are we going to be content and say that there is another proof here to confirm what that statement invalidates? And then we will look for ways to make it invalid and show the place of error in it, if there is an error, by using the testimony of someone against the truth of a point of view, by his fame and by the testimony of other people on his behalf. As to the other argument by a syllogistic statement against the truth of the opposite of that statement, it is similar to the opposition of two proofs, one of which implies the opposite of what the other one implies. The same is true with the issue brought up by a person who asks, "Is it possible that what you believe in a matter is different from what the matter is?" He only means by that, "Is it possible that what you believe in a matter is in opposition to what the existence of the matter is outside the soul or not?" By this question, we seek to prove also, in such points of view as these, that they are opinions and not certitude. **253a**

Some of those who test their points of views in speculative matters by stretching them further, to the point that they do not find any opposites against them, exaggerate the value of their points of view to admit that they are opinions, but when they contemplate the matter, they find that their points of view are such, or that they are not certain that such points of view are in opposition to what the existence of the matter is. They respond to the question by giving the impression that their opinions are certitude, and they reject by their views what the questioner wants to impose. They do this by referring to the words used by the questioner and not to the meaning of the words in the questioner's mind.

And if someone asked them, "Is it possible that what someone believes to be such or not such is in opposition to what he believes?" they would provide a vague answer that gives the illusion that their point of view is **253b** certitude, which is "It is not possible that what I believe to be such or not such is different from what I believe." This is an ambiguous statement that can be used in different ways, one of which is that the meaning of the statement "It is not possible" is that it is not in the capacity or power of his mind to believe in that thing differently from what he has believed, given the fact that he has done his best to find true the opposite to his point of view, and that he has not found it true. This is not an answer that will make his point of view certitude, even if he was sincere.

It is also probable that he means by "It is not possible" that the belief of a person that something is such is identical to his belief that it is not such. This does not mean anything more than that two opposites cannot be identical to the same thing. This answer also does not prevent the point of view from being opposite to the matter itself. This was exactly the object of inquiry on the part of the questioner, and they have not answered "no" by one of the two opposites of the question; they have only pushed away what the question aimed to imply.

It is also probable that the ambiguous statement "It is not possible" means that it is not possible that when we believe that something is such, we believe in that thing itself at one and the same time that it is not such. In such case, there is nothing more than this: that it is not possible that we have two opposite beliefs about the same thing at one and the same time. This is an answer about something different from what they have been asked.

254a There are two sorts of opinion, one for which a person does not know an opposite, either because he did not look for it at all; or he did not examine it; or he did not try to find one; or because he attempted to find an opposite but did not find one; or because he refuted, according to his ability, whatever opposite he encountered. As to the other type of opinion, the person knows the opposite. The opinion whose opposite is known relates to a particular person, or to a particular group, or to all, at a certain time; or it relates to a person or to a group at a certain time. It is not impossible that the opposite of a point of view is hidden from a person at a certain time and appears to him at another time, or that it appears to another person at that time or after that time. The same thing goes with the group. It is not impossible also that a point of view, which is commonly known to everyone, is such that no one among them is aware of its opposite, and that some of them recognize that opposite at a later time.

A strong opinion in every person is one to which there is no opposite. This type has various degrees: The weakest is one of which we do not know the opposite, because we have not looked for one, for negligence, inattentiveness, distraction, or good faith. The strongest is one we have worked hard to examine and compare with its opposite and refute whatever opposites we have found.

An opinion that has more support than opposition prevails. An opinion whose support is less and is less apparent, and whose opposition is more and is more apparent, is called doubt and suspicion and is discarded. An opinion whose support is equal to its opposition in number and clarity is used with its opposite in the arts of conjecture, not that they are used in one thing at one time, but in two different situations and two different times; and from such opinions doubt and confusion may result, whenever they are used in sciences and we are not aware of what falsehood they may contain.

Doubt is when the soul stops between two opposite opinions, resulting from two things that are equal in clarity and firmness. Equal firmness is **254b**
when the two opinions are equal in the necessity of the consequence of what is deduced from each one of them and when they are equal regarding the necessity or the possibility of their existence. Their clarity is equal when they are commonly known, or when a person knows about them or has an opinion about them in an equal manner. And if a person does not have an opinion on either one of the opposite propositions, this calls for research and it is not a doubt.

An opinion is authentic when it is an object of inquiry and is examined until we do not sense any opposite to our point of view. This may be done by rhetorical as well as dialectical means. A person is aware of rhetorical means before he is aware of dialectical means because he is used to rhetorical means since childhood and since his first experience observing the first things that a person can see. As to dialectical means, he is aware of them later. Demonstrative means are even less apparent than dialectical means, because a person is almost not aware of them spontaneously. Philosophers in antiquity used rhetorical means in their study of speculative matters for a long period of time because they were not aware of any other means, until they finally became aware of dialectical means, and as a result, they rejected rhetorical means in philosophy and used dialectical means instead. Several of these philosophers used sophistry and continued to use it until the time of Plato, who was the first to become aware of demonstrative means, for he distinguished them from dialectical, sophistic, rhetorical, and poetic means. However, he only **255a** distinguished them one from the other in usage, in diverse disciplines, and according to the right course that spare time and higher instinct would show, without prescribing any universal laws for them, which Aristotle later did in his *Kitāb al-Burhān* (*Posterior Analytics*) and its canons.

In fact, Aristotle was the first to possess these means, for which he framed universal laws, arranged in a technical manner, and which he firmly put in logic. Philosophers refused since then [to use] the old ways that the ancients used in speculative matters as a means of seeking certitude. They used dialectic in mathematics, sophistry for tribulation and warning, and they used rhetoric in the general matters common to all the arts, namely, those matters in which we cannot use a method proper to an art without the other arts. Thus rhetoric is common to all the arts, and it is for teaching the public several speculative matters, and for teaching a person who is not versed in a particular art those things that are proper to this art, whenever he needs that, and also in the discourses used for civic matters.

The arts of conjecture are those from which opinions are obtained in their topics that have been determined. Those are rhetoric, prudence, and practical arts, such as medicine, agriculture, navigation, and other similar arts. Each of these arts, except rhetoric, takes pains to pursue what is right in everything that a person has to do or where he has to do it. The right point of view is a sort of true opinion. Each of these arts has a special topic. He only invents what is right or persuades in its special topics. Rhetoric is a separate art.

255b In fact, rhetoric has been instituted for persuasion only, not for reflection, nor even for discovering the matter about which one persuades. The other arts of conjecture use reflection in discovering the thing that is their object of persuasion. Rhetoric does not have a special domain for persuasion, but we look for persuasion in all types of matters. Also, the business of rhetoric is the invention of opinions either in the domain where there are opinions—that is, the things possible in themselves—or in the domain where there is certitude—that is, the things necessary. From the other arts, we only have opinion in matters of opinion, not certitude, since their topics are about things possible.

Each of these arts is used in a person's reflection when he seeks to discover the right point of view in what he should do in such and such thing concerning a particular topic, which is governed by the laws that he has acquired from his art only. When he wants to persuade others, if those others are versed in his art and have the same degree of knowledge of the laws governing that art, the means that he has available is to use, in order to persuade, those same laws by which he discovered that right point of view. If they are not versed in his art, he will need to use rhetoric, which is common to all. He will not use the particular method of that art, unless it is agreed that that art is also common to all. If he is not able to follow the method that is common to all and wants to persuade others, he will commission an orator to do the job for him.

As to rhetoric, it uses, for persuasion, the means common to all, **256a**
since it aims at persuasion in all types of matters. It does not use particular means, except when those are also common to all. That is why it is possible to use persuasion in medical matters, not by the means that are particular to a doctor, but by those means that are shared between the doctor and those who are not doctors. The same goes with each of the other arts. That is why [rhetoric] has the power to persuade all people in all matters. That is why when someone professing an art, speculative or practical, aims at removing an error from one of the points of view of another person who is not versed in that [particular] art because he does not have free time, or is not fit to study that art, he will need to have the skills of an orator or commission an orator.

An a priori shared point of view is that which, when it suddenly presents itself to a person, will appear as it is, before the person conducts any inquiry about it. To conduct an inquiry about a point of view is for a person to search, with all his capacity, for the things that reinforce and strengthen that point of view. If he finds those things, his point of view will be stronger and he will grow confident in it. If he encounters things that are opposite to his point of view, he will seek to refute them. If he refutes them, his a priori point of view will confirm itself. If they are not refuted, either he totally rejects his a priori point of view, or his attention is drawn by the opposites regarding his a priori point of view to the condition or conditions that may have been neglected in the first place. This is what we mean by examining the a priori point of view.

Rhetoric has this in common with dialectic and sophistic, for they all proceed with investigation, and as a consequence, false points of view are exposed.

An enthymeme is a statement composed of two conjoined premises **256b**
that we use by omitting one of the two premises. It is called an enthymeme because the person using it hides certain premises and does not declare them; the person also uses the enthymeme in relation to the speaker's

knowledge of the premises that he has omitted. The enthymeme becomes persuasive in the shared apparent point of view only because of an omission, and without that omission, it will not be persuasive.

We have an example when we verify the existence of something in a certain matter so that we bring out the existence of that thing in a similar matter. The example is called an enthymeme by the public. In each of these two [the enthymeme and the example], the business of the premises, considered by themselves, by their number and by their composition, is persuasion in the a priori known point of view, whether they are real syllogisms or apparent syllogisms.

In the other arts that produce opinion, the number of premises and the composition of propositions by means of which the correct point of view is invented and by which persuasion is achieved must be syllogistic in truth and [when they are judged by comparison with other premises]. In this manner, rhetoric is also different from the other arts that produce opinion. Therefore, if the orator wants to persuade an audience in a matter belonging to one of these other arts, the moment he is persuading in that matter, he must turn away from the method that is particular to that art; instead, he must use the method according to the a priori known point of view. A point of view may also be prior to each in particular, and this one the orator must not use in anything of his art. A point of view may also be known to an entire nation, shared among its members, and proper to them only.

There are three types of listeners: those we want to persuade, the
257a opponent, and the judge. Those we want to persuade, either they have started the dispute and demand that the speaker persuade them about a particular thing, or the speaker started the dispute, demanding that the others accept a particular thing or listen to what he has to say. The goal of the person demanding persuasion is to hear the arguments so that he hears an argument that confirms a matter that he likes or to accept the most effective argument from two opposed arguments.

The opponent is either an adversary who stands up against the speaker whose discourse aims to persuade the listener, impeding persuasion, or an apparent adversary, examining what the speaker says and giving profound thought to what the speaker advances. His intention is to make the arguments [that] the speaker advances more persuasive.

One of the conditions for being a judge is the ability to distinguish well which one of the two opposing arguments is more persuasive. It is clear that the manner in which the judge addresses each of the two opponents is different from the manner in which they address each other. A judge who does not conform well to what the judges use may well become a hostile opponent, and this happens when he uses in his discourse by which he judges one of the adversaries the arguments that each of the adversaries uses with the other. This is why a person who does not have the ability to conform to the condition of judgment must not be raised to the status of judge.

If the argument of one of the opponents about an issue was less persuasive because of the weakness of that opponent, and if the judge had things about the issue by which he could reinforce the argument of that opponent, so that it could become more persuasive, and if [the judge] wanted to judge for that opponent by what he knew to be persuasive about that matter, not by what was apparent in the argument of the opponent, that would be a place for doubt. Will he judge according **257b**
to what is apparent from the argument of the opponent, or according to what he knows about the force of persuasion in that matter? But if the judge is judge in that matter only according to those two opponents, he must not judge according to what he knows about the matter without the two opponents. If he is judge in that matter according to the matter itself, or according to what is considered good in the city, or according to what is better for the two opponents in addition to what is good in the city, and what he knows is the best, he will judge according to what he knows in that matter.

All this must be known from the position of the judge exercising his power of judgment. It must be known from his rank in the judiciary. At that moment what is entrusted to the judge from the judgment in this case will be according to the rank of the judge. By what power and by what faculty and art a person becomes judge between two opponents by means of rhetoric is what we must summarize later.

Of the things that constitute persuasion, we have enthymemes and examples. The status of the enthymemes in rhetoric is similar to the status of proofs in the sciences and syllogisms in dialectic. The enthymeme is a rhetorical syllogism and the example is a rhetorical induction.

The enthymeme is a proposition composed of two conjoined premises and gives us by itself, first according to the apparent point of view, persuasion about the conclusion resulting from the premises. It becomes persuasive since the speaker hides one of the two premises and does not state it. For this reason, it is called the enthymeme or that which is hidden, since the fact of hiding one of its two premises has been the reason for making it persuasive.

258a This is why we do not call enthymemes the dialectical proofs and syllogisms when they are used in correspondences and letters; most of the time, one of the two premises is omitted for the sake of brevity or because what is omitted is apparent to the listener.

There is also the moral excellence of the speaker and the faulty character of the opponent standing against him. This is one of the things that cause belief in the words of the speaker. It helps achieve excellent persuasion even if the speaker does not use with it enthymemes or examples or any other thing, except that he gives pure and simple information about the issue, after he has established himself a good reputation of moral excellence among his audience, and his opponent has been exposed for his lack of moral excellence. If he uses enthymemes and examples with moral excellence, his words will be more persuasive and more acceptable to his audience. If his moral excellence is not well established, he will need arguments to show his superior moral character and the lack of moral excellence in his opponent, and he will also need to present the thing by means of which he aims to persuade his audience.

People often make mistakes and use all this in the sciences, especially when they oppose their opponents in their points of view, as Galen did when he wanted to refute the views of his adversaries. He proceeded by showing the superiority of his moral character over the character of his adversaries in the matter about which he was contradicting them.

The orator may also seek to show the superiority of his moral character and the faulty character of his adversaries, not in the matter about which he is speaking, but he shows his superior moral character and the faulty character of his adversaries in other things that are outside of the matter about which they are discoursing, as Galen did when he showed his superior moral character by talking about the excellent moral character of his father and his country and the lack of moral excellence in his opponents by mentioning the lack of moral excellence in their ancestors
258b and countries. In fact, he mentioned this in the book *Ḥīlatu al-Bar'*,[12]

12. The reference is most likely to *Ars Medica*, one of Galen's major medical works translated into Arabic by the physician and translator of Greek medical works Ḥunain ibn Isḥāq (809–73). On Galen and Menodotus of Nicomedia, see V. Boudon, ed.,

when he refuted Thales the doctor by evoking the disreputable character of his father's profession. Also, in the last book of his treatise regarding the views of Hippocrates and Plato, he refuted "Mendaberius,"[13] who had critiqued something from his treatise. He showed the disreputable moral character of "Mendaberius" by saying that he grew up in a village far from the big cities, whereas he showed his superior moral character by saying that he lived in Greater Rome, which, as many poets had said, was the microcosm.

There is also the appeal to the emotions of the audience, whose hearts lean toward believing the speaker and not his opponent. From there comes the appeal to the judge and the audience to be in favor of the speaker and not the adversary. From there also comes the attempt to firmly implant in the soul of the opponent an emotion that will weaken his stance against the speaker and his opposition to him, such as a burst of anger that will distract him. From there, finally, comes the speaker's effort to influence the soul of the listener he aims to persuade by provoking some emotions so that the listener is persuaded, such as flattery, anger, pity, cruelty, or any other emotion that the speaker believes will succeed at that time.

This type of mode of persuasion is more effective in reinforcing views and arguments in the souls of the listeners, in producing enthusiasm and fanaticism, and in making the character and views of the speaker more imposing, to the degree that the souls of the listeners will yield. The views that the speaker will advance will assert themselves to the point that they reach the degree of certitude.

This type is oratorical, but it may also be used in sophistic discourses. The dialecticians themselves may have used it, either by mistake on their part or by sophism.

There is also the stirring of the audience and the incitement of their **259a**
points of view so that they believe what [the speaker] says by moral propositions. These are arguments that urge them to follow certain moral values, even if they do not have such values, [and] that make them identify with those who know and emulate the acts of virtuous and knowledgeable people, even if they do not possess any of those things. This type is

---

Galien, Tome II: Exhortation à l' Étude de la Médecine; Art Médical (Paris: Les Belles Lettres, 2000). On the life and works of Ḥunain ibn Isḥāq, see Max Meyerhof, "New Light on Ḥunain Ibn Isḥāq and His Period," *Isis* 8, no. 4 (1926): 685–724.

13. Most likely empiricist physician Menodotus of Nicomedia.

oratorical. It may be used in sophistic discourses, and it is never used in dialectic, except by mistake or by sophism. Galen has often used it when he says, "Only those who are clever and favor the truth can understand my discourse, appreciate it, and accept it; those who have never been inclined by nature to follow any whims; those whose minds have not been corrupt[ed] by false views and other such arguments." We find this kind of discourse in speeches addressed to the public and in books written by several ancient and modern scholars.

There is also the amplification of the issue, or its diminution, or its embellishment, or its defamation. If the speaker glorifies what is true and good in his speech and belittles what is false and bad, and if he magnifies what is false and bad in the discourse of his opponents, his argument will be well received, and that of his opponents will be rejected. This mode is used in sophistic. In dialectic, it is used by mistake or by sophism.

There is also the falsification and distortion of the opponent's argument to make it appear offensive and easy to refute, such as when a speaker distorts several of his opponent's arguments and renders them null and void, or when he smoothly slips the opponent's arguments into
259b the places where they are allowed to be. This mode [of persuasion] is also powerful in reinforcing points of view, especially when emotions, such as fanaticism and zeal, and sympathy and love, are detrimental.

There is also the use of written statutes that one cites as pieces of evidence. A person in whose favor these statutes are introduced needs to buttress them, whereas his adversary needs to show, if he can, that they are forged or interpret them to the advantage of his own arguments. As to the use of these citations by a speaker to support his claim, you will find it more in the books of many of those who turned to the sciences incorrectly or to multiply their proofs, as Galen did when he attempted to show that the sensual appetites were in the liver and based his claim on the fact that there was a custom instituted in their country to punish the lecherous by removing his liver, and also as some ancients did when they attempted to prove that the soul never died and that it continued to live after it left the body because there was a custom that allowed the visitation of tombs.

There are also witnesses, as when a person takes as a witness another person whose words he trusts, or a group of people he trusts, whenever they give their testimony or when the things they are supposed to say buttress his argument and prove the arguments of his adversary wrong.

Galen maintained, in his book *Akhlāq al-Nafs*,[14] that reason was in the brain, using as evidence the expression people use when they refer to an idiot by saying, "He is brainless." [Galen] also argued that courage was in the heart, using [as evidence] the expression people employed when they described someone as a coward [by saying], "He has no heart."

There are [also] the speaker's desire and fear. A speaker's desire for [something] good manifests itself if he says the truth; his fear of [something] evil manifests itself if he tells lies. And if it is known that he fears something evil for getting caught telling a lie and says something, his words will be truthful, as when someone confesses under torture. He says **260a**
the truth to get rid of that evil, for fear that if he is found out telling a lie, he will be put under torture again. Also, if he expects something good for telling the truth, he will tell the truth. Also, if he wishes something good and changes his words, or fears something evil will befall him if he keeps his words, and does not change his words and we see that he keeps those words, we will think that he is sincere. Also, if a person is threatened that some grave evil will befall him for making a statement and endures the evil that will befall him and makes that statement, we will think he is sincere. Also, if he wishes some great good on the condition that he says something and remains silent about something, and scorns that good and does not remain silent, or says something that contradicts his first statement, his words will be more acceptable to his audience. Also, if he makes a statement from which he does not draw any benefit and prefers it to an opposite statement in which there is benefit, he will be more persuasive in the eyes of his audience.

There is also challenge in the form of pledges and contracts. Galen said that he pledged ten thousand dinars to anyone who would show him by way of dissection that the nerve principle was in the heart. There is also the speaker's oath when making a statement.

There is also the person's facial expression, or appearance, or the shape and look of his body, or what he does when he speaks, as when he announces a terrible thing approaching and shows the face of someone terrified and fleeing, or when he recommends something and he himself does what he recommends to someone else. This will show that he is

14. The reference is most likely to the Arabic translation of *Kitāb al-Akhlāq* (*Book of Moral Characteristics*), a treatise attributed to Galen. Ibn al-Nadīm indicates that the Arabic translation was done by ibn Hubaysh.

260b sincere. This type is used with discourses on virtue and vice. The facial expression, the appearances, the shape, and the action suggest a state that makes the statement credible and also suggest in his adversary a state that makes the statement rejected.

Finally, there is the manner of speaking, the voice quality, and intonation, which suggest the matter about which there is discourse, as when a person speaks of tragedies that have befallen him and uses a tone showing that he is moved, or when he threatens a person and uses a tone showing that he is angry.

But enthymemes and examples are primary rhetorical modes of discourse, for they are the first to produce persuasion. They come, by far, before the other persuasive types, for they are rhetorical. The son of Nicomachus calls the other types extrinsic persuasive types.[15] Enthymemes and examples are by far nobler, for they alone constitute the art of rhetoric. But the other extrinsic modes alone do not constitute an art, for they are used as accessories to enthymemes and examples and as means of display.

Of the emotions, some cut the adversary short and buttress the enthymeme and example, such as shyness, the inability to express oneself effectively, and fear. As to the judge, they make him lean toward one of the opponents, and this happens either through incitement or intimidation, or prejudice, or love, or other emotions. For this reason, the emotions need to support the enthymemes and examples when they do not effectively persuade an adversary.

261a [Aristotle] says that some orators in some nations did not allow the use of nonessential things in speeches and thought that only enthymemes and examples were permitted in speeches. He himself thinks that they are permitted. It is not necessary to draw conclusions from things outside the enthymemes and examples, only if we get them by chance and second intention.

Enthymemes and examples are syllogisms from which we draw conclusions the same way we draw necessary conclusions from syllogisms themselves, except when they depend on an a priori known point of view, since all people believe that nonessential things can only be persuasive. Some people have wanted to stop using examples and use enthymemes only. But it is absolutely not possible to cancel enthymemes, because if

15. "The son of Nicomachus" is a reference to Aristotle.

they are canceled, they are only canceled by enthymemes—that is, by themselves—and that is impossible.

We must explain enthymemes and examples and discuss each one of them—that is, their condition and general composition, the number of types of each, and the composition of each type, and the manner in which they are used.

Enthymemes come before examples, since examples are established by enthymemes. Examples are also closer to syllogisms and more necessary with regard to drawing conclusions from them. This is also evident in *Kitāb al-Qiyās* (*Prior Analytics*).[16]

Some people have considered examples weak; others in both ancient and modern times have considered the use of examples null. In fact, those among the theologians and dialecticians who are known today as "those who eliminate the syllogism" are only those who consider the use of examples null. They only use the term syllogism to refer to examples, and by that **261b**
term they mean examples because of the resemblance in meaning. For the public, the term means, first, comparison between two quantities so that one knows if [the two quantities] are equal or if one [quantity] is superior to the other, and [if the latter,] which of the two [quantities] is greater than the other; [the term] also means comparison between two other things so that one sees which one is better, or stronger, or any other thing—that is, anything else where it is possible to see which one is better. That is why, whenever exemplification between two things was closer to comparison between two quantities, the term syllogism was more appropriate.

However, logicians use this term to indicate joint premises that have necessary conclusions, whether they are attributive, conditional, or proceeding by the absurd. They call it syllogism, excluding induction and comparison. For them, enthymemes are worthier of the term syllogism than the term comparison, contrary to what the public and many dialecticians believe. They also call sophistic arguments syllogisms, not in an absolute manner, but they call sophistic arguments sophistic syllogisms and they call the enthymemes rhetorical syllogisms. As to the term syllogism, they, in an absolute manner, use it to refer to a statement from which a conclusion is necessarily derived.

Enthymemes consist of real syllogisms and apparent syllogisms. Enthymemes, in the immediate common sense, are syllogisms, and the

16. *Prior Analytics* is known in the Muslim philosophical tradition as *Kitāb al-Qiyās*.

262a common sense is a point of view that has not been examined. However, if the use of points of view of common sense were imperative as a condition of rhetoric, we should not trouble ourselves if the enthymemes were real syllogisms or not, provided that they were arguments, joined either by force or by act, and persuasive to everyone.

The first divisions of enthymemes are the same as the first divisions of syllogisms, because they are attributive or conditional. They must also be persuasive in substance and form; the same thing goes with the quantity of each one of them, its arrangement, and its quality, following the example of syllogisms mentioned in *Kitāb al-Qiyās* (*Prior Analytics*).

Every syllogism is composed of two premises, not more, not less; their conjunction is that they have one element in common, and their arrangement is that one of them is minor and the other one is major. One of them gives the syllogism the property by which a conclusion is necessarily drawn. The other one acts as a link between the conclusion and the one that makes the conclusion necessary. The quantity of each is that it is universal or particular. The quality of each is that it is affirmative or negative. As to the materials of these, they are the existing matters about which and in which there are issues. If they are joined, they become premises. Necessary premises have the highest degree of confidence in their being. Possible premises are the most inconsistent. Those indeterminate are between the two. For this reason, some of them are known with certitude; others are objects of opinion; and others are felt. Those that are known have the highest degree in comprehension; those that are objects of opinion are the most inconsistent in comprehension; those that are felt are between the two. It follows that the certitude we
262b have of something felt lasts only as long as we feel that thing. When it disappears from our senses, we do not know if it is still in the state [in which] we have felt it or not. Of premises, some are entirely true or entirely false. Some are partly false and partly true. Of these in particular, there are premises the biggest part of which is false; there are also premises the biggest part of which is true; and there are premises whose parts are equally true or false.

Then, after this, premises are distinguished from one another according to the ten different genera in which and by which issues exist, and according to the different types of each of these genera. For example, there are premises in which each of the two parts is in the essence, as when we say, "Man is an animal." There are those in which each of the two parts is in the quantity, as when we say, "These surfaces are of the number of ten." There are those in which each of the two parts is in the quality, as when we say, "Every square is a shape." The same thing goes with the other categories. Some of them happen to have one of the two parts under one category and the other part under another category, as when we say, "Man is white."

Also, premises differ according to the different arts that contain each particular type among the types of beings. These are types of materials of enthymemes and of syllogisms in general.

Enthymemes produce persuasion by their forms and by their materials. They become persuasive when there remains in them a point of opposition; and when there is no point of opposition, they are outside of the limit of persuasion, of its rank, and they enter the rank and bounds of certitude.

Attributive enthymemes enter the bounds of persuasion only when we consider first the attributive syllogisms, which are in truth syllogisms, and when we know from each one of them the premises that give them the necessity in the consequences of their conclusion, and those from **263a**
which it was evident in the first place that they produced necessity, as in the first of attributive forms, which were deleted, hidden, and from which only those that established conjunction between them and the conclusion were declared. For example, the universal major premises in the modes of the first form clearly give the necessity of the consequence of their conclusions. In the syllogisms of the first form, if we want to make them enthymemes, we ought to delete the major premise and hide it, and we declare the minor premise only. If we think that we ought to declare it sometimes, we take it in an indeterminate manner.

This is one of the ways in which syllogisms become persuasive from their forms: either, first, in the proposition there remains a place for opposition as to the necessity of the conclusion, and this happens only when the premises that give necessity are not declared, and if they are declared, they are not declared in the state by which the premise is essentially made necessary in its consequence; or, second, the proposition is probably untrue, its untruth being evidently clear, and the hearer feels it is false and the persuasion of the argument ceases. If the speaker keeps quiet about it, his silence gives the illusion that he is quiet about it only because it is evidently true. If it is true, he does not believe that it is partly true only; and if the speaker has to declare it, it is mentioned in an indeterminate manner. An indeterminate premise takes the place, in the immediate common sense of the public, of a universal premise, and the object of untruth in it is concealed, and it becomes persuasive since a point of opposition remains in it.

But in the syllogisms of the other forms, the places of the necessary
263b premises in each of their modes are hidden; however, it never happens that the major premises are necessary, but it may happen that the minor premises give the necessity in the consequence of the conclusion. There is no harm to declare in them the two premises after they have been rendered indeterminate, so that there remains in the composition the place of opposition. If we keep quiet about the necessary premises and mention the other ones in an indeterminate manner, they become more hidden and there can be opposition.

But if we declare all the premises, make the necessary one universal, and fulfill in each one of them the conditions of the syllogism, we will move from the degree of persuasion to the degree of certitude, and there will not be a place for opposition in their forms. However, persuasion ceases in another way—namely, when we suspect that the person using it has won, not by means of rhetoric, but by a logical art by which he has carried out an investigation about the discourse, or by a different art, not by the ability to use well the method that he shares with all speakers addressing their discourses to him and with all his adversaries. When a person is believed to have won because he has gotten into an art other than the art that is common to him and his adversaries, his discourse is not persuasive by the fact that we think that the thing by which he achieves persuasion is not the force of the matter or the propositions that he uses in his discourse, but by a superior force that he has acquired from another art, as two wrestlers, when one of them uses against the other, in addition to his strength, a weapon or other means that his adversary does not match. This shows that he is weak in this art or that he does not belong to the category of wrestlers. So it is with two persons involved in a dispute by common means.

Then, after this, we examine the modes of conjunction that are not
264a syllogistic, and we distinguish what we consider from its appearance a syllogism and use it. Thus there is the conjunction mode whose premises are all positive in the second mode. At first glance, it appears like a syllogism whose premises we have declared, whether these have been taken as universal or whether they have been put as indeterminate. If one of them has been deleted and the other one has been mentioned in an

indeterminate mode, the matter of falsification is more concealed, and in truth there will be more places of opposition in it. There are also the universal syllogistic modes of the third form; their conclusions must be taken universally. And even if they are syllogistic, they produce not universal conclusions, but particular ones. Therefore, they are not syllogistic with regard to the conclusions that are put for it in this art, and which are the universal conclusions. Their premises must be taken as indeterminate so that the place of opposition in them may be hidden a little. And there are also the nonsyllogistic modes, one of whose premises is positive and the other negative, when one of them is universal. For example, A contains all B, and B contains nothing of C; this does not necessarily produce that A is not in C, although A may not be in C. But if we reverse the premises entirely, the result is [that] C is not in A. For this reason, we can induce in error in this manner and make believe that we can deduce [that] A is not in C, except that this is an imperceptible means of persuasion, and therefore it is almost never used.

How are conditional enthymemes composed? And what are the ways in which they become persuasive, given that some of their forms are conjunctive and others disjunctive? Conjunctive enthymemes become persuasive only when we declare those that are conditional in them and
hide those that are objects of exception. Then we give the conclusion. **264b**
The conclusion of the conditional conjunctive in this art may be opposite to what is subsequent and it may be opposite to the antecedent, and this is according to what the speaker considers more useful for him; by keeping quiet about what is the object of exception, he hides the place of sophism in all these conclusions. That is, he is almost not aware, in the a priori point of view or with respect to the audience, of the manner in which he will need to use exception or of which exception produces which conclusion. All these are hidden from the public.

If the conclusion is opposite to what is subsequent, the minor [which is the object of exception] is opposite to the antecedent. This composition produces a conclusion in appearance, not in truth. If we declare that which is an object of exception, we are not sure that the listener is aware of it, and there will be no persuasion; that is why we must keep quiet about it and hide it. If the conclusion is the antecedent itself, we will only think that this comes from the fact that what is subsequent has been an object of exception as it is put. This in truth does not produce a conclusion. This composition is rarely used, and when it is used and the speaker prefers to

give it a persuasive force, in this case he must hide the object of exception so that we do not feel its bad composition, and its persuasive force fails. If the conclusion is opposite to the antecedent, it is clear that what is an object of exception is the opposite of what is subsequent. This composition is correct, but it becomes persuasive only when what is an object of exception is deleted. Here, if we declare what is an object of exception, we must keep quiet about the conditional so that there remains in it a place for opposition or interrogation. If the conclusion is what is subsequent, what is an object of exception is the antecedent. This composition is also sound, except that what is an object of exception in this is put in a manner that is not clear, and it will need clarification. If we declare it, we are not sure that we are aware of the fact that it is hidden, and the persuasive
265a force of the syllogism will cease, and then we must hide it also. Or else what is an object of exception is put in a manner that is not clear, and to make the conclusion sound, we will need to clarify what is an object of exception; if we do not do that, the conclusion is not sound. Aristotle explained this [point] in *Kitāb al-Qiyās* (*Prior Analytics*).

In sum, we delete only that which is apparent and declared. And to give it a sound composition, we will need a logical art so that this composition is made valid. We do not have recourse to a logical art for what has been deleted for the sake of brevity and concision. That is the reason why the major premise in the first of the attributive forms must be deleted, and the reason why the minor premise in the conditional conjunctive must be deleted, these two reasons being one and the same thing.

The conditional conjunctive premises are, in this art, used more in oppositions when we seek to refute the statements of the adversary.

As to the conditional subjunctives that we use by way of division, we normally do not delete anything from them, neither the conditional disjunctive nor that which is the object of exception. But if it is agreed that the oppositions in them are more than two, it is possible that the speaker has not treated exhaustively, at their division, all their kinds, and there remains in it for the adversary a place to speak. It is probable that the speaker has not treated exhaustively, in addition to that, the exception of all the oppositions, but makes an exception of some rather than others. Then there will also be for the adversary in what is an object of exception a place to speak.

If we limit ourselves to conditional premises only, our statement will not be persuasive; the statement will be an object of inquiry or a doubtful statement that does not have a solid point of view. If the oppositions are fulfilled in this conditional premise, and the exception is fulfilled in anything that truly needs to be made an exception, no place of opposition in it on the part of composition will appear. We will then look for opposition on the part of the material.

Perhaps one limits oneself in this mode to the conditional premise **265b**
and conceals the other. And the conclusion will help us understand what an object of exception is when it is very clear, or when there are things present, either for the senses or for the mind. The conclusion is as when the speaker says, "One of us," with the purpose of misleading the opponent. The force of this statement is similar to the force of this other statement: "The person at fault is either myself or this one. The person at fault is not myself. Therefore, the person at fault is this one." Statements such as these are used in allusions.

The matter may become problematic unless it is made clear in what is an object of exception. Therefore, it must be fulfilled, except when what is an object of exception is very clear. If a person is sometimes obliged to do that, he will have to declare what is made an exception or the conclusion, so that we know what the object of exception must be.

As to the mode in which the conditional disjunctives are used in the negative, as when we say, "Zayd is not in Iraq since he is in Syria," the situation is the same as in the conditional conjunctive, as in most cases we are limited to the conditional premise only, and we hide the one that is an object of exception, because the one that is an object of exception may render invalid necessity, which is at first sight necessity in the conclusion. That is why we pass over it in silence, so that the listener is not aware of it. If that which is an object of exception is made the opposite of any one of them, the conclusion will not follow necessarily, or at first sight, in which case we must hide that which is an object of exception. If the speaker seeks to draw the consequence or the antecedent, he will draw that only if he makes an exception of the opposite of the other. If we have that in mind, we must not limit ourselves to the conditional,
but we must declare it in the conclusion and hide that which is an object **266a**
of exception. Or else there will be no persuasion, since it will be up to the listener to make an exception from what you have provided of the thing that will render your conclusion null and void; or the listener does not know the conclusion you want to draw, since it is possible for him to suspect that you have hidden that which is an object of exception that

leads to a conclusion other than the conclusion you wanted to draw, and your statement is from the very beginning problematic, and the force of its persuasion fails. But if someone wants to draw a conclusion contrary to one of them, he will draw that conclusion only by making an exception and state the conclusion. His statement will then become more concise. And its force will be the force of what is in truth a syllogism, since it can demand a mode of constraint.

Everything that persuades and has in it a place for opposition, or interrogation, or inquiry is more appropriate to rhetoric. And so is the case with the conditional conjunctive, if we change it and put it into the negative, as when we say, "There is no day; or the sun rises"; and "There is no sole; or there is leather"; and "This human being is not a man without being an animal"; and "Zayd will not go until ᶜAmr speaks." These and similar propositions stem from conditional conjunctive statements. The error is often made in what should be made an exception in such examples and in what the conclusions should be in truth. The conclusions drawn at first sight from these propositions may be the thing and its opposite, whether it is an antecedent or a consequence. The speaker must put as a conclusion, in such examples, what he thinks is not acknowledged, and he must be careful not to declare that which is the object of exception, especially if the fact of declaring that which is the object of exception shows a flaw in the composition, and eliminate the necessity of the consequence.

266b Such conditional propositions may be used in the form of the predicative or in the form of the imperative, as when we say, "Zayd, don't go without ᶜAmr speaking."

As to conditional disjunctives, we more often must not fulfill all the parts of their oppositions; rather, we must limit ourselves to those that are more apparent and leave those that are more hidden; then we will see which of their parts alerts the listener to the place of opposition in the conclusion or in the composition of the speech and make sure not to declare it.

As to the absurd syllogism, it is more often used to make statements and oppositions invalid, as when we say, "If every human is not sensitive, then every animal is not sensitive, which is absurd." In an absurd syllogism, we must declare the position, which is the thing that we doubt, then the absurd that results from it, and we hide the true premise, which is added to that which we doubt. The speaker may be obliged to state the true premise when the constraint is not apparent. He must put that statement at the end of his speech, as when we say, "If every human is not sensitive, then every animal is not sensitive, since a human is an animal; and that is absurd."

Then we show how persuasion works from the part of its materials. **267a**
Since the premises, the property of which is to give statements correct binding conclusions from them, are more dominant in a speech than the rest of premises and must be given more attention, and since the other premises are meant to give up their property of being tangible, or certain, complete, or persuasive, the persuasion that the enthymeme acquires from the part of its materials must come from the fact that the premises that give the necessity of consequence are first. If such is the case, the premises of enthymemes whose role is to give them correct binding conclusions drawn from them must be universally known in the a priori point of view common to all. We have already explained the meaning of the a priori point of view.

These premises include those that are in truth universally known, those that are universally known in appearance only and not in reality. Universally known premises include those that are true and those that are not true. But if rhetoric uses them, it does not use them because they are true; if such is the case, it will use true premises that are not universally known when it finds them. But it does not do that; it rejects premises that are certain if they are not universally known. Also, if rhetoric uses universally known premises that are in truth universally known, it does not use them because they are in truth universally known, the way the art of dialectic does, but because they are at first sight universally known to all, and it is agreed that they are in truth universally known premises. Also, when [rhetoric] uses premises that are universally known in appearance only, it does not use them as they are, the way sophism does it, but as they are universally known, in the immediate point of view known to all, and as it is agreed that they are universally known in appearance. It may be agreed that these premises include several other premises that are true and certain; they may also include premises that are totally true or partially true, presumed or known, necessary, absolute or possible; **267b**
they may also include premises that are concerned with mathematics, or natural sciences, or any other arts, theoretical or practical. But this art [of rhetoric] does not use any type of premises because they are of such type, but because they are universally known in the immediate point of view. But some of them are marked by these other qualities.

As to premises that are universally known in the immediate point of view, some are commonplaces and others are types. The commonplaces are premises whose parts we use as major premises in each particular syllogism. The types are used [as a whole] as major premises in each particular syllogism. The types are the ones that are used as they are, as major premises in each syllogism in particular. In the commonplaces, there is nothing particular to a being at the expense of another being, or a species at the expense of another species, or a science at the expense of another science. Each one of them is common to numerous sciences and numerous species. They also include categories of particular cases, each category being particular to a species at the expense of other species, or a science at the expense of other sciences. As to the species, each one of them is appropriate to a particular syllogism and a particular enthymeme. And each of their categories is appropriate to a particular species at the expense of other species or a particular science at the expense of other sciences.

There are two sorts of particular premises of commonplaces: in one, the predicate is particular to the predicate of commonplace, and its subject is particular to the subject of commonplace; in the second one, the predicate is particular to the predicate of commonplace, and its subject
268a is itself the subject of commonplace. As to the premise whose subject is particular to the subject of commonplace and its predicate is itself the predicate of commonplace, it is not considered in the force of commonplace or in its parts. But it is the conclusion resulting from a syllogism whose major premise is put as the commonplace itself, and its minor premise is composed of (*a*) the subject of the premise, which is particular to the subject of commonplace, and (*b*) the subject of commonplace. The subject of commonplace is then the medium limit.

As to the types, some are preferences or laudable things in the immediate point of view, and second, essential things and signs in the immediate point of view common to all. Their subjects are universal meanings in which we find something existing for another thing, or not existing for it with absolutely no condition, and they are also taken in an indeterminate manner. Those in which there is something existing or not existing at the most in the future show that they produce probable conclusions when they are taken as major premises. As to laudable things in which something is taken as existing for another thing, or not existing for it absolutely and with no condition, they are taken in an indeterminate manner and as universal premises. Among them are those whose individual subjects are tangible and natural and those whose individual subjects are intentional. As to those whose individual subjects are tangible, what the sense corrects is true. And when nothing but the fact of being universally known holds the proposition that is universally known, that proposition is probable, and the syllogisms resulting from it produce probable conclusions. If it is agreed that it is certain, and nobody is aware of that, its certainty is then accidental. This is why [Aristotle] stipulated in *Kitāb al-Burhān* (*Posterior Analytics*) that certitude must be certain in a manner that is not accidental.

The proof and the sign have this in common: each one of them, by its **268b**
existence, necessarily causes the existence of the other. When the thing by whose existence the predicate is in a subject is more general or more particular than the predicate and the subject altogether, it is called a sign. And when the thing is more general than the subject and more particular than the predicate or equal to it, it is called proof.

The proof is composed in the first form only.

There are two types of signs. The first is one in which the common term is more general than the predicate and the subject. The second is one in which the common term is more particular than the predicate and the subject. The one whose common term is more general than the two extremes is composed in the second form and cannot be taken back to the first form, because if it is taken back by conversion, the one of the two that is converted will have its predicate equal to its subject, and it will not be more general than each of the two extremes. It will be converted only if it is in one of the two modes: either one or both premises are universal positive premises whose subject is equal to the predicate, or they are universal negative premises. If we put the medium term as more general than the two extremes, there is not one of the two premises, whether they are universal negatives or positives whose predicate is equal to its subject.

As to the second type of sign, it is one whose common term is more particular than the two extremes. It is necessarily composed in the third form. The more general and the more particular make believe, apparently by their existence, the existence of the predicate and the subject, without this being the case. This is due to the fact that the composition of the more general is absolutely not syllogistic in truth, neither according to the
conclusion nor according to another. As to the composition of the more **269a**
particular, even if it is a syllogistic composition, it is still not a syllogism

on the thing for which it has been made a sign as it has been made, even if it is syllogistic and produces something different, because it has been made a sign only for the existence of something in every matter. There is nothing in the modes of the third form that absolutely produces a universal conclusion.

But that which is more general than the subject and more particular than the predicate or equal to it is sound proof, since its composition is a syllogistic composition and it is also a syllogism based on the thing for which it has been made proof. Proof whose composition is correct is of two types. The first type deals with the thing by whose existence something exists, and by whose suppression that thing is eliminated, or the thing by whose existence something exists, as predicate in a subject, and by whose suppression that thing is eliminated from that subject. This proof is the proof of equality.

The second type deals with the thing by whose existence something exists and by whose suppression that thing is not eliminated, or the thing by whose existence something exists as predicate in a subject, and by whose suppression that predicate is not eliminated from that thing; this proof is the more particular proof. Both proofs are authentic.

The most authentic proof is one by whose existence something must necessarily exist, wherever that is, and in whatever subject that is, and at whatever moment that is. Then there is also the thing by whose existence something exists, either in the largest number of things about which we use proof or at most times when we use proof.

After these two types of proofs also comes the proof by whose existence something must necessarily exist, and by whose existence also the opposite of that thing must necessarily exist, to the extent that this first thing is proof for both the thing and its opposite. It is not improper that what proves one of the two opposites more firmly than what proves the
269b other opposite, or what proves both in an equal manner, belongs to this category. All these proofs are composed in the first form in a syllogistic manner, except that the weakness found in this syllogism comes from its material, not from its composition.

The proof and the sign are said in the first place about this only thing whose business is to make a medium term. But the thing that by the existence of proof must itself exist, either absolutely or in a given subject, is what is proved. It is the major term in any form and any mode. The same thing goes with the sign and with the thing for which a sign is a sign. The sign is the medium term. The thing for which or about which there is a sign is the major term in any mode or any form it can be.

Proof varies according to things. Thus proof may be taken as a thing that comes after what is proved, the way things tied to causes prove the causes. Those that come from causes or are tied to causes can be proofs of those causes.

There are three types of universally known causes: the agent, the material, and the purpose. Form is also one of the causes, except that it is not universally known. What exists by the agent is proof, just as art proves the artist. And the state of an effect indicates the state of its agent. The effect of a material indicates its material. What we see in the state of fabric indicates the material of the yarn—that is, what type of yarn it is and what type of material. It also indicates the state of the person who has woven it. All in all, the effects of materials indicate their agents and their materials.

Also, several things indicate their ends—what ends have been assigned **270a**
to them—and their consequences, what the consequence is.

The types of proofs are according to the types of causes, as when the rain is proof that there are clouds, and when smoke and combustion sensed are proof that there is fire, even if we do not see it.

The proof may come before what is proved, the way the causes of things come before the things themselves. The causes of things may indicate the things also, as when the fire indicates that there is something burning in the place where we see fire, if we do not see the burning. It may also be attached to what is proved, occurring neither after it nor before it, being neither a cause for it nor something resulting from it, as when the dark cloud indicates that there is rain. The darkness of the cloud is not a cause of the rain; it is an accident in a rainy cloud, either permanently or more often.

After this, the premise that is composed of proof and of what is proved is also called proof, as when we say, "Where there is smoke, there is fire," or "Where there is fire, there is burning." After this also, the syllogism whose major premise is this premise and whose minor premise is its connection is also called proof. The conclusion from this syllogism is what is proved. Likewise, we use the term sign first to refer to that common term that is more general and more particular than the two extremities, and we use the term "that which is known by the sign" to refer to that which makes that medium term a sign of the two extremities. Then we

also call sign the premise that is constituted from that medium term and
270b from the thing that is known by that sign. A syllogism whose medium term is a sign is also called a sign.

It is plain that all these are proofs in the immediate point of view. Whatever has been in this way, it is possible that it is not real proof, or that it is real proof but that we are not aware that it is so, if it is taken according to the manner in which it is universally known only. They give us from what is proved an opinion, and by these the enthymemes are persuasive.

Comparison is persuading a person that something exists for a particular matter, because of the existence of that thing in a similar matter, when its existence in something similar is known more than its existence in the matter itself. It is evident, based on the previous condition, that the thing similar must be a thing similar in the immediate point of view of all. Also, we must declare the thing similar and hide the thing by which the two things resemble each other, and it must not be declared, only if necessary, either because it is very much hidden or because of trouble caused by the opponent who will deny the resemblance between the two matters.

Resemblance may be in the words or in the form of the words only, or it can be in the meaning. Resemblance in the meaning happens when two things share one meaning that is common to them, either by accident or by something else. Or when the two matters are attributed to one thing or to two similar things; that is, either their attribution to one thing is one, or the attribution of one of the two to another thing is similar to the attribution of the other to another thing. Each of the two bears a close or remote resemblance, as with Zayd and ʿAmr. The two men resemble one another by human, animal, and physical characteristics. If we find something in one of the two matters, we must find that same thing in the
271a other matter. The most powerful resemblance is that in which we find that thing in one of the two matters through the meaning by which it resembles the other, considering that the thing exists for that meaning, either entirely or in a greater part; if such is the case, comparison is almost an enthymeme or a syllogism, and it gets out of the definition of comparison.

Moreover, if the second thing resembles the first thing by any meaning that can make two things similar, even if that element does not exist in the first thing from the part of that meaning, if this mode is not very much hidden in the comparison, the places of opposition in it become numerous.

In addition to this, there is resemblance of two things in the words. The speaker must especially choose what will conceal his matter from the audience. All these are modes of persuasion, and they are used in rhetoric.

As to the composition of comparison, it is first attributive, since its force is the force of an attributive syllogism, as has been explained in *Kitāb al-Qiyās* (*Prior Analytics*). It also happens that the person using it constructs it by way of a conjunctive conditional, but most of what is used based on the form of the conjunctive conditional is used in opposition, refutation, and blame; in the affirmative mode, the composition of comparison is very often made attributive.

As to the premises of comparison, when attributive, if the thing by which two things resemble one another is apparent, we must declare the model, follow it by the conclusion, and hide the resemblance. If the resemblance is not apparent, then we must declare it. When we declare the resemblance, three premises follow as a result. One takes for a subject the subject of the second one itself, and that is the first thing. Its predicate **271b** is the predicate of the conclusion. The second one takes for a predicate the thing by which two things resemble each other; and the third one takes for a predicate that thing itself and for a subject the second thing.

End of the *Book of Rhetoric*

Praise be to Allah, truly.

2. Avicenna's *Compendium, or Al-ᶜArūdī's Philosophical Treatise on the Meanings of the Book of Rhetoric*

Avicenna (980–1037)

The biographical information that we have available about Abū ᶜAli ibn Sīnā, known in the West as Avicenna, comes from an autobiographical note that the Persian philosopher himself dictated to his disciple Abū ᶜUbaid al-Juzjānī, who later took up his master's story and recorded the episodes of the philosopher's life up to the time of his death. We find this autobiographical note in al-Qifṭī's *Ikhbār al-ᶜUlamā' bi-Akhbār al-Ḥukamā'*,[1] edited by Muḥammad Amīn al-Khā'ijī in 1906. Al-Khā'ijī's edition was based on Julius Lippert's 1903 edition. However, Lippert's edition bears the name Ibn al-Qifṭī and the title *Tā'rīkh al-Ḥukamā'* (*History of Philosophers*). We find a similar biographical note about Ibn Sīnā in Ibn Abī Uṣaibiᶜa's *ᶜUyūn al-Anbā' fī Ṭabaqāti al-Aṭibbā'* (*Essential Information about the Generations of Physicians*). Al-Qifṭī (1172–1248) and Ibn Abī Uṣaibiᶜa (1203–70) were well-known and reliable Arab historians in the history of Islamic culture. William Gohlman has made available a helpful critical edition and annotated English translation of this autobiographical note, and L. E. Goodman and Soheil Afnan have provided very helpful biographical accounts, mostly based on Avicenna's autobiography and what al-Juzjānī wrote about his master.[2]

1. For a full biographical account, see Jamāl al-Dīn al-Qifṭī, *Ikhbār al-ᶜUlamā' bi-Akhbār al-Ḥukamā'* [History of philosophers], ed. Muḥammad Amīn al-Khā'ijī (Cairo, Egypt: Dār al-Kutub al-Khaddīwiyya, 1906), 313–25.

2. William Gohlman, *The Life of Ibn Sina: A Critical Edition and Annotated Translation*

According to these accounts, Avicenna was born in a village near Bukhara, in Persia, in 980. His parents were of Persian origin. His father, who was a high public official, was from Balkh, an important metropolitan center that hosted diverse religious traditions and afforded a rich intellectual life. We also learn from these accounts that Avicenna was introduced to a wide range of sciences at a very young age, for he studied the Qur'an, Arabic literature, logic, the natural sciences, mathematics, medicine, and metaphysics. At age twenty-one, Avicenna wrote his first comprehensive book, which he called *Kitāb al-Majmū*ᶜ (*Compendium*). Avicenna spent all his life traveling in search of higher political recognition in the courts of Persian rulers. Afnan seems to suggest that Avicenna was suspected of Ismāᶜili leanings and that his wanderings from town to town came as a result of what he describes as "the persecution of the followers of the Ismāᶜili heterodoxy and the ruthless repression of all forms of unorthodox movement and belief."[3]

Avicenna died in 1037 at the age of fifty-eight. However, the outcome of his trips and wanderings is a rich body of publications on several subjects. Among his most influential works are *Kitāb al-Shifā'* (*Book of Healing*), *Kitāb al-Najāt* (*Book of Deliverance*), *al-Qānūn fī al-Tibb* (*Canon of Medicine*), *al-Arṣād al-Kulliya*,[4] *al-Ḥāṣil wa al-Maḥṣūl* (*The Available and the Valid*), *al-Birr wa al-Ithm* (*Piety and Sin*), *Al-Ishārāt wa al-Tanbīhāt* (*Remarks and Admonitions*), and *al-Mabda' wa al-Maᶜād* (*The Provenance and Destination*). As Richard Walzer explains in *Greek into Arabic*, Avicenna was "the most influential and most revered of all the early Muslim philosophers."[5] Most of the works in the Islamic philosophical tradition that mention Avicenna are full of praise for his exceptional intellectual ability, for, as Afnan explains, Avicenna "rendered a great service to the development of philosophical style and terminology."[6] Avicenna came after al-Kindī, al-Rāzī, and al-Fārābī—that is, at a time when a strong Islamic philosophical tradition was already established. Paying tribute to the important contribution of Avicenna, historian of Arabic

(Albany: State University of New York Press, 1974); L. E. Goodman, *Avicenna* (New York: Routledge, 1992); Soheil M. Afnan, *Avicenna: His Life and Works* (London: G. Allen & Unwin, 1958). Gohlman's annotated English translation of al-Juzjānī's *Sīrat al-Shaikh al-Ra'īs* is a very reliable source of information about Avicenna.

3. Afnan, *Avicenna*, 76.

4. The English translation of this title is unknown.

5. Richard Walzer, *Greek into Arabic: Essays on Islamic Philosophy* (Cambridge, MA: Harvard University Press, 1962), 23.

6. Afnan, *Avicenna*, 79.

philosophy Nicholas Rescher rightly calls the eleventh century the "Century of Avicenna."[7]

From the note dictated to al-Juzjānī, we learn that Avicenna, who was then twenty-one years old, was commissioned to complete a collection of summaries of some of Aristotle's treatises for his neighbor Abū al-Ḥasan al-ᶜArūḍī. One of these summaries is titled *Kitāb al-Majmūᶜ aw al-Ḥikma al-ᶜarūḍiya fī maᶜānī kitāb rīṭūrīqā* (*Al-ᶜArūḍī's Philosophical Treatise on the Meanings of the Book of Rhetoric*).[8] Avicenna explains how he came to put together his compendium:

> I had a neighbor whose name was Abū al-Ḥasan al-ᶜArūḍī. He asked me to compose for him a compendium in this science and I composed this summation, which I named after him and in which I discussed all the sciences except mathematics. I was then twenty-one years old.[9]

The summary is limited to Book I of the *Rhetoric* since, as Muḥammad Salīm Sālim explains, Muslim Arabic-speaking philosophers in general did not go deep in their examination of style in their study of Greek philosophy because of the wide linguistic and stylistic differences between Greek and Arabic. Avicenna's compendium may be broken down into the following chapters and sections.

Part One: General Principles of Oratory

1. Definition of rhetoric
2. Relationship between rhetoric and dialectic
3. The scope of rhetoric
4. Divisions of rhetoric: epideictic, deliberative, and forensic
5. The speech, the subject matter, and the audience
6. Types of listeners: the opponent, the judge, and the jury members
7. The ethical appeal
8. The emotional appeal
9. The enthymeme and the example
10. Signs and proofs

7. Nicholas Rescher, *The Development of Arabic Logic* (Pittsburgh: University of Pittsburgh Press, 1964), 50.

8. Avicenna, *Kitāb al-Majmūᶜ aw al-Ḥikma al-ᶜarūḍiya fī maᶜānī kitāb rīṭūrīqā* [Al-ᶜArūḍī's philosophical treatise on the meanings of the Book of Rhetoric], ed. Muḥammad Salīm Sālim (Cairo: Maktabat al-Nahḍa al-Miṣrya, 1950). See Jamāl al-Dīn Al-Qifṭī, *Tā'rīkh al-Ḥukamā'* [History of philosophers], ed. Julius Lippert (Leipzig, Germany: Theodor Weicher, 1903).

9. Al-Qifṭī, *Ikhbār al-ᶜUlamā' bi-Akhbār al-Ḥukamā'*, 316 (my translation).

Part Two: Rhetorical Statements in Deliberative Oratory

1. Ways and means
2. War and peace
3. Food supply
4. Income and expenditure
5. Legislation (types of government)

Part Three: The Things That Constitute a Good State of Being

1. Good birth
2. Plenty of friends
3. Plenty of children
4. Wealth
5. Honor
6. Good deeds and good judgment
7. Happy old age
8. Good health
9. Beauty
10. Endurance
11. Strength
12. Glory and majesty
13. Happiness

Part Four: Rhetorical Statements in Epideictic Oratory

1. The Constituents of Virtue
    - Courage
    - Temperance
    - Liberality
    - Magnanimity
    - Generosity
    - Prudence
    - Gentleness
2. Noble Deeds

Part Five: Rhetorical Statements in Forensic Oratory

1. Definition of injustice
2. Definition of the law
3. The conditions that lead to wrongdoing
4. The conditions that make a person a victim of injury

Compendium; or, Al-ᶜArūḍī's Philosophical Treatise on the Meanings of the Book of Rhetoric

In the Name of Allah, the Merciful, the Compassionate

On the Meanings of the Book of Rhetoric; Namely, Political Oratory

[INTRODUCTION]

1. Rhetoric is a faculty whose object is persuasion in any particular matter.[10]
Persuasion is the belief that something is true, with the conviction that it may face opposition and disagreement.

2. Rhetoric resembles dialectic, for each one of them is geared toward public address; they both encompass all purposes and are concerned with general matters, and they both are concerned with opposites. Rhetoric is different from dialectic, since dialectic is concerned only with general issues, which are its subject matter. Rhetoric is based on syllogisms that lead to necessary conclusions, and its materials are premises that are in truth praiseworthy. Rhetoric not only is concerned with general issues, but it is also almost entirely concerned with particular issues and optional facts.

3. An orator is effective by the faculty of his oratory, and he has, if he wishes, a purpose outside oratory. As to the sophist, he is a sophist not by faculty but by choice. A dialectician is a dialectician by faculty only. He does not have choice outside his faculty.

4. In rhetoric, there are sufficient syllogisms whose conclusions are persuasive without being necessarily stated. There are also materials that are praiseworthy in an apparent point of view that is not an object of investigation without being praiseworthy in truth.

10. Avicenna brings together the terms *balāgha* (rhetoric) and *khaṭāba* (oratory) to render the meaning of the Greek concept *rhetorica*, which he transcribes in Arabic as *rīṭōrīqā*. In this translation, I use the two terms interchangeably. The word used by Avicenna to render the meaning of persuasion, *al-iqnāᶜ*, also means inducing conviction; the word *qanāᶜa* carries the meaning of contentment. See chapter 1 for further discussion of these terms.

5. Rhetoric has many benefits in civic matters more than any other arts. Ordinary minds are more disposed to it, they are more perceptive of its exigency, and they all practice some of it.

6. Those who consider dialectic must also consider rhetoric. Those who came before Aristotle did not lay down logical principles for oratory; they laid down only general principles and what are known as extrinsic principles. Their classification of these principles depended on particular cities and particular times. However, they did not examine or set down anything for praise or blame. They had nothing more than tricks by which to deceive judges.

7. Rhetoric is sometimes used in propagating religious beliefs; sometimes it is used in advocating natural beliefs according to what suits the minds of the general public; sometimes it is used in promoting moral beliefs; sometimes it is used in appealing to the emotions for the purpose of provoking sympathy, indulgence, satisfaction, anger, incitement, fear, and so on; other times it is used in disputes that happen over particular incidents that humans may cause. The aim of rhetoric is manifest in such many cases and among many people. There are three divisions of rhetoric:

a. Matters of display (epideictic)
b. Matters of deliberation (deliberative)
c. Matters of dispute (forensic)

8. The aim of epideictic rhetoric is praise of the praiseworthy or blame of the blameworthy. It is concerned with the present time, for it could not be concerned with any other time.

9. The aim of deliberative rhetoric is to grant permission to do something advantageous or to refuse permission to do something harmful, and it is concerned with the future.

10. The aim of forensic rhetoric is to accuse someone of injustice or free someone of guilt, and it is concerned with the past.

11. If people do not follow these principles, they are in error.

[EXTRINSIC MEANS OF PERSUASION]

12. There are three things that constitute the art of oratory: the speech, the subject matter, and the audience.

13. There are three types of listeners: the opponent, the judge, and the jury members.

14. Assent occurs with nonartistic means like witnesses and contracts, and it also occurs with artistic and crafty means, which is rhetorical assent.[11]

15. Assent is produced by the following three rhetorical appeals: the character of the speaker, the character of his opponent, and the ability to persuade the listeners. These belong to extrinsic means of persuasion. But the speech itself is the rhetorical discourse designed to achieve the desired goal of persuasion.

16. The types of the first appeal consist, first, of the virtuous character of the speaker or the defective character of his opponent. If the speaker has the reputation of being truthful, or of mastering the power of persuasion, or of possessing all the rest of the virtues, and if his opponent has the reputation of possessing the opposite of all those qualities, the speaker will gain more credibility. Second, they consist of the speaker's ability to challenge his opponents and invite them to measure up with him, and he does that by laying a wager or displaying a miracle that nobody will be able to perform and that will prove the truth of his discourse. Third, they consist of the speaker's power to commend his own speech and demean the speech of his opponent, for which he will recommend better thought and more research, and his claim that his speech makes sense only to those with sound judgment and minds free from devilish insinuation, like the sharp thoughts and sound mind that Galen used in his discourse on medicine. Fourth, they consist of the speaker's use of reliable testimony and his oath. And there is also the outward appearance of the speaker, the tone of his voice and his gestures.

17. As to persuading the audience, it is done through the appeal to their emotions with words that create in their souls such effects as affection for him, or attraction toward him, or interest in him, or anger and rage toward his opponent.

18. For this purpose, the rhetorician must be familiar with ethics. He must also understand the emotions, how they are constituted and of what substance they are constituted.

19. In this way, rhetoric is composed of dialectic and ethics.

20. As to the speech itself that causes assent, there are two parts in it—the enthymeme and the example—just as in dialectic, in which there are two parts, deduction and induction, or in sciences, which consist of inductive instructions and universal syllogisms.

11. Avicenna appropriates the adjective from the Greek *al-rītōrīqī*, which he transcribes in Arabic.

[The Rhetorical Syllogism]

21. We have an enthymeme when the two premises in a syllogism are not declared. Only the minor premise is declared, and the major premise has been suppressed because it is plainly false and its opposite is clear. When it is declared, it is only implied and it looks as if it is not stated. For a syllogism to be rightly constructed, the major premise, or anything to which all the predicates refer, must be stated first. If there is no predicate, it will be basically similar to a suppressed premise. And the syllogism will look like anything but a syllogism. The purpose of a rhetorical statement is not necessarily its conclusive character, but its persuasiveness. And persuasion occurs with the enthymeme. And in a syllogism, the enthymeme is never from predicative premises. It is from exceptions suppressed from conditional premises. This way is more appropriate when the intention is blame and not affirmation.

22. An example of an enthymeme is when we say:

> *This young man is always roaming around in the dark at night.*
> *Therefore, he must be waiting for the opportune moment to break in.*

This syllogism contradicts the major premise and conceals it. If the premise was stated and we said, "Every person who is frequently roaming around in the dark at night is waiting for the opportune moment to break in," in this case it would be a false statement, and its opposite would be easy to figure out. And consequently, there will be no persuasion.

23. As to the example, it is used either when there is a shared general meaning or when there is a relationship of similarity. Commonality and relationship may exist in truth, or they may exist according to a widely known opinion. Or they may exist according to an apparent opinion that is not an object of investigation. And perhaps the example is what does not have any shared meaning, but only a shared term, and this term is not known according to the apparent opinion that is not an object of investigation.

24. The enthymeme resembles the syllogism in dialectic, and the example resembles induction in dialectic also. The example is what our scholars today call analogy [*qiyās*]. Of rhetoricians, some abandon the example and use the enthymeme only. Of those who reject analogy in theology, the Rawāfiḍ and the Dāoudids follow this method, [which is the enthymeme].[12]

---

12. The Rawāfiḍ were a Shiᶜit sect known for having left Zayd Ibn ᶜAli. According to al-Aṣmaᶜī, they showed allegiance to Zayd Ibn ᶜAli and then said to him, "Forsake the two masters and we will fight on your side." He refused their request and said, "They were

25. A powerful example is one in which the term of comparison leads necessarily to the judging of the like.

26. These are the different means of persuasion, some of which are extrinsic and some of which are intrinsic.

27. Many people use only the extrinsic means of persuasion and leave the essential ones, as most people do in most of their beliefs. They take those extrinsic means of persuasion from those who established them, since those same individuals who established those extrinsic means of persuasion use them in their practices such as asceticism, abstinence, and also verbal and practical miracles. They have confidence in those extrinsic means and abandon the use of essential means of persuasion. Several early orators were against this method and disdained the use of nonessential means of persuasion.

28. As to "the master" of logic [Aristotle], his view, and what an excellent view it is, is that in rhetoric, one must use all the means of persuasion, since the purpose of rhetoric is not to achieve clarity but to reach persuasion by any means.

29. We must first examine more thoroughly the essential and appropriate means of persuasion. We begin with the enthymemes and say:

30. Of the principles by which we reach the syllogistic art on a given issue, there are principles that are not set up to discover the parts of a syllogism, and in this case they are called the topics. There are also principles themselves set up to constitute the parts of a syllogism. These are called particulars. And they are obligatory and proved in an apparent point of view. Or they are general statements omitted from the parts. There are also proofs. When there are proofs, there is a predicate in a subject. The proofs do not concern the subject, but perhaps they concern the predicate. There are also signs, and they resemble proofs, except that either they are more general than both the predicate and the subject, or they are more particular.

An example of enthymemes taken from proved premises:

So and so committed adultery.
He must be punished.

---

my grandfather's ministers, so I will not forsake them." So they deserted him and were called the Rawāfiḍ (the defectors). Ibn Manẓūr, *Lisān al-ʿArab* [The tongue of the Arabs], vol. 7 (Beirut: Dār Ṣādir, 1955–56), 152. In *Al-Fihrist*, chronicler Ibn al-Nadīm explains that the Dāoudids were the followers of Abū Suleymān Dāoud Ibn ʿAli Ibn Khalaf, who was the first to have used denotation (*qawl al-ẓāhir*) and dropped everything apart from the Qur'an and the Tradition of the Prophet, including opinion and analogy. A devout and virtuous man, he died in the year A.D. 795.

An example of enthymemes taken from proofs:

This maiden has given birth to a baby;
Therefore, a man has impregnated her.

An example of enthymemes taken from signs:

This maiden has not menstruated;
Therefore, she is pregnant.[13]

31. Proofs could be cause, and they could be effect, and they could be apposition. Proof can be a symptom, and it becomes visible only after it is ready for the appearance of another symptom, as the white color of urine that appears in the case of acute fever. In this case, it is proof of a cerebral disease or other illnesses of the brain.

32. It has been said that the enthymeme is divided into two classes. The first one is composed of proved premises, and the second one is composed of proofs. There are two types of proof: signs and what is from a similar matter. Signs are of the first type, which is the most complete form, and it is called the more similar matter. The other two forms are called signs.

33. As to the example, it is when judgment is passed from one topic to another topic that is similar in meaning either in truth or in appearance, or when there is a shared name when the meaning does not show in the apparent point of view. That meaning is either general, covering the two, or has the aspect of a similar relationship. And the relationship is either disjunctive or conjunctive.

34. Opposition to an example is when there is a similar meaning in which that rule does not apply, or when we have a similar meaning that is not clearly the cause for that rule, but there is another cause that made similarity obligatory.

35. Enthymemes and examples are also needed in external means of persuasion, if one wants to show that they are persuasive or if one wants to show that they exist, as, for example, when a speaker wants to show his virtuous character, or when he wants to lead his audience to [logically] accept his discourse, or when he appeals to their emotions so that they promptly accept his discourse.

36. All dialectical topics are useful here.

37. We have said enough on the general principles of oratory.

13. The Arabic manuscript edited by Muḥammad Salīm Sālim, from which I am working, says, "inna hādhihi al-jāriyyata qad ḥāẓat, fa 'idhan hiyya ḥāmil." The sentence literally means "This maiden has menstruated; therefore, she is pregnant," which I believe was an error on the part of the copyist.

[DELIBERATIVE ORATORY]

On the Composition of Particular Types of Rhetorical Statements in Deliberative Oratory

38. Let us show the particular types of these statements.

If the aim of rhetoric is persuasion in theological, physical, and moral matters, and in determining the emotional responses in the souls, and also in deliberative, forensic, and epideictic matters, and the theological and physical matters are interpreted differently by the inhabitants of cities, and the legislators of those cities bring the people to take different lifestyles, it will not be favorable to enumerate in them the universal premises that are useful for rhetorical purposes.

39. As to moral matters, the ultimate goal is for the orator to call upon his audience to embrace them or to keep away from them. They are included in matters of deliberative oratory. It will be sufficient if we introduce in deliberative oratory premises that are useful for permission and premises useful for prohibition.

40. Therefore, what we ought to count from the particular types is the kind by which to state the emotions, the deliberative kind, the forensic kind, and the epideictic kind.

41. These kinds are necessary, since they all have in common the good and the evil, the noble and the base, or the beautiful and the vile, or the just and the unjust.

42. In deliberative oratory, the orator, when speaking of possible things, dissuades or persuades and says, "This has never taken place or will not take place." He has to have premises on what is possible or what is not possible, or what exists and what does not exist.

43. Let us begin with deliberative oratory and say, of matters of deliberation, some belong to the general good of the city and some belong to the good for some people. The ones that are of the general good are five: ways and means, war and peace, national defense, imports and exports, and legislation.

44. As to ways and means, the political speaker will need to know the number and extent of the country's sources of revenue, so that if they have diminished, he will manage to increase them, and if they have increased, he will manage to secure them and keep them for times of need. As to the unemployed and the extravagant in the city, he will need to put aside the former or encourage them to learn trades and keep the latter from being more wasteful. Further, he will need to know old accounts about a similar situation.

45. As to war and peace, the political speaker must know how serious the matter is and its consequences. He also must know the extent of the military

strength of his city and the special warfare equipment, the beasts of burden, and weapons available. He must also compare the military force of his city at the present with the military force of the enemy and what could a second time happen in numbers and weapons. He must contemplate the situation of people who live at the outskirts of the city and what potential harm they may endure and which could lead to injury to the people inside the city. He must know the historical accounts of wars in his country and in other countries and the way each type of war ended. Similar causes are likely to have similar results.

46. With regard to national defense, the political speaker must know the extent of the defense of the city and the methods of defense. He also must know the inlets, the garrisons, and the number of the police force, in order that it may be increased or decreased. He must also know the intentions of the defensive force, so that if one of them is working for the enemy, he may eliminate him and replace him with someone else. If there is someone giving good advice, he may recommend him for a reward.

47. The political speaker must also know the food supply of his city and the method of acquiring it.

48. As to income and expenditure, they vary according to the people in the city: the wealthy, the poor, and the middle classes.

49. As to the study of legislation, it is the most beneficial part and the most serious matter. The political speaker must know the four kinds of constitution and the special characteristics of each one of them, the good and bad in each one of them.

50. Of these four kinds, there is democracy. It is a type of constitution in which the citizens—both the noble and the lowly—are equal when they deserve punishment, honor, and leadership. The leader is chosen by consensus or appointed by their first leader.

51. Then there is the mean form of government, and it is gained by the accumulation of wealth. Of this type of government, there is plutocracy, in which case someone who rules by virtue of his wealth holds power over his people. There is also oligarchy, in which case those who are distinguished by their wealth, not by mastery, hold power over their people. The government of the wealthy does not stand firm when there are several rulers in it. As to oligarchy, as long as it remains an oligarchy, it does not endure any harm with a bigger number of rulers, except when it changes into another form of government.

52. There is also autocracy. In this form of government, the ruler's goal is to impose obedience and servitude on his subjects. He gains possession of this privilege by virtue of the size of his body or by his style of management that gives them protection from the enemy, or by virtue of straightening their lives,

or by inheritance. The purpose of this form of rule is dignity, and whenever it is agreed to increase the number of rulers, it never occurred that this government went bad or changed into other forms of rule, especially plutocracy.

53. There is also aristocracy. This is a virtuous and wise form of government, and that is when the ruler is more virtuous than the rest of the nation and when the citizens are ranked according to their virtues, either virtues of the mind or virtues of skills. The head of state [*ra'īs al-madīna*] is more virtuous, wiser, and more pious. From the head of state, other forms of rule branch out. For example, the leadership of craftsmen goes to the most skilled one of them, the most knowledgeable of the areas of their craft, and the most tactful. The leadership of the police force goes to the most courageous one of them and the most knowledgeable of the states of combat. Other forms of government branch out until it gets down to the last individuals, and then everyone in the city has a limited position before and after another leader, according to the degree of his virtue.

54. This form of government, if constructed according to the virtues of knowledge and work, is called government by selection. This form of government follows divine government in its arrangement of the parts of universe and also in its arrangement of the parts of the human body, for there is nothing in it that is idle and useless. This form of government is rarely found in the world; and if ever it is found, it is hard to overthrow; and when it is overthrown, it changes into a government of dignity and then a government of force. In this form of government, there may be a number of individuals in power, and the group is like one person, since they all aim toward one goal.

55. These are simple forms of civic government, the best of which are the monarchy, then government by selection, and then government by honor. The lowest forms are government by domination, then the oligarchy, then government by a large group. These forms of government constitute civil societies.

56. As to the form of government in our country, it is a mixed form composed of government by domination, oligarchy, and government by honor, and some government by a large group. If there is some government by selection, it is very minimal.

57. The political speaker giving counsel on legislation must know all these forms of government. He must also know that they are subject to change, and when one of them changes for a known cause, he must know what form of government it changes into. He must know that corruption of civic governments comes as a result of citizens being too lenient or too argumentative, or as a result of domination.

58. As to deliberation about hostile countries, the written accounts give information about them.

59. These are the kinds of deliberation on serious and important matters.

60. As to those kinds that deal with individuals or a group of individuals on private matters, and have no benefit for the city-state, but the purpose of which is intimidation, incitement, and prohibition, these are the kinds that we want to talk about. We say, the rhetorician aims at that which is believed to be good or is in truth good, [and] the means to achieve that good, which is called beneficial, [is] by favoring some means over other means because they are more beneficial. This may be available in what is discussed in the meanings of the *Topics* in the part on the most advantageous and the most desirable.

61. The end of rhetoric is everything that is or is believed to be the general good. And that may be defined as good actions resulting from a virtuous mind, a longer life, affection for loved ones and enjoyment of affection in a state of good health, prosperity, nobility, and the strength to gain it and keep it.

62. As to a good state of things, some of it is obtained through determination, some of it happens by chance, and some of it is gained by nature.

63. The constituent parts of a good state of being are noble birth, which is fortuitous; plenty of brothers, which may be obtained by will or by chance; plenty of children, which may be obtained by will and nature; wealth, which may be obtained by will or by chance; nobility; good actions; a happy old age; good health; beauty; endurance; abundance; strength; glory; majesty; happiness; and virtue.

64. As to good birth, it means that the people are indigenous, or ancient, or leaders, or wealthy and free and notable, either in actions or in words, of great deeds.

65. As to plenty of friends, it means that he has among people those who do good deeds that he obtains willingly, and the number of friends is large.

66. As to plenty of children, it means that they are male, healthy, enduring, strong, obedient, hardworking, and brave. If they are female, they are chaste, well rounded, and beautiful.

67. As to wealth, it means solid abundance of gold, silver, land, slaves, goods, furniture, beautiful household effects, and livestock. All these kinds of property are secure, safe, and useful. The crops and revenue are obtained without toil. If enjoyment comes in addition to these kinds of property, the conditions of wealth are complete. Wealth consists in enjoying things by using them rather than in owning them.

68. As to honor, it is justly deserved by the man who earns it after devoting his attention to it. Also, a man gains honor for his wealth and other things.

69. The constituents of honor are sacrifices, commemorations, front seats at celebrations and pleasant events, invitations to public feasts, and presents. The

conditions of honor are fulfilled when these privileges are voluntarily offered and well deserved.

70. As to good deeds and good judgment, they must show in his words and actions in the sense that they please the public and men of good sense.

71. As to a happy old age, it means to live a long life, free from grief and pain.

72. As to health, it means that the body is naturally free from disease, and when affected [by ailments], it quickly recovers from them.

73. As to beauty, it varies with the age of the man. In a young lad, beauty is the appearance of a body that is fit to endure exertion of contests of strength, wrestling, and swiftness. In a man in his prime, beauty is a pleasant appearance with fitness for sports that prepare for warfare and at the same time make him look formidable.

74. As to endurance, the man has the strength of performing actions smoothly and naturally.

75. As to excellence in size, the man surpasses other people in height, thickness, and breadth, and his movements are smooth and natural.

76. As to strength, the man has the power to move someone else at will.

77. As to glory and majesty, it means that the man is of noble birth, that he does good deeds, and that he is virtuous.

78. As to happiness, it means the man acquires good things fortuitously and not through his will or the will of his ancestors or his followers.

79. As to good moral character, it will be defined in the section on epideictic rhetoric.

80. We have explained the aim of deliberative rhetoric.

81. As to useful things, they may be good things in themselves, or they may be bad, or they may have lesser good in them, except that they are somehow useful as part of a good condition. If they are virtues or pleasures, they are more conducive to accepting deliberation or something of what aims at a good condition or what is more pleasant, such as wealth for some and power for others.

82. When people deliberate about these useful things with the aim to reach a good condition, they do it voluntarily. When they deliberate about what is more beneficial, that falls under the desirable.

[EPIDEICTIC ORATORY]

Of the Types That Prepare for Epideictic Oratory

83. Let us discuss the useful types that belong to epideictic oratory.

Praise is directed at the beautiful for its own sake. It is praiseworthy and good, and it is pleasant for the sake of being good. For this reason, virtue is the most praiseworthy. Virtue is a faculty of providing truly good things or things supposed to be good. It is a faculty of conferring many great benefits in all aspects and for all things.

84. The constituents of virtue are righteousness. Righteousness is a virtue of justice by means of which an individual gets what he deserves by law, and the opposite is injustice.

85. Courage: it is a virtue that disposes an individual to do good and useful deeds in situations of war, in accordance with and in service of the law. Cowardice is the opposite.

86. Temperance: it is the virtue that disposes an individual to obey the law where physical pleasures are concerned. Incontinence is the opposite.

87. Liberality: it is a virtue that disposes an individual to spend money for the good of other people. Illiberality is the opposite.

88. Magnanimity: it is a virtue that disposes an individual to do great deeds. Meanness of spirit is its opposite.

89. Generosity: it is a virtue that disposes an individual to be noble by giving away food to others. Depravity is its opposite.

90. Prudence: it is a virtue that disposes an individual to have a good sense of understanding and deliberation that enables men to come to wise decisions about great matters. Foolishness is its opposite.

91. Gentleness: it is a virtue that disposes an individual to control his temper. Insolence is its opposite.

92. Wisdom: it is a virtue that disposes an individual to have a reasonable amount of knowledge of things that exist. Ignorance is its opposite.

93. This has been an account of the constituents of virtue.

94. A person is praised not only for those virtues, but also for things that are productive of virtue and tending toward virtue, such as virtuous contentment, and also the signs of its presence, such as good deeds and acts of courage and effects of courage and acts of justice.

95. However, acts done impulsively in reaction to an injury, even when they are intended to restore justice, are not praiseworthy; they are blameworthy.

96. The same is true of the effects of other virtues and noble deeds for which the reward is greater honor.

97. Reward with honor is better than reward with money. Deeds are noble when they are done not for one's sake, but for their own sake or someone else's sake, and when they do not necessarily benefit us. Noble are the deeds that are done for the sake of being enjoyed after death. Noble are the deeds done for the

sake of other people and for which we refuse to be rewarded. Noble are the deeds done as a service to family members and [they] are not wasted and are beneficial to family members and other people. Those deeds are done not by chance, but are done through acquired knowledge. Then there are virtues by which evil people are exposed. It is noble when a man is ashamed of saying shameful things, which are the opposite of virtuous things. Also, a man is not ashamed of saying virtuous things for the sake of honesty, as when Alcaeus offered to tell the wise Sappho about a shameful thing and said:

> *I want to say something to you.*
> *Only shame restrains me.*

She neither was embarrassed by what he said, nor was she angry with him, nor did she feel the need to scold him.

98. It is noble for a man to avenge himself on his enemies and for a brave man to be victorious and not defeated. It is noble to do things that are made memorable. It is noble to do things that are exceptionally gained by one man alone. It is noble to have the qualities that are distinctive of the noble only, such as long hair, which the Macedonians in Greece had. It is noble for a man not to be deceived, but also to be of those who are deceived and err in small matters because of their old age.

99. Of the signs of nobility, we find the constituents of good conditions. The noble bring forth the noble. When a noble man attains wealth and comfort easily, he only attains what he deserves. Seriousness is aided only by worthiness.

100. When people wish to praise a man of ill repute, they go around and praise the characteristics that are favorable to them and similar to their depravity, as when they say that a deceitful man gives good advice, an adulterer gives pleasant company, a stupid man is mild tempered, a coward is a gentle-hearted man, a man with poor judgment is modest, a reckless man is brave, an unjust sultan has a good sense of government and discipline.

101. A speaker ought to consider in his praise the things that are exalted and aggrandized. For example, a man performed the great action alone; or he is the first one to perform such a great action; or he performed a great action in such a fast manner; or he performed so many great actions; or he performed a great action in such difficult circumstances; or he set a good example by performing such a great action; or he inspires people by his great action to the extent that they take him as a model and become better people; or he becomes famous, like other famous people, in his great action.

102. These are the materials out of which speeches of praise are made; the opposite of these materials are used in speeches of blame.

[FORENSIC ORATORY]

On the Types That Prepare for Forensic Oratory

103. Forensic oratory is concerned with accusation and defense. Accusation is about an unjust act; defense is about justice or an act that is not unjust.

104. Let us first treat of accusation, and a discussion of defense will follow. Let us first treat of an act of injustice. It is an injury inflicted willingly and in voluntary violation of the law—that is, an act done deliberately by the wrongdoer for the sake of his pleasure, not induced by external things.

105. The law is either general unwritten principles that are acknowledged by the public or special written principles that regulate the life of a particular religious community or a particular nation. And the two may be different, in the sense that most of what is permitted by a written law is not necessarily permitted by an unwritten law. For example, the written law among Arabs and Hebrews permits a man to marry three women in addition to a suitable and caring first wife, but the unwritten law does not permit that if those marriages are harmful to the first wife.

106. Let us now discuss the conditions that lead to wrongdoing so that people are aware of them, and that can help in framing an accusation.

107. Wrongdoing may be caused by wickedness, and it may be caused by poor judgment.

108. As to wrongdoing caused by wickedness, it is a deliberate, calculated, and purposeful act on the part of the wrongdoer. Wrongdoing caused by poor judgment is as when drinkers and ill-mannered people are impudent and do wrong to others, but not deliberately or intentionally; and like the man who shows his mean character and does wrong to others in matters of money; and the ravenous in matters of physical pleasure; and the weak in matters of idleness; and the cowards in times of adversity, for many times they desert their fellow men and abandon them in the face of danger; and the stupid who cannot distinguish right from wrong; and the shameless because of his lack of desire to show gratitude.

109. The characteristics of wrongdoing are limited to these points; that is, all actions are due to chance or to nature, or to compulsion, or to habit, or to anger, or to appetite, or to reasoning.

110. The things that happen by chance or by nature are not subject to blame; also, the things that happen through coercion are not subject to blame; and all other things are considered unjust. In some cases, the degree of injustice depends on the vicious nature of the act, and that is when the act is done deliberately. In the other cases, the degree of injustice depends on the poor judgment of the wrongdoer.

111. These are the things that constitute in a man's actions the principle of injustice.

112. There are motives and goals that induce a man to do wrong, and the speaker must consider them. The goals are three: what is good, what is beneficial, and what is pleasant.

113. The beneficial resembles what we mentioned in our detailed discussion of the constituents of the state of happiness. As to what is pleasant, we must discuss in detail its constituents. By this I also mean the types of pleasant things. We say that pleasure is a movement of the soul, a condition by which the soul is suddenly and consciously brought into its normal and appropriate state of being. Everything produced by this movement and condition is pleasant, and what is produced contrary to it is painful and harmful.

114. Of the appropriate states of being, some are appropriate by nature, some are appropriate by habit, and some are appropriate by nature and habit, like indolence, relaxation, freedom from toil, rest, and sleep. The pleasant things that we desire through imagination, the senses, and the intellect are similar to the things that we are induced to possess.

115. Not all pleasant things are acquired through the senses. Pleasant things are acquired through imagination also. If pleasant things are hardly attributed to the senses, those who remember them draw pleasure from remembering them. People draw pleasure from remembering the industrious efforts by which they reached pleasure. They also draw pleasure from remembering the tricks they used to free themselves from evil. Those who hope to get some pleasure also experience pleasure. Thus anger becomes pleasant, since there is hope in it for revenge. There is no pleasure in seeking revenge on someone inferior to us or someone much superior to us. Pain and pleasure may be felt together, as it is the case in funerals. People feel saddened by the loss of someone close, but they draw pleasure from remembering his company. It is pleasant to seek vengeance and bring failure down on the enemy.

116. Victory is pleasant, and not merely to those who like victory, but to everyone. Victory by means of justice is pleasant, and victory by means of disturbance is pleasant to those who are accustomed to it.

117. Honor and majesty are pleasant, especially what constitutes good repute. What is present is much better than what is absent; fellow countrymen are much better than strangers; things of the present are much better than things of the future; sensible people are better than ignorant ones; a large number of people is much better than a small number.

118. Loved ones belong to the class of pleasant things, for it is pleasant to love and it is also pleasant to be loved. It is also pleasant for a person to be admired.

Flattery is pleasant. Repetition of the same thing is pleasant. Habitual things are pleasant. Also to do new things is pleasant. That is why lifetime occurrences are pleasant. Learning and the desire to learn are pleasant. Beneficent acts and good deeds are pleasant. Being self-sufficient is also pleasant. To set people right and take care of them is pleasant. Imitation must be pleasant. Skillful imitation of favorite products is pleasant. Things of the same nature are pleasant. What a person does, if done through skillful imitation, is more pleasant to him than what another person does. Power is pleasant. Wisdom is pleasant. Amusement in words and deeds is pleasant. If you understand pleasant things, you will understand harmful things. Since we have explained wrongdoing and the conditions and motives that make men do wrong, we must explain now what makes it easy for men to do wrong.

119. Men do wrong, thinking their wrongdoing may be ignored or forgotten; or that the loss will be less than the gain for themselves; or that the punishment will be a fine and not corporal; or, as for some, the punishment will be corporal and not a fine; or if they have a great number of friends and a great deal of money; or if their friends share the benefits with them, and also the friends of their friends and their servants. Also, it makes it easier for men to do wrong when they are on friendly terms with those to whom they do wrong, so that it becomes easier for them to deny their wrongdoing and the accusation is weakened, and the way is paved for them to express an apology before a fight breaks out.

120. Friends do not guard against friends, so it is easier to do them wrong. Or they may be on friendly terms with the judges who will stave off a trial or use a trick to avoid sentencing them or impose a light sentence. It is easier for the weaklings to do wrong, because nobody guards against them and because they inspire pity. Public and open injuries are the easiest to do, because there are no precautions taken against them. It is easier to conceal the places or the conditions in which they are committed. The wrongdoer may feel that the gains to be gotten by wrongdoing are clear or great or immediate, and that the disadvantages are small or uncertain or distant and slow. Those whom injustice leads to praise are—just like the wrongdoer who takes vengeance for justice—quick to do wrong. Of weak-minded people, some are quick to do wrong, expecting profit to be easily gained and forgiveness to be easily granted. Some insist that they have done wrong because they have failed several times to do right rather than actually doing wrong. Some are led to do wrong because of the gain and the pleasure that come with it, even if the loss that follows is enormous. People of strong character do not do such things.

121. These are the conditions that lead to wrongdoing and make it easy to commit acts of wrongdoing.

122. The conditions that make a person a victim of injury are the following: when a person is not aware of the injury done to him; or when the public is not aware of an injury being done; or when a person does not have many friends or supporters; or when a person is weak; or when a person acts slowly and carefully; or when a person is on friendly terms with the wrongdoer or is related to the wrongdoer; or when a person is too lazy to seek justice; or when a person is bashful and does not stir up mischief; or when a person is fearful of the judge; or when a person is reputed for being a liar when committing an injury; or when a person himself has done previous wrong to those who have done him wrong; or when a person is a stranger, for the wrongdoer finds pleasure in doing him wrong even though the wrongdoing does not bring any gain with it; or when the wrongdoers are evil characters and do wrong voluntarily or involuntarily; or when the injury is done by the wrongdoers' associates who are happy with their wrongdoing or by the friends of wrongdoers, and also by those who are on the point of being wronged or of being openly punished by others or are on the point of being destroyed.

123. Among the kinds of wrong done to others are those that are easy and sordid and quickly change, like food, and which we can change as when we change clothes, and those that can be mixed with other things so that nobody can tell the difference. There are things or things of that nature that the wrongdoer has that make it easier to do him wrong. There are wrongs done to wrongdoers and about which they cannot speak for fear of being exposed, as in the case of a scandal involving women.

124. Injury is found in three situations: in dominion, in honor, and in safety.

125. Injury happens with violation of the law. The law is either written or unwritten; it is also either special, having to do with particular individuals, or general, having to do with a nation or city. Violation of the law does not go beyond that.

126. As to the man who makes excuses and refuses to take responsibility, either he does not in the least admit to having done wrong, or he admits the act but frees himself from wrongdoing or modifies it as when he says, for example, "I took [something], but I did not steal; I communicated with the enemy, not to betray the city, but to trick them; I had a relationship [with a woman], but I did not commit adultery." And also, the man might admit the act and ask for forgiveness and grace.

127. The wrongdoer refusing to take responsibility for an act comes up with the following kinds of excuses: Do not use the written law against me, but treat me according to my conduct; do not take his words at face value, but look at

what they mean; do not look at my act, but look at my intention; do not look at one thing I have done, but look at many acts from me; do not look at me here and now, but look at my things past; remember beautiful things, and you will forget my mistake; do not be excited about the favors you have bestowed on me, but remember the favors I have done in return; go slow with the penalty, for a lot of unpleasant things follow pleasant things; look at the words and not the action; forgive an evil act with nice words; show love for gentleness, and do not make argument lead to enmity, as the proverb says, "Let your presence at banquets be more preferable to you than your presence at disputes."

128. The plaintiff needs ways by which to show the enormity of the injury. An enormous act of injury is when a powerful man seizes something of which he is not in need. A ruler is in that category. Hence insignificant things are considered enormous acts of injury, like, for example, those who sold Joseph at a cheap price, or the one who pointed out Jesus for thirty dinars.

129. An enormous act of injury is when a man plunders the wealth of someone else and tortures him; or when a charitable man is punished and tortured, as when the pious man was killed by ibn ᶜUrs; or when the wrongdoer is the only man, or the first man, to do wrong, or the man who has repeatedly done wrong. To sever family ties is an enormous act of injury. Breaking obligations and oaths, and violation of trust, committing adultery with someone else's spouse, are enormous acts of injury. The opposite of these acts are not unjust acts or are less unjust by which a man evades responsibility.

[CONCLUSION]

130. So much, then, for the discussion of the meanings of the *Book of Rhetoric*. Praise be to Allah, the guardian of praise.

3. Averroes's *Middle Commentary on the Book of Rhetoric (Book I)*

Averroes (1126–98)

In *ᶜUyūn al-Anbā' fī Ṭabqāt al-Aṭibbā'*, Ibn Abī Uṣaybiᶜa informs us that Abū al-Walīd ibn Rushd, known in the West as Averroes,[1] was born and raised in a family of magistrates and physicians that lived in Córdoba and Seville, Spain, during the reign of the Almoḥads. He was trained in jurisprudence (*al-Fiqh*), the science of the tradition of the Prophet Muḥammad (*ᶜilm al-Ḥadīth*), theology (*ᶜilm al-Kalām*), and also the sciences, medicine, and philosophy. He was known in his time as a magistrate (*qāḍī*), physician, philosopher, and commentator. Toward the end of his life, he experienced a brief but trying misfortune (known in Arabic as *al-miḥna*) that culminated in disgrace and exile, after which the caliph Abū Yūsuf Yaᶜqūb al-Manṣūr called him to Marrakech, Morocco, where he died in 1198.[2]

1. On the reception of Averroes in the Latin tradition, see Harry A. Wolfson, "The Twice-Revealed Averroes," *Speculum* 36, no. 3 (1961): 373–92.

2. For a succinct and very informative account on the political context in which Averroes grew up and lived, see J. Langhade and D. Mallet, "Droit et philosophie au XIIᵉ siècle dans al-Andalus [Law and philosophy in the twelfth century in Islamic Spain]: Averroes (Ibn Rušd)" *Revue de l'Occident musulman et de la Méditerranée* [Journal of the Muslim West and the Mediterranean] 40 (1985): 103–21. ᶜAbd al-Wāḥid al-Murrākushī gives some details about this misfortune in *Al-Muᶜjib fī Talkhīṣ Akhbāri al-Maghrib* [The admirable in an outline of the history of the Maghreb] (Casablanca, Morocco: Dār al-Kitāb, 1978), originally published in the first quarter of the thirteenth century.

From some of the works of Averroes, Ernest Renan has gleaned a number of statements that reflect what he describes as Averroes's "superstitious admiration" for Aristotle.[3] For example, Renan informs us that in the preface to his commentary on Aristotle's *Physics*, Averroes looks up to Aristotle as "the wisest of the Greeks, who founded and completed logic, physics, and metaphysics." For the Andalusian commentator, Aristotle "completed" these sciences because not one of those who came after him was able to add anything to his writings or find any significant error in them. Averroes notes that since all this wisdom is found in one man, it must be "an unusual and miraculous thing." Thus he comes to the conclusion that "such a privileged being deserves to be called *divine* rather than human."[4] Elsewhere, Averroes expresses his gratitude to Allah, who "predestined [Aristotle] for perfection and placed him at *the highest degree of human excellence* that no one in any time has ever been able to reach." In this manner, Averroes not only brings Aristotle into the Islamic philosophical tradition but also puts him in the most distinguished position. He aptly quotes from the Qur'an, "It is to [Aristotle] that Allah refers when He says: 'This higher position, Allah gives it to whomever He chooses.'" Averroes remarks that Aristotle is worthy of such a privileged position because his doctrine is "*sovereign truth*" and his intelligence has been "*the limit of human intelligence*." The reference to the sacred text to back up these claims is significant because it occurs in a work written with a definite audience in mind and for a definite purpose. Also, such words of praise addressed to Allah for having sent a "pagan" philosopher to enlighten his creatures in the Islamic world almost inevitably seem to imply the intention of Averroes to undo a well-established priority in the Islamic belief system. That is, by proposing a form of divinity for Aristotle, who has been "sent to us by providence to *teach us* what is possible to know," Averroes enthusiastically puts Aristotle right next to the Prophet Muḥammad and almost offers an alternative to the dominant discourse in the Arabic-Islamic tradition. Put simply, Averroes, who ascribes absolute sovereignty to the philosophical doctrine of Aristotle, astutely promotes the idea of a shift from thought based on revelation to thought based on Aristotle's universal concept of demonstration.

The Moroccan historian al-Murrākushī tells us how Averroes came to be commissioned by the Almoḥad caliph Abū Yūsuf to embark on a huge intellectual enterprise:

3. These works include Averroes's *Commentary on Physics* and *The Destruction of Destruction*. The quotations are from Ernest Renan, *Averroès et l'averroïsme* [Averroes and Averroism] (Paris: Maisonneuve & Larose, 1997), 54–55 (my translation from the French).
4. Emphasis mine in all quoted material in this paragraph.

> Ibn Rushd says: One day Ibn Ṭufayl called me and said to me: "Today I have heard the Commander of the Faithful complain about Aristotle's obscurity of style. 'God willing,' [the caliph] said, 'someone would want to comment on [Aristotle's] works and clarify their meaning to make them accessible to men.' You [Ibn Rushd] have all the potential for such a task. Do it. Given your high degree of intelligence, your profound lucidity, your solid determination to work, I hope that you yourself will do it. My age and my numerous commitments to the monarch prevent me from doing such a job."[5]

In this highly intellectual society, where he received support and encouragement, Averroes produced a rich body of commentaries, which earned him the esteemed title of the commentator (*al-shāriḥ*). The task was indeed enormous, for, as Jorge Luis Borges ingeniously tells us in his remarkable fictional story "Averroes' Search," the "slight preoccupation [that] darkened Averroes' felicity . . . was not caused by the *Tahāfut*, a fortuitous piece of work, but rather by a problem of philological nature related to the monumental work which would justify him in the eyes of men: his commentary on Aristotle."[6] In fact, the Aristotelian corpus available to the commentator was surrounded by a complex body of functions—copyists, translators, and commentators spanning around fourteen hundred years—all of which contributed to a large amount of unease of expression caused by numerous distortions and omissions. One could easily imagine how far the Andalusian commentator trusted such translations and commentaries and the enormous difficulties he must have encountered in working from them. Also, the commentary tradition left by al-Fārābī and Avicenna must have served little purpose for Averroes, as it was written for different audiences and purposes at different times in the history of the Islamic state. Muḥammad ᶜĀbed al-Jābrī reminds us that the philosophical school in North Africa and Andalusia was almost totally independent from the philosophical school in the eastern part of the Islamic state, and as a consequence, the philosophical school

5. Al-Murrākushī, *Al-Muᶜjib fi Talkhīṣ Akhbār al-Maghrib*, 354 (my translation). This is reminiscent of Byzantine rhetoricians' reaction to Aristotle's style. As Thomas Conley informs us, Byzantine rhetoricians such as John Doxapatres, Theodore Prodromos (in the twelfth century), and Michael Acominatos complained about the density of Aristotle's ideas and the obscurity of his style. Thomas Conley, "Aristotle's *Rhetoric* in Byzantium," *Rhetorica* 8, no. 1 (1990): 30–31. In the Islamic tradition, Avicenna openly admits that he read Aristotle's *Metaphysics* forty times and could not understand it until he came across a commentary on it by al-Fārābī.

6. Jorge Luis Borges, "Averroes' Search," in *Labyrinths: Selected Stories and Other Writings*, ed. Donald A. Yates and James E. Irby (New York: New Directions, 1964), 149.

of Averroes in particular was interested in a new reading of the Aristotelian corpus as part of a large revolutionary intellectual project led by Ibn Tumart, founder of the Almoḥad dynasty.[7]

So one wonders how Averroes must have read the works of Aristotle and what the commentary tradition that he left can tell us about the historical formation of the reading practices of that period. In *Faṣl al-Maqāl* (*On the Harmony of Religion and Philosophy*),[8] Averroes uses the example of "a sharp knife" that a Muslim can borrow from any person, regardless of his religious beliefs, for the purpose of sacrificing an animal. This analogy clearly allows Averroes to highlight the universal character of logic, as if it were an instrument free of all ideology. He writes:

> But if someone other than ourselves has already examined that subject, it is clear that we ought to seek help toward our goal from what has been said by such a predecessor on the subject, regardless of whether this other one shares our religion or not. For when a valid sacrifice is performed with a certain instrument, no account is taken, in judging the validity of the sacrifice, of whether the instrument belongs to one who shares our religion or to one who does not, so long as it fulfills the conditions for validity. (46)

"One who does not [share our religion]" evidently refers to those ancients who studied these matters before Islam. Perhaps it is worth mentioning that logic was part of the scientific corpus considered "intrusive sciences" (*ᶜulūm dakhīla*), since it came from the Greeks and made its way into the Arabic-Muslim scientific scholarship.[9]

This instrumentalist approach to exegesis clearly emphasizes the importance of what Averroes describes as "a code of ethics in reading classical texts." He goes on to say:

> From this it is evident that the study of the books of the ancients is obligatory by Law, since their aim and purpose in their books is the purpose to which the Law has urged us, and that whoever forbids the study of them to anyone

7. Muḥammad ᶜĀbed al-Jābrī, *Naḥnu wa al-Turāt* [We and the tradition] (Casablanca, Morocco: Al-Markaz al-Taqāfi al-ᶜArabī, 1993), 211.
8. Averroes, *Faṣl al-Maqāl Fī Taqrīri mā bayna al-Sharīᶜa wa al-Ḥikma min al-Ittiṣāl* [On the harmony of religion and philosophy] (Beirut: Markaz dirāsāt al-waḥda al-ᶜarabiyya, 1997) (my translation). Text references are to page numbers from this edition.
9. On the relation of logic to other disciplines, see Nicholas Rescher, *The Development of Arabic Logic* (Pittsburgh: University of Pittsburgh Press, 1964), 50–52.

> who is fit to study them, that is, anyone who unites two qualities, (1) natural intelligence and (2) religious integrity and moral virtue, is blocking people from the door by which the Law summons them to knowledge of God, the door of theoretical study which leads to the truest knowledge of Him; and such an act is the extreme ignorance of and estrangement from God the Exalted. (48)

The work of Averroes carries in it the trace of what J. Langhade and D. Mallet describe as the quality of "a philosophical mind leaning toward the universal."[10] In the eyes of Averroes, the universal validity of such an instrument makes the study of classical texts obligatory, because it guarantees a universal and cumulative character of knowledge and ensures a strong sense of continuity. Averroes continues to explain:

> If this is so, then whenever we find in the works of our predecessors of former nations a theory about beings and a reflection on them conforming to what the conditions of demonstration require, we ought to study what they said about the matter and what they affirmed in their books. (48)

Averroes calls for an appreciation of the works of ancient philosophers, and he reminds us that if by any chance such works should show errors of judgment, their authors should be exonerated:

> And we should accept from them gladly and gratefully whatever in these books accords with the truth, and draw attention to and warn against what does not accord with the truth, at the same time excusing them. (48)

Clearly, *Faṣl al-Maqāl* spells out the intellectual and moral qualities and obligations of a Muslim philosopher and commentator.

Commenting on the body of works left by Averroes, Harry Wolfson informs us that there are thirty-eight commentaries on Aristotle, in addition to short treatises on special topics in Aristotelian philosophy.[11] Regarding Averroes's commentary tradition on the *Rhetoric*, we have available today a short commentary (*mukhtaṣar*) in an English translation by Charles Butterworth. This translation is based on two Judeo-Arabic manuscripts. In this short commentary, Averroes generally assumes authority, since he talks freely about Aristotle's text and does

10. Langhade and Mallet, "Droit et philosophie," 114.

11. Wolfson, "Twice-Revealed Averroes," 374. P. M. Bouyges gives a comprehensive inventory of the works of Averroes in "Inventaire des textes arabes d'Averroès [Inventory of the Arabic texts of Averroes]," in *Mélanges de l'Université Saint-Joseph* vol. 8 (Beirut: Imprimerie Catholique, 1922), 1–54.

not necessarily feel constrained by the structure of the primary text. Also, the short commentary often includes new material to help us relate the philosophical discussion of the subject of rhetoric to contemporary theological and legal matters. In addition, we have a middle commentary (*talkhīṣ*), which is available in two Arabic editions, one prepared by Muḥammad Salīm Sālim in 1969 and another one by ᶜAbd al-Raḥmān Badawī in 1959. The middle commentary is naturally longer and tends to come closest to the primary text itself. In this type of commentary, we notice a textual reproduction of the Aristotelian text. The commentator begins each section with "[Aristotle] said," quotes Aristotle very briefly, and proceeds with paraphrase and explanation of the primary text. Often in the paraphrase it is hard to tell who is speaking, as Aristotle's voice and that of the Muslim commentator blend in one authorial voice. Averroes follows the order of the argument in the primary text, although he elaborates on the points that he deems important, and this makes the commentary look longer than the treatise itself. We do not have a large commentary on the *Rhetoric* available, and if Averroes had composed one, it must have been lost. Generally, Averroes's large commentaries (*sharḥ* or *tafsīr*) stay close to the primary text. That is, Averroes goes into lengthy explanations of the primary text and covers each paragraph in some detail, and he often stops at the terms that Aristotle uses and explains them. In sum, as Ernest Renan points out:

> Although Averroes never aspired to a glory other than that of a commentator, this apparent modesty should not mislead us. The human mind always knows how to claim its independence. Chain it to a text, and it will know how to find its freedom in the interpretation of that text. It will distort it rather than surrender the most inalienable of its rights, which is the exercise of individual thought.[12]

The English translation of Averroes's Middle Commentary on Aristotle's *Rhetoric* that I make available in this book is based on ᶜAbd al-Raḥmān Badawī's 1959 Arabic edition. However, I have compared as often as possible my rendering of the text against Maroun Aouad's excellent French translation of Averroes's commentary, as well as W. Rhys Roberts's English translation of Aristotle's *Rhetoric*, whenever the Arabic text seemed unyielding.[13] As I indicated earlier, because the commentaries of al-Fārābī and Avicenna are limited to Book I of

12. Renan, *Averroès et l'averroïsme*, 77–78 (my translation).

13. Averroes (Ibn Rushd), *Commentaire moyen à la Rhétorique d'Aristote* [Middle commentary on Aristotle's *Rhetoric*], ed. and trans. Maroun Aouad, 3 vols. (Paris: Vrin, 2002); Aristotle, *Rhetoric*, trans. W. Rhys Roberts (New York: Modern Library, 1984).

Aristotle's treatise, I make available in this book Averroes's commentary on Book I only, for the sake of consistency. The commentary on Book II includes the following topics:

2.1. The emotions that make the judge lean toward a position when making a judgment and the reasons for which a speaker gains the sympathy of his audience
2.2. On anger
- Definition of anger; the pleasure that accompanies anger
- Definition of contempt; various types of contempt
- The things that cause anger, the states of mind of the person who gets angry, and the states of mind of the person with whom one gets angry

2.3. The things that appease anger
2.4. On friendship and love
2.5. On fear; on courage
2.6. On shyness and shame
2.7. On owing thanks and denying them
2.8. On concern
2.9. On the relationship between concern and other emotions, such as jealousy and indignation
2.10. On jealousy; on joy
2.11. On sorrow and regret
2.12. On matters of moral character
- On the moral character of young men

2.13. On the moral character of older people
2.14. On mature age
2.18. On the difference between the judge and the disputant
- On the character specific to every political regime
- On the premises common to the three types of oratory

2.19. On premises by which one persuades on possible and impossible things
2.20. On examples
2.21. On maxims
2.22. On enthymemes

2.23. On topics
2.24. On sophistical topics in rhetoric

The commentary on Book III includes the following topics:

3.1. On words and meanings
3.2. On the excellence of rhetorical and poetic words
3.3. Cold Words. On the use of rhetorical and poetic variations of words
3.4. The example is a type of variation
3.5. On conjunctions
3.7. Discourse becomes beautiful only when there are words that excite the imagination
3.8. On pauses and intonations
3.9. On the divisions of rhetorical discourse
3.10. On variations and analogy
3.11. On hyperbole

- On homonyms

3.12. Word choice and oratorical types
3.13. On the parts of speeches
3.14. On the exordium
3.15. On embellishment and topics of defense
3.16. Topics common to praise and deliberation

- On narration

3.17. On deliberation
3.18. On the question

Exposition of the Meanings of Book I of Rhetorica, Which Is Aristotle's Book on Rhetoric

In the name of Allah, the Merciful, the Compassionate

May Allah bless our lord Muḥammad and grant him and his family salvation.

1

1.1.1. [Aristotle] said: The art of rhetoric is analogous to the art of dialectic, for both aim at the same goal, which is to address other people, since a person does not use these two arts to converse with himself, as it is the case in the art of demonstration, but he uses them only with other people. Both are related, in some way, in the same subject, since both are concerned with all things and are used by all people. I mean every person naturally makes use of dialectical and rhetorical statements. And things are such only because neither of the two arts constitutes a definite science. In fact, sciences have special topics and are used by a special category of people. However, since dialectic and rhetoric look into all existing things, and also since sciences look into all existing things as well, the two arts, in some way, are related to them. Since the two arts are related, their examination must belong to one art, which is the art of logic.

1.1.2. Every individual person makes use of some manner of rhetoric and to a certain degree, in either of the two types of statements, one of which is disputation and the other is instruction and, in most cases, in special topics such as complaints, apologies, and all other statements used in particular matters. Several people achieve their purpose through this practice. Some do this by chance; others do it through habit and a steady natural disposition. Of course, those who practice this art through a steady natural disposition are superior to those who practice it by chance. And since that is the case, a person who practices this art by a steady natural disposition and knowledge of what he is doing achieves his goal and is superior. This is something the general public knows, let alone the elite. For this reason, it was deemed necessary to put the parts of this art in a book, and not to be limited to things acquired by a natural disposition or by habit only, as it is the case in several syllogistic arts.

1.1.3. [Aristotle] said: Those among our predecessors who have spoken about this art have not said anything about essential parts or about artistic matters,[14] for those are the things that produce rhetorical assent, especially syllogisms, which in this art are called enthymemes, and which constitute the pillar of persuasion in this art. I mean they come first and foremost. These predecessors have not spoken about the things that produce rhetorical assent in general, or about the enthymemes, which are most proper to this art. They have spoken in excess only about matters external to assent, for these things only help produce assent, such as the discourse on fear, pity, anger, and other similar emotions that are not geared toward the matter to be proved in the first place; they are used only as appeals to the jurymen and opponents. These [nonessential] things only pave the way for assent, but they do not produce it.

1.1.4. [Aristotle] said: If anything of the parts of rhetoric existed as they now did in some states, these predecessors would have nothing useful or beneficial to say about rhetoric. If they ever said anything good, it was something that existed in states in which it was not allowed to speak in front of jurymen about things that would win them over to one side. In such states, only matters that induce assent are permitted. In effect, the inhabitants of these cities in this time are divided into two groups: those who believe that the laws by which the inhabitants are educated should be firmly established in the souls of those citizens in all matters that affect assent, whether they are matters that cause assent or whether they are external matters. There are also those who forbid speaking of external matters especially in front of judges, as it was the case in the government in Athens and in the country of the Greeks.

1.1.5. [Aristotle] said: The view that advises the use of all the things that have an impact on assent in establishing the things that one wants to establish by means of rhetoric is a sound view. If someone used this principle, it would be proper that by using it, he would become in this art an intelligent and refined man.

1.1.6. That external things are useless in this art is evident in the fact that the person who seeks to establish something before the judges either ascertains that something exists or does not exist—I mean something has either existed or has not existed—that is, when the legislator has

14. Did Averroes read Aristotle's *Rhetoric* historically? Clearly, Aristotle had the Sophists in mind when he talked about "these framers of manuals of rhetoric."

determined whether the matter about which there is accusation is important or unimportant, just or unjust. Or he establishes both matters, and that is when the law does not determine that which is discussed. The use of emotions to determine whether something is just or unjust is not possible, since emotions such as pity or anger are only for partial things, whereas justice and injustice are general matters. Also, the use of emotions to show that something has or has not happened has some effect; however, it does not necessarily imply that something has or has not happened. It is only used to appeal to the judges so that they say that he speaks the truth in what he claims or that he does not, without there being for the judge or the opponent any more conviction in what is being discussed.

1.1.7. [Aristotle] said: The laws must determine what is just or unjust and give full power to the judges to decide if something has or has not happened. In sum, the laws give full power to the judges to decide upon small matters for two reasons: First, because it is rare to find a judge who is capable of probing the essence of things in a manner that will allow him to decide that this matter is unjust or this matter just, if not rarely. Quite often most judges in the cities do not have that capacity. Second, because the legislator, to determine what is just or unjust, needs a considerable amount of time, which is not possible in the short amount of time in which the dispute takes place before the judges. For these two reasons, it is difficult to delegate full powers to the judges so that they decide what is just or unjust, beneficial or harmful. They can decide only if something has or has not happened, since it is something evident and because it is a matter that is impossible for the legislator to institute.

1.1.8. [Aristotle] said: Since that is the case, it is evident that those who have spoken about the external things in the subject of rhetoric, such as the exordium, the narration, the emotions, and what is analogous to them, have not spoken about anything that takes the same course as the part in rhetoric; they have spoken only about things that take the same course as accessories. As to the things by which artistic convictions take place and that are, in the first place, the enthymemes, they have said nothing.

1.1.9. Because we think the enthymemes constitute the pillar of this art, we believe that the discourse following the mode of disputation and argument in the presence of judges and the discourse following the mode of instruction and teaching belong to the same art, which is this art [of persuasion]. Those who have spoken about this part of rhetoric should have attributed to this art only what follows the mode of disputation and argument, and not all the types about which there is argument, except the meanest type—that is, the vulgar matters that people quarrel about before the judges. As to the disputes over the making of legislation, there is no benefit in the part of rhetoric that these [handbook writers] have talked about, since they have said nothing about enthymemes. But when they have spoken about things that serve to denigrate or aggrandize something, they have thought that they have explained everything in which rhetorical statements are used. To use things that are external to rhetoric and not things that are proper to rhetorical statements is an improper act.

1.1.10. One must not say that in the statements used in disputes one can be content with external things and disregard the things essential to the matter of dispute, since the laws in most cities prescribe what is just or unjust, and what is great or small, in such a way that in this type of rhetoric one needs only the things that influence the judges as opposed to the statements used in deliberative rhetoric. Statements that give advice about what is to be done, either expedient or harmful, regarding those guilty of crime are easier for the orator to make than forensic statements about these individuals. I mean the statements that maintain that they are unjust or just. This is not about those guilty of crime only. This is the case in speaking about deliberative matters as well as forensic matters. The judges give their ruling, in matters of advice, about matters known to the public—that is, that something is beneficial or harmful—and the public is not afraid that the judges are going to be misled in deciding on it. If this is so, the person speaking in front of them does not need to establish more than this: that the matter is useful or harmful. The judges then will agree, for it will not be possible for them to disagree with him, since what the public knows about what is useful and what is harmful is the same as what the judges know. As to the person speaking before a judge on matters of dispute, he must be mindful of the judges' ruling on what is just or what is unjust, since the knowledge of what is just or what is unjust is foreign to the public, and only lawmakers have that knowledge. Therefore, the judge may permit the speaker to make his case, and he may not decide in the speaker's favor on what is unjust or what is just, for the person speaking before the judges needs to know the things that are unjust and those that are just and the things by which one establishes what is just or what is unjust. This is why the law in many cities forbids speaking about things that may make the judge lean favorably toward one of the litigants. Litigants are allowed to speak only about the things that are prescribed by the lawmaker. As to the speaker on deliberative matters, he does not necessarily need such caution. Judges show extreme caution against saying that something is beneficial when it is not, or that something is not harmful when it is harmful, since that will be disgraceful to them in the eyes of the public, since the public has the same knowledge that the judges have. If things are such, the speaker in forensic matters then needs to know about the things that induce assent more than what a speaker in deliberative matters needs.

1.1.11. **[Aristotle] said:** Given that things related to this art are meant to produce assent and acknowledgment from the part of the person being addressed of the thing about which there is allegation, assent happens only by firmly establishing in him the thing acknowledged, since we only acknowledge something when we are convinced that it has been firmly established in us. The means by which things are firmly established in rhetoric is the enthymeme, since it is the foundation of assent and its pillar in matters that induce this type of assent. I mean rhetorical assent. The enthymeme is a kind of syllogism, the knowledge of which is part of the art of logic. The logician must look into this art, either as a whole or in some of its parts, for clearly a person who understands from what elements a syllogism is composed and when it is composed will be more capable of producing the enthymeme than a person who understands the enthymeme only, but does not understand how the syllogism, which is its genus, operates. A person who, in addition, understands the enthymeme and sees the distinctions between the enthymeme and all syllogisms in other arts will be even more capable than these two.

1.1.12. Such knowledge only belongs to the art of logic, for only this art itself has the power to show what is true or approximately true. Rhetorical convictions, even if they are not true, resemble the truth. Also, people are by instinct predisposed to know the truth itself, and in most cases, they usually tend to aim at the truth and act on it. Laudable premises, and they are the ones from which the enthymemes are derived, resemble the truth because they substitute for truth among the public. That which resembles the truth may belong to the science of truth, which is the science of logic.

1.1.13. If things are such, it is now clear that the limitations of those who spoke of rhetoric are explained by the fact that they did not have any knowledge of logic. All those who have spoken of rhetoric and those who use rhetorical statements only without prior knowledge of these things, which constitute the pillar of rhetoric, have spoken only of things that, in relation to eloquence, take the same course as ornamentation and embellishment, which are superficial, and not of things essential, even if they believe that they have achieved their goal in persuasive statements and that they have followed the right and just course.

1.1.14. **[Aristotle] said:** Rhetoric has two benefits, one of which is to urge citizens to do virtuous deeds, for people naturally tend to do the opposite of what is virtuous and just. If they are not controlled by rhetorical discourse, they tend to be carried away by unjust actions, and that is something blameworthy and the person who does such deeds deserves reprimand. I mean the one who leans toward unjust things or the leader who does not control the citizens by rhetorical discourse so that they do just and virtuous things. By just and virtuous things, I mean those virtues involving one person and other persons; I mean virtuous things between him and his associates no matter what the domain of association may be, not those concerning a relation between a person and himself.

1.1.15. As to the second advantage of rhetoric, one does not have to use proof in theoretical matters to persuade all types of people, since some people either grow up with popular beliefs that are not true, and therefore they are easily persuaded when they are led toward the beliefs they grew up with; or by instinct they are essentially not predisposed to accept demonstration at all; or it is not possible to demonstrate truth to them in a short period of time and expect to obtain assent from them. Therefore, to induce conviction, we have to use premises that we have in common with the audience. I mean we have to use laudable premises.

1.1.16. The art of rhetoric shares this benefit with the art of dialectic, as we have observed in *Kitāb al-Jadal* (*The Topics*) when we have spoken of the things by which to demonstrate different topics.

1.1.17. This art [of rhetoric] can produce persuasion on two opposite sides of an issue, just as in dialectical syllogism. Thus we can persuade an audience that the defendant is guilty or not guilty. I do not mean that we do both things at the same time. We do one thing at one time and we do another thing at another time as we see fit, for most often something may prove to be useful in one time and its opposite useful in another time. Also, when we have available means by which to establish something and its opposite, and we hear a speaker use persuasion to prove something unjust, we can with this power [of persuasion] refute him. These two benefits are found in the ability of this art to persuade for and against something.

1.1.18. This power exists in no other syllogistic arts except in these two—namely, the art of rhetoric and the art of dialectic. Both arts are naturally and equally predisposed to persuade the two opposed sides; I mean that neither is more prepared than the other to persuade one rather than the other of two opposed sides. The ability to persuade both sides is found in both arts equally.

1.1.19. As to the things laid down for these two arts—that is to say, the things about which they persuade and by which they persuade—their ability to receive persuasion is not equal and the benefit of persuasion in them is not equal. But when the things about which these two arts persuade are true, the rhetorical and dialectical statements employed in them are superior and more eloquent.

1.1.20. **[Aristotle] said:** It is not necessary that we consider it bad that a man is incapable of doing damage with his hands and that we do not consider it bad that he is incapable of doing damage with his words, causing damage being a property of man. I mean that he is incapable of causing greater damage by his words, not only the damage that is just but also the damage that is unjust.

1.1.21. [Aristotle's] opinion is that this is common in all the virtues, one of which is this art, with the exception of theoretical and moral virtue, especially in greater, useful matters, such as strength, health, wealth, power, and other similar benefits. I mean that each of these benefits is available for the person acquiring them to benefit other people greatly, provided that he is just. He can also cause greater harm when he is unjust. Health, strength, and power may be used to cause harm or to be useful—and such is the case with rhetoric.

1.1.22. It has been made clear that this art [of rhetoric] does not examine one of two opposite sides. Rather, it examines both sides in an equal manner, just as in dialectic, and that it is very useful for this matter.

1.1.23. The act of this art [of rhetoric] is not inevitably to persuade. I mean that its act is not necessarily followed by persuasion, the way the act of a carpenter is necessarily followed by the making of a chair when there are no external obstacles. The act of rhetoric is to make all the means of persuasion known and available, even if persuasion does not take place.

1.1.24. In this sense, the situation in this art resembles the situation in several arts, such as the art of medicine. The function of medicine is not inevitably to cure, but rather its function is to reach the highest degree of what is possible to do in the case that one is trying to cure. That is why a person who does not belong to these arts may sometimes be associated with the acts of these arts. For example, someone may cure without being a doctor or persuade without being a rhetorician. But the true act [of persuasion] is done by the expert in the art [of rhetoric]. In effect, the goal follows in most cases the act of this one and in the least cases the act of that one.

1.1.25. And since in dialectic there is what is syllogistic and what is believed to be syllogistic when it is not syllogistic, which is the sophistic syllogism, so in persuasive discourses used in this art there is what is truly persuasive and what is believed to be persuasive when it is not. But as the sophist is not a sophist by the fact that he has the power and faculty by which he produces sophistic statements, but he is a sophist by the external honorable and good qualities that he aims to achieve by those statements—and he does this because he gives the illusion that he is a sage of some sort—and as the dialectician is a dialectician only by the faculty that he acquires from this art, it is therefore necessary that the sophistic statements are not part of the art of dialectic; I mean those statements that are believed to be dialectical syllogisms when they are not dialectical when they are used for this purpose; but when they are used by means of proof, they are part of this art. As to the rhetorician, since he sometimes becomes a rhetorician because of external things, such as honor and other good qualities, and he sometimes becomes a rhetorician by the faculty of this art, the statements [that are] believed to be persuasive, but are not persuasive, become part of this art, because the purpose of such statements in this art may be the same as the purpose of the sophist. Things are such because the purpose of this art, with respect to the audience that one wants to persuade, is to provoke an action or excite an emotion. When that happens, there is no difference whether that happens through statements that are truly persuasive or through statements that are believed to be truly persuasive and are not persuasive. If the action or emotion that one aims to obtain from the audience is to a certain degree better for it, not for the rhetorician, the statements that are believed to be persuasive but are not persuasive belong to this art, the same way the statements that are believed to be dialectical, but are not dialectical, belong to the art of dialectic since they are not meant to be sophistic. If the aim of the rhetorician is to obtain a good thing from the good things that sophists aim to obtain, the discourse that is believed to be persuasive but is not persuasive, since it is sophistic, is part of this rhetorical art, because the rhetorician shares the same purpose with the sophist. Thus sophistic statements belong to this art of rhetoric and not to the art of dialectic.

1.1.26. [Aristotle] said: The art [of persuasion], whose benefits we have mentioned and which has not been sufficiently discussed by those who have talked about it, is what we have intended to speak about in the first place, to show of what and how it is composed. What we have first spoken about has not been our primary purpose.

1.1.27. This is why we must resume our discussion of this art and return to our purpose as if we were making a fresh beginning. Let us first begin and define what this art is, so that we explain what it is and make clear its relative kind and its specific division, and then accordingly we proceed with a classification of its parts, following the mode of analysis of definition.

2

1.2.1. [Aristotle] said: Rhetoric is a faculty that takes upon itself persuasion that is possible in any of the individual things.

1.2.2 By "faculty," [Aristotle] means the art that acts on opposites and the purpose of which does not necessarily follow its action. By "takes upon itself," he means to make an effort to find the available means of possible persuasion. By "possible," he means persuasion that is possible in that which is talked about and that is by the highest degree of what is possible. And by saying "in any of the individual things," he means in any of the individual statements existing in each of the ten categories.

1.2.3. This is the part that distinguishes this art [of rhetoric] from all the other arts that are believed to be persuasive in the matters that may be considered. In effect, each art instructs—that is to say, it is demonstrative and persuasive, only in the kinds of things that it considers proper to it, and not in all the other kinds. For example, medicine instructs and persuades by means of demonstration only in matters of health and illness and in their kinds. So is the case with geometry. It instructs by means of demonstration and by means of persuasion in matters of magnitudes and forms found in bodies. As to rhetoric, it takes upon itself persuasion in all matters, in any category and any genre, and therefore it is not concerned with any special genre.

1.2.4. As to the things that produce assent in this art, some are artistic, and these are the ones whose existence depends on our choice and our deliberate reflection and of which we are the doers. Some are not artistic, and they are the ones whose existence does not depend on our choice and our deliberate reflection, such as witnesses, torture, contracts, and similar things that will be mentioned later.

1.2.5. Of artistic things that we do, some have already been produced by others before us, such as argument by means of current examples that have been laid down and have become well known. Some are invented by us when we talk about the thing in which there is persuasion and are discovered by us.

1.2.6. As to the modes of persuasion that we invent, they are of three kinds.

1.2.7. One is when the speaker establishes the excellence of his moral character, which makes him worthy of being credible, as when Allah the All Highest said, reporting the words of Hūd, "And I am to you a sincere and trustworthy adviser."[15] Also, the speaker, from his facial expression and his body posture, is in a disposition that produces assent regarding the subject about which he is talking, as when he carries himself slowly and deliberately, and with dignity, and so on and so forth. This type of excellent moral character of the speaker is what Aristotle refers to as "the manner and disposition," and that is what he means by "appearance."

1.2.8. That men of excellent moral character are quickly believed without having to make an effort in what they say is a sign that excellence of moral character has an effect in producing conviction. This happens only in matters that are apparent to the senses that they claim to have felt. For example, one has drunk or one has killed. But as to giving information about matters hidden to the senses—and they are those that one believes that what men of excellent moral character have felt about them or have fancied them when it is possible that the senses have an erroneous impression about them—they are not going to be believed in the things that they claim without using discourse to establish those things.

1.2.9. **[Aristotle] said:** It is not true, as those whom we have mentioned and who have spoken of rhetoric believe, that perseverance and excellence of moral character are useful only in the section on emotions.

15. Qur'an, *Surat al-Aʿrāf,* verse 68.

1.2.10. As to the second kind of conviction, it is the kind that occurs when the hearer has, through discourse, a certain emotion that necessitates assent about that which is talked about. Our conviction and our assent are not the same when we are happy or when we are sad. And the same is true when we are angry or when we are pleased. These are the things that those we have mentioned and who have spoken of rhetoric have talked about.

1.2.11. As to the third kind of conviction, it has to do with determining the thing, with speech that is persuasive or is believed to be persuasive, in the particular cases about which there is persuasion.

1.2.12. Since the convictions exist in this art only according to these modes, it is evident that a speaker who can possibly cause persuasion in any particular case is only a person who knows three things. First, he must know persuasive arguments; second, he must understand moral character and virtues; and third, he must understand the emotions—that is, the nature of each emotion, where it comes from, and when and how it happens. When such is the case, this art [of rhetoric] is composed of the art of discourse and the art of ethics, by which I mean civic discourse.

1.2.13. The predecessors in this art have not spoken of its divisions in a comprehensive manner, either because of their ignorance or because they kept back from other people what they knew for benefits coming from outside.

1.2.14. This art [of rhetoric] is a branch of logic, and it resembles dialectic in that it examines the two opposite sides. Also, the two arts do not treat of a specific subject in a manner to attain certitude; the two arts only attain by their examination what is below certitude. [Aristotle] has spoken earlier about this subject in a sufficient manner.

1.2.15. Now we must begin by defining persuasive arguments and what is considered persuasive.

1.2.16. **We say:** Just as in dialectic the arguments by which we affirm [something] or annul [it] are of two types, one of which is induction or what is believed to be induction and the other is a syllogism or what is believed to be a syllogism, so it is with the arguments by which we affirm [something] or annul [it] in this art of rhetoric. They are of two types, one of which resembles induction, and it is called the example, and the other resembles the syllogism, and it is called the enthymeme. The enthymeme that is believed to be an enthymeme, but is not an enthymeme, resembles a syllogism that is believed to be a syllogism, but is not a syllogism. In the same way, the example that is believed to be an example, but is not an example, resembles induction that is believed to be induction but is not induction. The enthymeme is a rhetorical syllogism, and the example is a rhetorical induction. When we carefully consider the methods followed by orators, it is clear that they produce all the convictions that exist in discourse by using these two types. I mean they use either the example or the enthymeme, because by doing so, they aim to obtain something that resembles induction and the syllogism. What they do from this they only do by what is in truth an example or an enthymeme or what is believed to be so and is not so. It has been made evident from *Kitāb al-Qiyās* (*Prior Analytics*) that every conviction is achieved by the syllogism and that induction and the example give conviction only because of the force of the syllogism that they both have.

1.2.17. As to what the syllogism is, and how it differs from demonstration, it has been discussed in *Kitāb al-Jadal* (*The Topics*). The difference between the syllogism and induction has also been made clear in this book. Both induction and the example prove that something exists in this way or does not exist in this way because of the fact that this thing exists or does not exist in what resembles it. The enthymeme and the syllogism have in common the fact that each one of them is a proposition that must be followed by another proposition.

1.2.18. Since that is the case, it is evident that in each of these two genres of discourse there is a rhetorical type, a dialectical type, a demonstrative type, and a sophistic type, so that as induction and the syllogism are found in these arts, in a similar manner, the example and the enthymeme are found in rhetoric. The difference in these arts is in usage—namely, in the art of demonstration and the art of dialectic. In dialectic, the syllogism is more dependable than induction. In rhetoric, the example is more persuasive than the enthymeme, since the enthymeme is more open to opposition than the example. We shall discuss later the reason why these things happen and how they are used.

1.2.19. But now we must define these two modes of persuasion—namely, the enthymeme and the example. We say, a persuasive statement is persuasive either to one person, or to a group of people, or to the majority of people. Also, a persuasive statement is persuasive in a universal matter or in a particular matter. Also, in both cases, a persuasive statement is persuasive because it is self-evident or because it is proved from other persuasive statements. Statements proved from other statements in particular cases are of two types, one of which is when someone says that something is such only because of such, as when somebody says, "Drinking oxymel is beneficial for so and so because he has a fever." This is what we call the enthymeme. The second type is when someone says that something is such because it resembles such. For example, someone says, "So and so is taking oxymel and it is helping him because someone else took it and it helped him." This is what we call the example.

1.2.20. The statements that are persuasive for one individual person only are not used in this art, because they are not infinite and they are not known to the person using them. For this reason, this art does not use from among laudable premises, by which I mean acceptable, what is acceptable to one individual person only—and those are opinions that occur to people when they experience longing and fancies—but only uses what is laudable to most or all people, the way it is used in dialectic.

1.2.21. Since that is the case, what distinguishes the syllogism used in the art of dialectic and the art of demonstration from the enthymeme, which is used in this art [of rhetoric], is that the syllogism is arranged in such a way as to draw a necessary conclusion, whereas with the enthymeme, its premises are arranged in a manner familiar and acceptable to the general public, and that is different from technical arrangement.

1.2.22. People tend to be suspicious of statements resulting from technical arrangement and see that the results have been reached only from a technical point of view and not from the point of view of the matter itself. Also, a technical arrangement requires that all necessary premises be expressed in making the purpose evident. And people will not be able to understand a conclusion drawn from several premises. Also, people do not establish a distance between the conclusion and the thing from which the conclusion is drawn; I mean they do not state in the syllogisms the two premises together with the conclusion; they provide only one premise and follow it with a conclusion. For example, they might say, "This man is roaming around the street at night; therefore, he must be a burglar." They do not say, "And every man who roams around the streets at night is a burglar," which is the major premise.

1.2.23. Moreover, because the enthymemes are in most cases produced technically in possible situations—which is evident in deliberative matters, since no one ever suggests to anybody else something the existence of which is necessary or something the existence of which is impossible—and the major premise in such matters is partly false, people do not declare [the major premise] in the syllogisms that they use in this art of rhetoric for fear that its falsehood may be discerned.

1.2.24. In addition, because technically well-produced syllogisms in this art are of only one type, either the syllogisms that are composed of premises whose persuasion is self-evident or premises that have been evident by other premises mixed with them, without which the character of laudable premises is not evident, it follows necessarily in this second type that it will be difficult to compose premises and to arrange them in an artistic manner because of their big number and the long period of time it takes to declare them all and arrange them in an artistic manner. That is something that the judges do not encourage; on the contrary, they urge the speaker to use language that is simple and not contrived, following the conventions of the general public. When language is not composed in this [simple and natural] manner, it is not persuasive, and this is, in the two cases, where persuasion takes place; I mean in the case where something exists or does not exist and, in the case [where] it exists, if it is laudable or not laudable. Also, when someone uses conviction by taking the method of similarity that he investigates and turns it into an inductive method, the difficulty that we have described with respect to the length of time and the excessive number of premises occurs.

1.2.25. When such is the case, the rhetorical syllogism, which is the enthymeme, and the example are only in the things where syllogistic and inductive [reasoning] absolutely exists. Such things are taken in a manner different from the manner in which the syllogism and the induction are taken. When those things are used in the manner that [Aristotle] explained in *Kitāb al-Qiyās* (*Prior Analytics*), the example becomes induction and the enthymeme a syllogism. When they are taken in the manner that we have mentioned, the induction becomes an example and the syllogism an enthymeme. That case consists in taking the syllogism and the induction by means of a few brief premises, since there is more persuasion with a few brief premises and also with premises that are absolutely clear and from which what is hidden has been deleted.

1.2.26. In addition, the laudable [thing to do] in this art is to delete the point from which the thing follows [the necessary premise] and to put forth what follows from [the necessary conclusion], for to inform about what is attached and about that with which there is attachment [i.e., both premises] is similar to mentioning the thing twice, which is considered prattle, according to the immediate point of view. Accordingly, the middle term in a syllogism is mentioned only once; so it is the case with induction. That which is similar is mentioned only once. Therefore, the syllogism is necessarily an enthymeme—that is, one of its premises is omitted. In this way, it is called an enthymeme since one of the premises is omitted. The induction is necessarily an example.

1.2.27. [Aristotle] said: The premises in rhetorical syllogisms may be necessary, and that happens in a few cases, or they may be possible, and that happens in most cases, because most public examination is about only what can possibly be and what cannot possibly be. And that is clear in the things about which we deliberate, for they are all matters done to humans, and it is not possible for things done to humans to be either necessary or impossible. Conclusions that are necessary are drawn only from premises that are themselves necessary; and conclusions that are possible are drawn only from premises that are themselves possible.

1.2.28. Some enthymemes come from laudable premises; others come from signs. By laudable premises, I mean those that are not signs. For example, we must thank a benevolent person and blame a malevolent person. By signs, I mean the things that indicate the existence of something for something else. These two types of premises—namely, laudable premises and signs—are found in necessary and possible materials. They do not exist only in things that are possible in most cases, but also in those things that are equally possible. These materials are those whose relation to possible premises in most cases is the relation of the whole to the part. In effect, truth in necessary things is in most cases more general than truth in possible things, since necessary things are found in universal subjects, and possible things in most cases are not. The relation of the equally possible to the possible in most cases is the same; I mean that possible things are believed to be true with respect to their subjects more than to equally possible things.

1.2.29. Of the signs taken as middle term, some are more general than the smaller term and more particular than the larger term; others are more general than both terms; and others are more particular than both.

1.2.30. A sign that is more general than the smaller term and more particular than the larger one is necessarily composed in the first kind. If it is of a more possible material, it is what the ancients define as "the more similar." An example of a sign of necessary material would be "This woman produces breast milk; therefore, she has given birth to a baby."

An example of a more probable material would be "So and so is preparing arms and assembling men and there is no enemy nearby; therefore, he wants to revolt against the king." An example of an equally probable material would be "So and so shows fatigue. A person who shows fatigue has a fever; therefore, so and so has a fever." This type is known as "doubtful."

1.2.31. As to that which is more general than the two terms, it is composed in the second form, except that it leads to a conclusion only in the immediate apparent point of view. An example of the more probable material [type] is "Socrates breathes hard. A person who has a fever breathes hard; therefore, Socrates has a fever." These two premises are true, but the conclusion may be untrue, since Socrates's breathing hard may be due to running. Since that is concealed to many people, when they see that such true premises produce false conclusions, they believe that such premises contain falsehood. Then they are inclined to refute the first premises but find it hard to do that because of the truth of those premises, and thus they become perplexed.

1.2.32. As to those signs that are more particular than the two terms, they produce conclusions in the third form, in a particular [and] not universal manner. But the conclusion is taken in this art as universal. An example of a necessary material is "All things are in the celestial world; and all things are in a time; therefore, time is of the celestial world." An example of a probable material is "Wise men are just because Socrates is wise and just."

1.2.33. Proofs of the second and third forms are called "signs"; those of the first form are called [complete] "proofs." Proofs of the second form are closer to being signs than those of the third form. Also, the more probable proofs are called "that which closely resembles." The equally probable are called "doubtful enthymeme."

1.2.34. From what has been said, we have explained probabilities, proofs, and signs and the differences among them. But in truth, what has been made evident with respect to syllogisms is only what has been explained in *Kitāb al-Qiyās* (*Prior Analytics*), because it is in this book that we have indicated what a syllogism is, the number of the types of syllogisms, and we have showed, in each of these types, what is a syllogism and what is not.

1.2.35. As to the example, it has been described earlier as a certain type of induction. But it differs from induction in that we do not move from the part to explain the whole, the way we do in certain types of induction. Nor do we move from the whole to the part, the way we do in certain types of induction. And that is when we explain, by the whole that we have established by induction, a part other than the parts by the induction of which we have established the whole. The example is similar to induction in that it goes from part to part because of their coming together in a whole. This is when we bring together in the induction the two statements at once. I mean when we go from part to whole and from whole to another part, because in this manner, we go from part to part by means of the whole, just as in the example. In the example, we go from part to part only because the two have in common a whole, since the judgment taken from one part to the other belongs to the most common part because of this whole, or that it is believed to belong to it from its part; otherwise, the transfer from part to part will not be appropriate. I mean if there is no whole because of which this judgment belongs to the more familiar part. An example of what happens in the induction—I mean the transfer from part to part by means of a whole—is, as someone has said, "Your Majesty, so and so has requested to be your bodyguard, and he is a former enemy. Do not let him be your guard, because he wants to kill the king. So and so made the same request to king so and so, and another man asked the same thing of king so and so—the speaker here talking about people that he enumerates—and they later murdered their kings." The speaker here has made in this statement the transfer from part to part by means of a whole—that is, anyone who asks to join the guard and has been an enemy of the king wants to murder the king. However, this whole, which inscribes itself in the soul so forcefully, even though not stated by the person using the transfer from part to part, is an induction if the transfer to it in the mind has more parts. If it is from one of its parts, or from less, then it is an example.

1.2.36. [Aristotle] said: Of the things that are called examples, we have said enough.

1.2.37. The discourse on the sections of enthymemes from the point of view of the things from which they are produced is vague and hidden, but it is very useful for our purpose here. The reason this discourse is vague is that the enthymemes exist in all the ten categories, just as the dialectical syllogisms. But of the enthymemes, some are in the materials found in the arts, like the enthymemes that are used in universal and particular matters in the art of medicine and the other arts. These enthymemes must be used in these arts like demonstrations used in that art, not in the manner they are used by a speaker in a matter concerning rhetoric when, for example, he uses them as part of a speech, and all the other things by which rhetorical statements become more effective, which will be mentioned later. Of the enthymemes, some are concerned with this art in accordance with what has been made evident of its usefulness, and they are voluntary questions. And these are the types that must be used following the manner in which speakers use rhetorical statements. These are the things that must be considered in enumerating the sections of enthymemes in this art, not the materials that are found in each one of the arts.

1.2.38. **[Aristotle] said:** The more general a statement is, the more appropriate and the easier it is to use in many things; and the more particular it is, the more adequate it is to be part of a particular art. For this reason, the topics are more general than rhetorical syllogisms and dialectical syllogisms, for the topics are common to logical, natural, and political matters, by which I mean voluntary matters, as in the topics "more or less" that have been enumerated in Book II of *Kitāb al-Jadal* (*The Topics*). For from these topics, we do not produce the syllogisms in one of the three arts that we have mentioned, but in all the arts, since we do not use these topics themselves, but we use their power. As to the types, they are special premises that apply to particular arts. For example, we do not produce syllogisms in ethical matters from premises from which syllogisms are produced in natural matters. In the same way, we do not produce syllogisms in natural matters from premises from which syllogisms are produced in ethical matters. Since that is the case, then syllogisms are not composed from the topics in a particular art, since what is conceived from these topics is common to more than one art. As to the types, it is from them that syllogisms are composed, and by these syllogisms the art to which these types are proper is consolidated.

1.2.39. But the types that we intend to mention in this book are not certain premises, because if that were the case, rhetorical syllogisms would be certain syllogisms and they would not be dialectical syllogisms, let alone rhetorical. The enthymemes used in this art are in most cases composed of these types, whether they are those that are proper to each of the three genres of rhetoric or those that are common to the three genres of rhetoric that we will define later.

1.2.40. **[Aristotle] said:** Here we must do in these things as we did in *Kitāb al-Jadal* (*The Topics*). Just as what has been mentioned there of materials of dialectical matters has been divided into topics and types, so here we must divide the matters from which enthymemes are produced into topics and types. Types are the universal premises used in each of the particular arts; the topics are the universal premises, whose particular ones are used in each art.

1.2.41. First, we must speak of the types and then the topics. But first, we must define the genres that are proper to this art [of rhetoric], by which I mean the types of subjects proper to rhetoric. When we have enumerated them, then we can enumerate their elements and premises separately.

3

1.3.1. There are three types of things that rhetoric looks into with respect to voluntary matters, just as there are three kinds of listeners. For a speech is composed of three parts: a speaker, who is the orator; the subject that is talked about, about which statements are produced; and those to whom the discourse is addressed, and they are the listeners. The purpose of a speech is to address these listeners. The listeners are undoubtedly a disputant, or a judge, or a person we intend to persuade. A judge may be a person looking into future things that are useful or harmful, or into past actions. Of past actions, some are found in a person by his choice, and they are virtues and vices. Some are found in a person, not by his choice, but are caused by another person, and they are injustice and justice. The judge looking into future actions is the leader; the judge looking into past actions is appointed by the leader, such as the magistrate in our cities, which are the cities of Islam. As to the disputant, he only uses the power of the faculty of rhetoric in disputation. The types of rhetorical discourse, then, are three: deliberative, disputative, and demonstrative.[16]

1.3.2. A deliberative enthymeme may be permission or it may be prohibition. When someone gives advice to a citizen on a private matter, or to all the inhabitants of the city on a public matter, his discourse is either permission or prohibition. Similarly, disputative discourse is of two

16. The Arabic verb *thabbata* carries the meaning of firmly establishing a fact or truth through demonstration.

types. It is either an accusation or an acquittal from an accusation. As to demonstrative discourse, it is either praise or blame.

1.3.3. The time that is proper for things about which we deliberate is the future, for a man only gives advice to another man on nonexistent things. The time that is proper for things about which there is disputation is the past, for we only accuse about things that have already taken place. And if we accuse about things that are expected to happen on the part of the person we are accusing, that is an accusation by way of giving advice on what is useful in that respect. In the same way, it happens that deliberation is about things that have already happened, but from the point of view of what is expected of them. Whenever accusation is about one thing and not about another thing, it is always about something that has happened. As for things about which there is demonstration, the most appropriate time is the present. I mean the time that is closer to now. People only praise or blame with reference to things that exist, at the moment of praise or at the moment of blame, in the person who is praiseworthy or the person who is blameworthy. Through artful use of exaggeration of virtues and vices, some people probably praise a person for the things they expect to happen or wish to happen from him and thus mix praise with a call on him to do those things.

1.3.4. These discourses have three goals in view. Deliberative discourse aims at what is beneficial or what is harmful, for the counselor approves what is beneficial or what is more beneficial and reproves what is harmful or what is more harmful. As to the discourse of disputation, the aim is what is just or what is unjust. As to demonstrative discourse, the aim is what is moral and what is immoral. If one of these discourses has in view the goal of another type of discourse, that is not its first intention; the intention is to aim for a special goal. For example, the counselor uses persuasion to shows that something is just or unjust, in order to approve a just course of action because of the benefit that it brings, and to reprove an unjust action because of the harm that is expected from it. Virtue and vice are used in the same way. I mean from the point of view of the good and bad that result from them. Since each of these three goals is proper to each type of discourse, by which I mean goals according to the first intention, the definitions that distinguish each of these three types from one another are provided by the specific differences resulting from these goals.

1.3.5. What indicates that these goals are proper to each of these three genres of discourse is that when one of them is used to persuade with the end of another genre in view, the opponent may not protest what is being said and may often concede, although he may not concede the goal proper to this discourse. For example, when someone makes an allegation that so and so has taken money from so and so, and that is undoubtedly harmful, the opponent will probably concede that it did happen, but he will not concede that taking the money from him was unjust. Similarly, the counselor may concede that a possible act is unjust, but he will not concede that it is harmful. Since these ends are mixed together, it so happens that counselors very often recommend, by way of deceit, harmful things and claim that they are just, or that they are not unjust, without admitting that they are harmful. They may even artfully claim that such things are beneficial. For example, they may advise [soldiers] to patiently accept death in battle and not to flee, because fleeing is considered by the law unjust. Also, when a nation defeats and conquers another nation, the counselor will probably advise people not to feel any resentment toward that conquest, claiming that it is not unjust, and he may even mislead them by suggesting that the conquest is not harmful. In a similar manner, a man who praises [an action] may admit that something is harmful, but he will also claim that it is virtuous, as when someone saves a man from death and knows that he will meet death by doing so. Thus the opponent concedes that death is harmful, but he will also see that it is virtuous. In a similar manner also, he may praise a despicable action, artfully claiming that it is beneficial, and not concede that it is despicable. On the contrary, he will claim that it is a virtuous action because of the benefit that comes in it. Thus each of these discourses uses the ends of other discourses by accident, and that is why there is no dispute about them, but there is certainly dispute about their ends. If a discourse uses the end of another type of discourse, that is a form of sophism.

1.3.6. **[Aristotle] said:** Since this art is syllogistic, it is evident that there must be premises in it. Its premises are the three that we have described: laudable premises, proofs, and signs. An absolute syllogism is composed of absolute propositions; a syllogism proper to each particular art is composed of premises proper to it. This is why an enthymeme is a syllogism composed of these premises, which we have mentioned.

1.3.7. Because of the subject matter about which we give counsel, we first need to know whether the action is possible, for impossible actions cannot be done either in the present or in the future. In a similar manner, in the two other kinds of this art, I mean the demonstrative kind and the forensic kind, we need to show first that something has happened. Therefore, the master of this art must have, other than the premises by which he demonstrates those three ends, premises by which he will persuade his audience that something is possible or impossible and that it has happened or has not happened.

1.3.8. Further, since orators do not limit themselves to praise and blame, approval and denial, accusation and defense, but they also take upon themselves the task to demonstrate that the matter is good or bad, significant or insignificant, honorable or disgraceful, appropriate or inappropriate, and that is either in an absolute manner or through syllogisms—I mean that it is greater and nobler or the opposite—it is evident that orators need to have at their command premises by which they demonstrate that the good or bad is greater or lesser, base or noble, appropriate to that which it is related or inappropriate.

1.3.9. Such are all the kinds of premises used in this art.

1.3.10. Since this has been made evident, we must now begin by enumerating the premises proper to each of these three ends and give an account of premises, first in deliberative oratory, then in demonstrative oratory, and third in forensic oratory.

4

1.4.1. The first thing we must consider with regard to matters about which we deliberate is, what is the good that we give counsel about? Deliberation is, in effect, not about everything good, but in the good things that may or may not be. As to the good the production or nonproduction of which is by necessity, there is no deliberation about it. Nor is there deliberation about all the possible good things, since herein are good things that possibly exist by nature, but there is [deliberation] about possible good things the production or nonproduction of which depends on us—they are the things the principle of the production of which is by choice and will—and among these things are the things whose existence or non-existence depends on our deliberate reflection and actions at the most. As to the things that come from deliberate reflection by chance and on a few occasions, they do not in most cases belong to the scope of deliberation, except when the other kind [of oratory] does not possibly exist. What indicates that counsel is indeed achieved by these things is that the person examines, first, if the thing he wants to do is possible or impossible. Then if such action is possible, he should consider the means by which it is possible and the manner in which it is possible. Once that becomes clear to him, he will proceed to work on it. But if it becomes clear to him that such action is not possible, he will abandon it. The things about which we give counsel are the things about which we deliberate.

1.4.2. What we have said evidently shows the good that we recommend and in what things it can happen, and these are the voluntary things the existence of which depends on us; they are not the necessary things the existence of which does not depend on us.

1.4.3. As to giving a complete account of the difference between voluntary and involuntary things and providing an exact enumeration of their types and the knowledge of the essence of each one of them, to the utmost degree of what their nature allows us to know, that is not the object of this art [of rhetoric] to know voluntary things; rather, it is the object of the art of philosophy, which is superior to this art [of rhetoric] in the formulation of concepts and conviction, and the premises used in it are more truthful and more accurate than those used in this art [of rhetoric].[17] In effect, here we are not concerned, in relation to the knowledge of these things, with the essential states relative to them, but with widely known matters.

1.4.4. Since such is the case, as we have described in these things, it is also evident from what we have said that everything we have said about the particulars of this art [of rhetoric] is true; I mean that it is composed of the science of logic and the science of ethical politics, and that there are in it things that are dialectical or that resemble dialectical things and also things that are sophistical or that resemble sophistical things. Things that exist in numerous arts become parts of one art only when they are all taken in [the context where] [the mode and state by which] those many things are collectively useful in the purpose of that particular art and from which the states that are different are discounted; I mean the things that are not considered useful for the purpose of that particular art. Since such is the case, ethical matters become part of this art [of rhetoric], because they are intended for public speaking. They are also part of the art of politics, since they constitute some of the things that

17. Whereas Aristotle leaves the reference to the other branch of knowledge vague, Averroes indicates that this branch is philosophy.

we intend to learn and study. Dialectical and sophistical matters become part of this art [of rhetoric], since what is used from them in this art is already familiar to humans and is not beyond their knowledge; for example, of the syllogism, it only uses the syllogism that is commonly known to the public, which is the example and the enthymeme. The same thing goes with sophistical matters. [Rhetoric] uses from them only the things that are ordinarily used by the public, such as absolutes and restrictions and other things that the public is naturally accustomed to use. This art [of rhetoric] differs from these [dialectical and sophistical] matters only by the degree of examination. This art also differs, by the degree of examination of voluntary questions, from the examination devoted to them by political science. I mean it devotes to the examination of voluntary questions only the type of examination that is previously known to people and leaves to political science the task of examining that area thoroughly.

1.4.5. Of the matters about which the orator gives counsel, some concern all the inhabitants of a city, and some concern particular individuals from that city or community. As to the important civic matters about which people deliberate, they are about five. The first of these is about money supplies for the city; the second one is about war and peace; the third one is about national defense; the fourth one is about import and export; and the fifth one is about legal obligations.

1.4.6. [The speaker] who gives counsel about supplies needs to know three things. First, he needs to know the city's sources of revenue; that is, whether they are plant, animal, metal [sources of revenue], or all these things together, or two of them, so that if any has decreased, he suggests that it be increased. Second, he needs to know all the expenditures of the people of the city. Third, he needs to know the types of people in the city, so that if there is a person in it that is unproductive, and that is a person with no virtue, or idle, and that is a person with no skill, he advises that this person should be turned away from the country. If there is a person who is extravagant in things unfavorable or unnecessary, [the speaker giving counsel] advises that the surplus be taken away from him, for wealth comes not only by increasing money but also by reducing expenses. It is said, "A small family is one of two ways to prosperity."

1.4.7. **[Aristotle] said:** From the necessity requiring these things and the degree of the need for these things, the orator gets to know what he needs to give advice about regarding each and every one of these things. He does not necessarily need to be a farmer in order for him to give advice about increasing crops or a shepherd in order for him to give advice about increasing farm animals, but it will suffice for him to know the degree of the need for these things. However, in addition to this, he needs to be knowledgeable of past ways and means in these things and what knowledge people have of them.

1.4.8. As to the speaker giving advice on war or peace, he needs to know the degree of the power of the enemy being fought, the degree of the power of the fighting army, as well as the degree of what will be gained from this war, whether it is small or large. He also needs to know the state of the city, with regard to its strength and fortification, the weakness or strength of its inhabitants, and the surface area of the city, whether it is small or large. I mean whether the number of its inhabitants is the number of people who can fight a war, if they have the qualifications of those who can fight a war or not. He also needs to know something about past wars so that he can show the people how to wage a war if he advises fighting a war and make the business of war look easy for them, or to make them understand what is detestable in a war if he advises them to abandon the idea of getting engaged in a war. He must know not only the facts about his countrymen, but also the facts about those who live on the border with his country and in the harbor. I mean facts about them in these matters as well as facts about how they deal with their enemy when they win a war or when they are incapable of winning. From these, the orator draws useful premises in giving his people counsel [as to] whether they should go to war or have peace. He also needs to know how to distinguish good wars from unjust wars. He needs to know the condition of the armies. Are they the same in strength, in courage, in judgment, and in the good accomplishment of each particular part of war that each division has been assigned? I mean that the armies become the same in that matter, for perhaps they have increased in number and multiplied to the point that some of them are not fit for war or for part of the war that they have been assigned. Additionally, he must study not only the outcomes of the wars that the armies of his country have fought but also the outcomes of the wars that all similar armies have fought in the past, for [it is] on similar things that we form a judgment on what is similar. I mean that if wars similar to theirs led to a misfortune, he should advocate peace. If they led to victory, he should advocate war.

1.4.9. As to national defense, the orator giving counsel needs to know about the methods of national defense, the degree of defense that is necessary in each and every emergency, as well as the number of types of defense available. In addition, he needs to know the [strategic] positions that are protected by men, which are called the forts, so that if the number of guards is small, it may be increased, and if the guards are not going to be useful, they may be removed, particularly those guards that do not intend to protect the city and intend only to care for themselves. He also needs to protect more the hidden points. I mean the points whose protection is very beneficial. An orator who knows all this is capable of offering counsel on national defense and of becoming an expert in questions of national defense for the country.

1.4.10. As to advice regarding food and all other essential supplies that the city needs, the orator giving counsel about this matter needs to know how much is available and how much will suffice; how much already exists in the city, and whether enough has or has not been imported; what articles must be exported, and that is the surplus in the city; and what articles must be imported, and that is what the city seriously needs. The orator needs to know all these things so that he may give appropriate counsel.

1.4.11. A person needs to protect his countrymen for two reasons: first, for the sake of the virtuous, and second, for the sake of the wealthy that are there for the sake of the virtuous. In general, those who protect cities need to know about all these five types when defending cities.

1.4.12. **[Aristotle] said:** As to the examination of the subject of legislation and giving counsel about such legal matters, they are not easy when the matter involves cities, for the safety and unity of cities are only guaranteed by the law. Therefore, the legislator ought to know how many different forms of political systems there are and which law is useful for a particular political system and which law is not useful; for which people a particular law or particular political system is suitable and for which people it is not suitable. He also ought to know the things that one would fear might introduce corruption into the city, either from external opposition or from the people in the city. All cities, except the virtuous city, may get corrupt by the laws instituted in them, and that is when those laws are excessively weak and lenient or excessively harsh, whether in matters of opinion, or morality, or action. A political system that is called freedom appears to turn often, for this reason, into a mean form of government; that is, a government of greed or a government of money. What [Aristotle] has said is evident to us in the forms of government whose histories have reached us.

1.4.13. [Aristotle] said: This form of government—I mean a free democratic form of government—does not in the end turn into a government of the vile, [an oligarchy], because of flexibility and laxity of laws, although that is often the case, but because of excess. For many things, when in excess, cease to exist, the same way they cease to exist from weakness and inadequacy. For example, a nose that is excessively snub is believed to be nearly not a nose at all. But if it is not excessively snub, it is close to being normal.

1.4.14. [Aristotle] said: [The orator] needs to know the laws that several people instituted and found useful in each of the notorious forms of government and in each nation so that he can use from them what is beneficial for him and the nation that is proper to him. Therefore, it is evident that the legislator's knowledge of the temperament of people, of their morals and their customs, is useful in instituting the laws. For from this, it is possible to institute laws that are beneficial to different nations with different customs.

1.4.15. As to corruption coming into the cities from outside—I mean corruption coming from enemies—it is a self-evident matter. People have written about the ways from which the victory of enemies is expected to happen and the ways by which one can protect oneself against such enemies. From these, the orator draws premises by which he gives counsel to his countrymen about protection from enemies.

1.4.16. What we have said about legislation and about the things the lawmaker ought to know is the business of political science and not of rhetoric. Here we have mentioned only what is sufficient for this art [of rhetoric].

1.4.17. [Aristotle] said: These are the most important matters about which orators give counsel to the people of the city. In such matters, there are things about which orators give counsel to particular individuals as well. Now we shall speak of things from which there is approval and disapproval when addressing each and every individual. We shall first begin by explaining the things about which counselors give advice, in such a way as to approve them or disapprove them.

5

1.5.1. It seems as if every person has a certain passion and a natural desire for the good that everybody wants for himself and recommends to others, without any one of them knowing what that good is, for them to choose it and prefer it to other things. When asked about it, they give an answer announcing its nature when it only exists in each one of them. And when asked, one by one, what its name means, each one will give a different answer. This good is preferred by everybody because of this passion that they have for it by nature. This good is, in general, the state of well-being and the constituents of the state of well-being. Therefore, we must first explain in general terms what is meant by a state of well-being, and then explain its constituents and their opposites and the things about which there is approval and disapproval, and they are the things that are advantageous or more advantageous, or harmful or more harmful, in a state of well-being. In this way, we will complete our discussion of the things from which statements of deliberative oratory used among people are achieved.

1.5.2. **[Aristotle] said:** Those who have spoken of this art [of rhetoric] have spoken only of things treated in the same manner as universals. For example, they have said, "The orator must exaggerate a small matter if he wants to make it look magnificent and diminish a great matter if he wants to make it look despicable; he must not approve of things that corrupt the state of well-being or the things that impede the state of well-being or extend to the opposite of the state of well-being." They have not mentioned the things by which a matter is exaggerated or diminished, or the things that necessarily cause the deterioration of the state of well-being, or impede the state of well-being, or extend to the opposite of the state of well-being.

1.5.3. **[Aristotle] said:** As to the state of well-being, it is a good action combined with virtue, a long life, a pleasant life with security, wealth, good standing among people, and, in addition, the things that preserve and cause these things. What proves that this is the well-known definition of the state of well-being is that all people consider this to be the state of well-being or something close to it.

1.5.4. Since the state of well-being is this, its constituent parts are good birth, plenty of brothers and children; wealth; good action; a good old age; bodily excellences, such as health, beauty, vigor, large stature, and strength; fame; majesty; happiness; virtue and its constituent parts, such as reason, courage, temperance, and kindness. The individual is, in this manner, more completely independent and more self-sufficient, by which I mean if he possesses external goods as well as internal goods, excellences of the soul and bodily excellences being internal. Good birth, brothers, wealth, and honor are external. It is believed that power and good luck—what people call happiness—are also external. With these things, the life of an individual becomes, in its course, the life of someone who is not lacking anything external and whose goods are not spoiled by anything bad.

1.5.5. Since things are such, we must now examine each of these constituent parts according to the view for which we aim, and that is the commonly known view.

1.5.6. As to good birth, it means that the people from whom the individual comes are indigenous or ancient in the city; that they are, in addition, rulers or leaders of good repute and great numbers; that they are, in addition, free citizens and have never been dispersed; or that they are of those who have obtained beautiful things envied by people even when they are not rulers or leaders. As to the examination concerning the question of whether good birth comes from males only or from females, it seems, as everybody agrees, that it is more perfect if it comes from both. The orator must use, with regard to this subject, what is notable in every nation. Of the conditions of good birth, the existence of the leaders and free citizens from the group famed for virtue and wealth and other such noble qualities does not cease in the group from the individual in question, in the group from which he comes; but there always exist, in this race, elderly men possessing this quality and who are followed by young men possessing those qualities. If honor ends in this race from which he comes, he is not of good birth; and if it does not end in that race, he is of good birth, even if it ends in those who are born from that race.

1.5.7. The good state of being with the possession of children and with their great number is something quite evident. Applied to a community, the good state of being with the possession of children means a great number of young men possessing excellences of the body as well as excellences of the soul. As to the excellences of the body, they are four. The first one is stature, which means that their figure is natural and by which they surpass many people; the second one is beauty; the third one is strength; and the fourth one is bravery. With these four qualities, the young men are good in their bodily excellences. As to the excellences of the soul, the young men are good with two, which are temperance and courage. As to what produces a good state of being for some people, it is a great number of male and female children.

1.5.8. The good condition of female children comes with excellences in the body and the soul. As to bodily excellences, they are two: [first,] a well-rounded body, which means a body whose parts are of natural shape and that has plenty of natural flesh, not fat, and [second,] beauty. As to excellences of the soul, they are three: temperance, love of congeniality, and love of hard work. With these excellences, the home gains perfection.

1.5.9. It is fitting that these excellences, which we have talked about, exist in all women from the lineage of that man [whom we are discussing] in general; in all men in general; in the children of males in particular; in the children of females, especially when these are close to [our man]. The orator must see if the excellences [that he is looking for] in his nation are the same excellences [that exist] in the eyes of the citizens in that nation—I mean in their children—or not. Several nations raise their children, male and female, with ornament and fatness. Aristotle says about these nations that they have missed half of the state of well-being because of their children.

1.5.10. The constituents of wealth are plenty of money, land property, real estate, furniture, goods, livestock, and all different kinds of property that are secure and owned with freedom and provide enjoyment and pleasure and are not just owned and accumulated.

1.5.11. **[Aristotle] said:** The useful and productive things in wealth are fruit trees and revenues. The enjoyable kinds of things are those we get without toil or expense. Security and acquisition of wealth mean that it is put in a place where it is not impossible for the person to have access to it, and that it is in the condition where it is possible to gain profit from it. For example, if it is land property, it should not be a salt marsh; if it is a horse, it should not be unruly. Freedom of ownership of wealth means that the person has the power to give away and sell and buy property. To enjoy wealth means to use it for pleasure. This criterion has been put so that wealth is used rather than owned, for to own wealth is the agent of wealth, whereas to use wealth is wealth itself.

1.5.12. As to a good action according to the right point of view, it is that which all people believe is an excellent action, and it is that which is desired by most people, or by the best among people, and by the fine and intelligent people.

1.5.13. [Aristotle] said: As to honor, it belongs, in our time, to the person who takes good care of doing good. The honor paid by people to those who take good care of them is a reward by means of justice and truth, since these acts are not rewarded by dinars and dirhams. Honor is not paid to those who take good care of people only, but it is also paid to those who are capable of taking good care—that is, to those who have the power to do that, although they do not do it at the time of being honored. The act of taking good care of people that requires honor is the care taken to release them from the evils that are not easy to be released from, or to donate goods to their benefits the acquisition of which is not easy. These good deeds are the ones that come from wealth, or power, or something similar that enables a person to do such good deeds. Many people are honored for doing a few good deeds, but such deeds become relatively numerous at that [particular] time and that [particular] circumstance. Honor is paid by accident for small things; that is, with respect to what happens by accident to those things, they become relatively numerous at that [particular] time or circumstance.

1.5.14. As to the things by which honor is paid, some are common to all nations, and some are limited to specific nations. The specific ones include, for example, sacrifices and offerings by which the Greeks traditionally honored the dead. The general ones include ranks in assemblies, the rush [to the front seats] in order to follow the words of the man who is honored, the restraint from opposing him, the presents that necessarily imply love and closeness. A gift represents two things: the bestowal of wealth and honor. That is why a gift is something favored by all people, and every man finds in the gift what he desires. In effect, there are three kinds of people. There are those who love honor; there are those who love money; and there are those who love them both. A gift represents what is desired by these three kinds.

1.5.15. [Aristotle] said: The excellence of the body is health. This means that people are absolutely free from disease and use their bodies, for a person who does not use his health does not enjoy it; that is, he is not in a good state of being and is far from performing all human acts or most of human acts.

1.5.16. [Aristotle] said: Beauty varies with age. In young men, beauty is when their bodies and their figures are such that they are not easily receptive of pain and emotion—that is, when they are not incapable of enduring injury. Beauty is also when they are pleasant to watch when they are running or winning [contests of strength].

1.5.17. [Aristotle] said: This is why people consider young men prepared for the five practices and games very beautiful. By the five practices and games, we mean the things by which the Greeks trained their boys, and they are sprinting, horse racing, fencing, wrestling, and boxing.

1.5.18. [Aristotle] said: People consider a young man who is prepared for these five practices beautiful only because he is prepared for nimbleness and victory.

1.5.19. [Aristotle] said: When such youth become men in their prime, they are pleasant to look at in the exertion of warfare, and that is depending on the appearance by which they are fit for the war.

1.5.20. As to beauty in old men, it is in the pleasure taken in their acts in activities that are serious, and they are the ones for which young boys exercise in these five games, which are the wars. In addition, beauty in old men is to be seen free from sadness and grief, since sadness and grief, when they appear in an old man, [cause one to think] that what has suddenly befallen him—such as poverty, disgrace, and the like—hurts his old age.

1.5.21. [Aristotle] said: As to strength, it is the power by which an individual moves someone else at will. When he pulls someone, or pushes him, or lifts him, or drives him from his ground, or holds him down, and he does so with anyone attacking him or with most of [his attackers], he has vigor.

1.5.22. [Aristotle] said: Excellence in size is for the man to surpass many people in height, breath, and thickness. And despite his size, his movements are not self-conscious, given the quality of this excellence, and his size is not caused by fat or something acquired.

1.5.23. The disposition that is called "strength in combat,"[18] it is composed of size, strength, and swiftness. When swiftness is joined with strength, a man can run fast and far, because if he is swift but not strong, he will run fast but not far. A man who combines size with strength is a wrestler; a man who combines wrestling with swiftness is called by [the Greeks] a name that is derived from the term (*ḥadq*) "skill in the usage of strength

---

18. I have borrowed this expression from Aouad's French translation ("*la force au combat*"). Roberts used the term "athletic excellence" in his English translation.

and swiftness."[19] A man who possesses all these qualities, [the Greeks] called him "the master" of the five games or "a well-rounded athlete."[20]

1.5.24. [Aristotle] said: Good old age is aging with freedom from sadness, for if death comes upon a man before he reaches the last limit of old age, he will not age well even if he is free from sadness. If he gets to live until the last limit of old age and is afflicted with grief and sadness, he will not possess a good old age. He is free from sadness only if he has good luck and excellences of the body. I mean he is healthy and no misfortunes come upon him and spoil his old age. For when he is in poor health and does not have good luck on his side, having been afflicted with misfortunes, he does not possess a good old age even if he lives longer. The same is true if he is in poor health. People wonder how a person lives longer despite illnesses. But it appears that the power of aging is other than the power of health, since we see that many people live longer despite the fact that they suffer from diseases. The exact examination of this subject belongs to natural science; its examination is not useful in this science. The orator learns only what is sufficient to know with regard to the things apparent in this subject.

1.5.25. [Aristotle] said: As to the possession of many friends and the good state of being resulting from the possession of brothers, that is also clear when the terms "friend" and "companion" are defined. That means that each one of them will do a good thing that he thinks will be good for the other and not good for him only. Since friendship and companionship are such, it is clear that the person is in a good state of being when he possesses a great number of brothers [and friends].[21]

1.5.26. [Aristotle] said: Good luck means that something good happens to a person by chance, and that is from the good things found in the individual himself or from the good things happening to him from outside. The cause of chance may be artifice and it may be nature, which is most often the case. An example of natural [pure] chance is when a person is born with such strength and disposition by which it is difficult to receive matters coming to him from outside. That a person is healthy is

19. Averroes does not give the Greek term. The Arabic term signifies "to be skilled and sharp."

20. This is Roberts's English translation.

21. The terms *khilla*, *ikhwān*, *al-khalīl*, and *al-ṣāḥib* are in the same semantic field and mean friends and companions.

due to natural [pure] chance, as, for instance, when he is born healthy. It may also be due to artifice, as, for instance, when he is administered a poison and [contrary to reasonable expectation] is cured of a disease. The fortuitous cause of beauty and stature is nature itself. In general, the good things that happen by good luck, which is good chance, are the good things that make a man happy and excite envy. Good luck may be the cause of good things that are not truly good but are considered relatively good in comparison with someone else, as when ugliness may be a good thing for someone when someone else is considered uglier, or when two men are standing on the same spot during the war and an arrow hits one of them and misses the other. The one who does not get shot is considered, in comparison with his friend, to have obtained a good thing, especially when the same man who does not get shot has usually seen many wars, while the other has only seen that war. Or when one of those searching for a treasure finds it is considered to have obtained a good thing, in comparison with the one who does not find it, even if the treasure is small. From this and what is similar to this, the orator examines happiness that is due to good luck.

1.5.27. As to excellence, the most proper place to mention it is when we talk about the subject of praise, because the definition of excellence is especially connected with the man who praises, and for this reason, it is essential that the man who praises is the one who defines it exhaustively.

1.5.28. Although, with respect to excellences, there is a future and a present, the man who praises examines them only as being present, and the one who gives counsel examines them as being future—that is, useful.

6

1.6.1. These are the ends for the sake of which the orator gives advice. From them, it is plain what their opposites are, and for the sake of which the orator deprecates—and they are the ones from which statements of disapproval are composed—since their number is that same number and their position with respect to deliberative statements is that same position.

1.6.2. Since the aim of the counselor, in the first place in his mind, is to propose a useful thing from which each one of these ends results, and that is because these ends are the beginning of thought and the end of action, and useful things are the end of thought and the beginning of action—and by beginning of thought, I mean the consequence, and by end of thought, I mean premises—the orator must possess foundations and laws by which he knows useful things in the ends, and they are the consequences, since they are the beginning of action.

16.3. Useful things, even if they are not absolutely good, are good because they are the means to good in an absolute manner. Absolute good is what is chosen for its own sake, whereas other things are chosen for it and that is what all people desire. And here by all, I mean people with good understanding and intelligence. And it may be good in truth; and it may be considered good according to every particular man's belief. Therefore, when the thing that a man believes is good exists and is available for him, he is content with it, obtains what he needs from it, and has no desire for anything at all.

1.6.4. In general, the things useful with respect to this good are of four kinds: things that are the agent of this good; things that maintain this good; what entails the things that maintain this good; and what entails the things that are the agent of this good. What entails something counts with the thing. Also, what entails the thing that corrupts something counts with the thing that corrupts. What entails the opposite of the agent of something counts with the opposite of the agent in the things prohibited.

1.6.5. The necessary connection between the end and the agent is sometimes simultaneous, as when praise requires the acquisition of things that are praised; and sometimes it is subsequent, as when knowledge follows the action of learning.

1.6.6. Things productive of other things are of three types: either 1) in essence or 2) by accident. The thing productive of other things in essence is double: either 1) close, as food produces health, or 2) distant, as the doctor. The type of things productive by accident is as the act of fatigue during exercise produces health. Since it is essential that the kinds of things productive of other things are these three, it is necessary that some useful things represent a good thing for itself, like the usefulness of food for health; some represent a bad thing in itself and also a good thing, given its usefulness, like taking medicine for health. The bad things that are useful are useful in two ways, one of which is that one gains a greater benefit than the bad thing that follow their use, as when one gains health after taking medicine and as when one gains a large amount of wealth after a little hard work. The other one is when one is saved from a bad thing greater than the bad thing one suffers, as when the travelers by sea are saved from injury when they throw their merchandise overboard from the vessel, for throwing their merchandise overboard is a bad thing that they suffer, but they gain safety from what is a greater bad thing, which is injury. Aristotle calls the good things gained from good things "absolute benefits." As to the other ones, he calls them "transition," and he means by that that they are a transition from evil to a lesser evil or a transition from evil to what is good.

1.6.7. [Aristotle] said: The excellences, even if they are ends, are also good things in themselves and useful in the production of good. Those who possess them are, by possessing them, in a good condition. In addition, these excellences produce good things and are used in producing good things.

1.6.8. [Aristotle] said: We must explain each one of these virtues, how they are good things in themselves and how they are productive of good things, and develop all these points in detail.

1.6.9. Pleasant things are also good things in themselves, since all living beings desire them. Pleasant things must be good when the person enjoying them is in a good condition. Upon a close examination, it is evident that they are good things and that they are also useful in producing good things.

1.6.10. In general, of the constituents of a good condition, some are ends only; others are considered ends, while they are also useful to the ends. To some constituents belongs an order in relation to others. I mean that some are the reason for the existence of others. For example, for the sake of courage, wisdom, temperance, greatness of the spirit, magnificence, and all such excellences of the soul, several things among the constituents of a good condition are chosen. Similarly, for the sake of health and beauty, which are excellences of the body, one chooses things that are constituents of a good condition and are productive of these excellences. In the same way, one chooses other productive things from the constituents of a good condition, such as the things that produce pleasure and things that produce good conduct. This is why one believes that wealth is a good thing if it is the cause of these two noble things, one of which is pleasure and the other one good conduct. The good condition produced by the acquisition of a great number of [brothers][22] is productive of many good

22. The term *ikhwān* does not necessarily mean biological brothers. Here the term is used to refer to friends and companions.

things, especially when the friendship that exists between two persons is for the sake of love itself, not when love between the two exists for another thing. Friends of this nature produce honor, glorification, and other similar good things. Such good things come from them in words and deeds, since the words and deeds by which honor, glorification, and other similar good things are produced are good and useful.

1.6.11. [Aristotle] said: Among the things that are useful in essence are natural faculties by which a man is apt for good things. Such faculties include intelligence, memory, learning, and swift movement. The same is true with perfections, such as sciences, arts, and laudable conduct. All these, in addition to being useful in other things, are good in themselves. And if another good thing is not associated with them, they are unique good things on their own, chosen for their own sake.

1.6.12. Gentleness also is a useful good thing.

1.6.13. [Aristotle] said: These are the good things that people recognize and agree to admit that they are good and useful. When it has been demonstrated in something of these good things that it is indeed a good thing, that demonstration is not done by way of pretense and deceit used in this art. But when it has been demonstrated in something of the opposites of these good things that they are good, when in fact they are bad things, that is done, in this art, by way of pretense—that is, by way of sophistic demonstration. In effect, evil is useful only by accident, as when an orator explains to the inhabitants of a city that cowardice is good for them, for if they become courageous, they will come out of the city, and the enemy will attack them and defeat them. But cowardice is absolutely not a good thing. It is only relatively good for the inhabitants of the city to whom this has happened accidentally.

1.6.14. A useful thing is in most cases and in essence good to man. Similarly, an evil thing contrary to good is useful to enemies. In effect, since cowardice is in essence an evil thing for the inhabitants of the city, it is useful to enemies. However, it so happens that an evil thing may befall a man and is harmful to his enemy; and a good thing that happens to him may also be good to his enemy. It is similar to cowardice that happens to the inhabitants of a city, who, when they come out of the city, they have no strength left to resist their enemy. Therefore, the orator must all the time examine what is useful in these things. Also, this proposition is not universal. I mean the one saying that everything that harms the enemy or constrains him is useful, and everything that is useful to the enemy and brings him joy is harmful, since most often the same thing is harmful to a man and to his enemy, and useful to a man and to his enemy. For example, what is useful to both of them and brings joy to each one of them is when the two enemies are separated from each other after a fierce battle and a resistance that put them on the verge of destruction, without victory for either one of them. When they are separated following this situation, each one of them rejoices; and for this reason, what is useful becomes also useful to enemies.

1.6.15. As to what is harmful to both of them, it often makes friendship with the enemy necessary, and that is when the two are equally affected by the evil that hits them, without one surpassing the other in this. For this reason, several nations have come to sign agreements, for it is said that evil often draws people together.

1.6.16. This is also one of the things by which evil becomes useful. I mean damage befalling a man also hits his enemy, which makes friendship with the enemy necessary. At this point, an external enemy desires the contrary of what each one of the first two enemies desires, for each of the first two enemies desires the friendship of the other because of their collaboration against an external enemy. The external enemy wishes their enmity to remain the same or get firm. Aristotle says, "For this reason, very often a great deal of money is spent and much labor is done for this kind of good by which a greater evil is pushed away. The soul finds it agreeable that money and labor are spent on such things only because what results from them and corresponds to the desired goal is evident to the point that when such things are found, the goal is also reached."

1.6.17. Excessive evil that hits the enemy is also a reason for the appreciation of the small amount of good that an enemy gets from his enemy, and without this excessive evil that hits the enemy, an enemy does not appreciate this small amount of good, as in what Aristotle reports about what happened to one of the kings who were enemies of the Greeks. The war that the Greeks waged against this king and the siege that they laid around him intensified for several years, and they killed his son during that siege. The king asked them to give him the body of his son so that he could burn it according to funeral custom. The Greeks did that, and he thanked them and showed his gratitude for them in front of all his people and his countrymen. Had a great evil not hit him, he would not have thanked them for this small amount of good that they allowed him, as Homer, the poet, reported.

1.6.18. [Aristotle] said: Of the useful things and deeds whose value is greater to the beneficiaries and by which the benefactor reaches a greater good, a man chooses, among a certain type of men, a man of great value who has an enemy of great value, from another certain type of men, and inflicts evil on the enemy of that man and does good to his friends. It is similar to what happened to Homer with the Greeks and their enemies. He went to a great man among the ancient Greeks and composed eulogies in his honor and his Greek friends and also composed satires about this man's great enemy and his people, who were enemies of the Greeks, during the wars that the two fought. Hence Homer became the master of grace among the Greeks, for they made him magnificent to the point that they believed he was divine and that he was the first master of the Greeks.

1.6.19. In general, to do evil to enemies and good to friends is a useful thing. A precondition for this deed of great impact is that what is done of it is considered as not possible or easier for the man to do otherwise—whether the deed itself is great or small—and that one believes that doing such a deed is motivated not by fear or by something one expects, but by the desire to do it. This way the deed is done continuously and easily. In fact, deeds motivated by fear are less tedious only for a short time, and when they take a longer time, they become tedious and come to an end. And when they come to an end, enmity ensues from the part of the beneficiary and is directed at the benefactor. Therefore, a precondition for this deed is that it must be easy for the doer to do it. Such are the preconditions for initiating deeds that are impressive and useful.

1.6.20. As to a reward that is not impressive, it is one given according to what the man giving the reward naturally desires with respect to most people. And that means the reward may be of less worth than the favor rendered to him, either in terms of quantity or in terms of beneficial use, or it may have become superfluous for the man giving the reward and he does not need it. It is a reward in which there is deceit. The man giving the reward is only naturally the one who desires the reward to be in one of these three conditions, since he is limited to giving. Hence all he desires is that the good that reaches him does not diminish or that the diminution is less than the good that reaches him. When the reward is not of this nature but is equal to the favor rendered either with respect to the kind, as when the reward for dinars is paid back in dirhams, or with respect to power, as when the reward for money is paid back in honor by which an equal amount of money is gained, that is a fair reward, but it is also considered a vulgar type of reward. When the reward is neither vulgar nor deceptive, but one believes that the choice, by the man giving the reward, of what is less does not exceed his choice of what is more—whether the reward occurs by what is less or by what is equal, or by what is similar—that is a beautiful reward, for the reward by less that he gives has not occurred from him by his own choice, but because it has not been possible for him to do otherwise. When it happens that there is, in addition to this, a surplus that will make friends happy—I mean the beneficiary's friends—and offend the enemies of the beneficiary, and that the surplus is, in addition, admired by the people, and that with respect to the person from whom the surplus comes, it then produces a great impression on the beneficiary, especially when the favor corresponds to the beneficiary's desire. It is like when the lover of honor is rewarded with honor, the lover of money with money, and the lover of victory with victory. This favor is not only pleasurable to the person to whom it was rendered or by which he is rewarded, but it is also an excellent thing. The same is true with all the other kinds of good.

1.6.21. The acts of favor and reward become for the person initiating the favor and for the person giving the reward easy and possible for them to continue doing only when they are, by their natural disposition, prepared to do such acts and have acquired the faculty by which those acts are issued from them. Of the small favors that one thinks do not diminish anything about the benefactor, there is the favor by discipline and exhortation.

1.6.22. **[Aristotle] said:** From these modes, the orator derives the premises for persuasion that the thing is useful or not useful.

7

1.7.1. Since the orator sometimes admits that the thing is useful but claims that there is something else more useful, he needs to have the grounds on which he is able to base his demonstration that the thing is more useful and superior.

1.7.2. Of these grounds, what is useful in all things is more useful than certain things; what is useful in a more permanent manner is more useful than what is useful in a shorter period of time; what is greater is more useful than what is smaller; what is more is more useful than what is less.

1.7.3. What has assembled more qualities of good or has assembled all its qualities is more useful. The qualities of perfect good is that the thing is chosen for its own sake and not for the sake of something else, that it is desired by all, and that it is chosen by men of excellence and reason. The thing that has assembled all these qualities or most of them is a good and useful thing and is the end. It is the end for all the things characterized as good. Characteristics of good related to this good that has assembled all these qualities are said to be more useful only when there is in one of them one of these qualities or more than one. And everything, among these things, that has a greater number of qualities of good is more useful as long as one quality is not more useful than two or three.

1.7.4. Again, if the greatest member of one class is superior to the greatest member of another class, the class in which the superior member exists is superior to the other class. And if one class is superior to the superior class, the greatest member of the superior class is superior to the greatest member of the other class, which is the opposite of the first case. Thus if males are superior to females, a man is superior to a woman. And if a man is superior to a woman, then males are superior to females. Things are such only because the relation of the greatest member to his class is similar to the relation of the other greatest member to his class, in such a way that the relation of class to class is the relation of the greatest to the greatest.

1.7.5. Again, when one thing accompanies another thing and the other does not accompany it, the one that is accompanied by the thing is better than the one that is not accompanied by the thing. For example, in the case of power and wealth, wealth accompanies power and power does not accompany wealth. Therefore, power is better than wealth. The same goes with harm. Poverty is accompanied by avarice and avarice is not accompanied by poverty. Therefore, poverty is more harmful than avarice. The thing that accompanies another thing exists in three ways. Either simultaneously—I mean the thing that accompanies another and the thing that is accompanied by another—as when white and whiteness exist simultaneously, and as when humans and animals exist simultaneously; or subsequently, as when knowledge is subsequent to the act of learning; or potentially, that is, one does the act of the other and not the contrary. I mean the latter does not do the act of the former. For example, in the case of poverty and avarice, poverty is accompanied by the act of avarice and avarice is not accompanied by poverty. Poverty hampers the acquisition of things more than the absence of use of money does, which is avarice.

1.7.6. Again, the doer of a more useful good is more useful than the useful good, like vigor and beauty, for both are useful and good. Vigor produces a greater good than beauty does; therefore, it is more useful. Likewise, health is more useful than pleasure, for with health one produces more good things than one does with pleasures.

1.7.7. Again, a thing that is chosen alone is better and more useful than a thing that is only chosen together with the thing that is chosen alone. For example, beauty is only chosen with health and health is chosen without beauty; therefore, health is better and more useful than beauty.

1.7.8. Again, when one of two things is perfection and the other is a means to perfection, the one that is perfection is better. For example, in the case of health and pleasure, health is perfection and pleasure is being, and being is a means to perfection.

1.7.9. When, of two things, one is chosen for its own sake and the other is chosen for the sake of something else, the one that is chosen for its own sake is better than the one chosen for the sake of something else. For example, in the case of wisdom and wealth, wisdom is chosen for its own sake and wealth is chosen for something else.

1.7.10. Again, the thing that makes a man, when he acquires it, less in need of his friends or people is better than the thing that makes him more in need. A man who is more self-sufficient and more independent is the one who needs a few things and that are easy to get.

1.7.11. Again, when, of two things, the possession of one implies the need for the second and the possession of the second does not imply the need for the other, the one whose possession does not imply the need for the other is better. In the case of wealth and children, for example, children make one need the possession of money, whereas wealth does not make one need the possession of children. Then wealth is better and more useful.

1.7.12. **[Aristotle] said:** It is plain that that which is a principle does not necessarily have to be greater than the thing of which it is a principle; in effect, willpower is a principle of good, whereas the act of doing good is greater than the willpower to do good, and the same with the act of learning and knowledge—although it is impossible that a useful thing exists without a principle.

1.7.13. When two things are [the beginning] of two other things and one of the two beginning things is greater than the second, the one that comes from the greater beginning is greater. Again, contrary to this, when two things are the beginning of two other things as agents and one of them is greater than the second, then the one that is the [beginning] of the greater is greater, and likewise when there are two [things] as an end.

1.7.14. When the efficient [cause] is compared with the end, it is possible to imagine that the efficient [cause] is greater than the end, since the efficient cause is that which produces the end and without which the end does not exist. And it is also possible to imagine that the end is greater than the beginning, and that without the end, the efficient [cause] is superfluous. An example of what makes the end greater than the efficient [cause] is the statement made by someone speaking of blame: "It is proper to relate so and so to injustice for having done this thing more so than so and so, who has advised him to do so, since if [the former] did not want to, that act would not have come from him." In effect, if he had not done that act, the harm would not have occurred. An example of what would make the efficient [cause] greater than the end is the statement "So and so is worthy of thanks for this act more than so and so, because it is [he] who has advised [the other] to do that act, and without his advice he would not have done that praiseworthy act." And in both situations, what precedes the end is produced only because of the end.

1.7.15. Further, what is rare is a greater good, like gold is better than iron. But if gold is more rare than iron, it is no longer more useful. Also, conversely, what is plentiful is a greater good than what is rare because we can make more use of it. Thus it is said, "Water is a good thing because it is plentiful and we can make general use of it." Also what is a hard thing to get is better, for what is hard to get is rare and what is rare is unfamiliar and provokes competition. Conversely, what is easy to get is better, for it is there every time we desire it.

1.7.16. Further, the thing whose contrary is the greater evil is better. Also, the thing whose loss is more harmful is more useful. And here we should not understand by greater and less the greatness of comparison in goodness only, but also in badness and in what is neither bad nor good.

1.7.17. Further, in relation to the ends and things for the sake of which acts are done, when some ends are better than others or worse than others, the things that come before those ends where more exists are of the order of more.

1.7.18. Further, in proportion as the faculties, excellences, and, in general, the agents are greater, the acts resulting from them are greater, since the relationship of the acts with their beginning is the relationship of the beginnings with one another. So if sight is better than the sense of smell, then the act of seeing is better than the act of smelling. This is the case of all the acts in proportion to their efficient causes—not only essential acts but also acts that happen by chance, since the chance by which a great act happens is also great—and of the chances existing in the thing. I mean the chance existing in a greater thing is also greater.

1.7.19. Again, to love a man who possesses wealth is better than to love wealth, since love for a human being is better than love for wealth.

1.7.20. Again, excellences are better than those who possess excellences.

1.7.21. Things the desire for which is excellent are better than those the desire for which is not excellent. For example, the desire for sciences is excellent, but the desire for food and drink is not excellent, because sciences are superior to food and drink. Again, conversely, that which is excellent, the desire for it is excellent. For example, wisdom is superior to sexual intercourse, so the desire for it is superior to the desire for sexual intercourse.

1.7.22. Further, the sciences that are better and superior, their acts are better and superior. For example, since [theoretical] sciences are superior to practical sciences, their act, which is the truth, is superior to the ones whose act is praxis. Conversely, those whose act is superior to [the act of] the sciences are superior; in effect, since knowledge of the truth is superior to praxis, scientific arts are superior to practical arts. These two accompany each other only because the relation of one art to the other art is the relation of the act of one art to the act of the other art.

1.7.23. **[Aristotle] said:** What all people, or the majority of people, or men of reason, or good men judge is better and superior is in itself absolutely superior when their judgment on things is in accordance with their natural disposition and they are men of reason, and not in accordance with the points of view that they have gotten from outside. In effect, among people, men of reason tell, from their natural disposition, what the excellences and good things are, how many they are, and on the occasion of what thing they are, even if what they know from their natural disposition is inferior to what is known of that in the sciences. What is meant by what has been said of the definition of good, that it is what everybody desires, is the good that everybody desires in accordance with their natural disposition. I mean their rational disposition. In effect, what rational dispositions desire—as rational dispositions—is absolute good, or good superior to another good. They know, for example, that courage, culture, and vigor are good things and they desire them.

1.7.24. What is relatively good to a man—as one of excellent men, who considers that to suffer wrong is better than to do wrong himself—people do not comprehend it in accordance with their natural dispositions, but only a man who, among people, is of the highest degree of justice and excellence has this point of view.

1.7.25. Again, of good things, what is accompanied with pleasure is better than what is not [accompanied with pleasure]. Of good things, what is more pleasant is better. Things are such only because all people rush toward pleasure and seek it, and their search for pleasure is for the sake of pleasure itself, not for the sake of something else. And of what has this characteristic—I mean to be desired by all—it has been said that it is a good thing and the end, and that therefore pleasure is a good thing.

1.7.26. More pleasant are the pleasures that are more exempt from harm and sadness and that last longer.

1.7.27. Beautiful pleasure is more pleasant than hideous pleasure, since the beautiful is what is often chosen for itself, even when it is not pleasant, and it belongs to the things that man chooses to be the cause of his being, either for himself or for his friend.

1.7.28. In general, all pleasant things that are superior are more pleasant than those that are more evil.

1.7.29. And all the things that are more lasting are more pleasant than the ones that are more fleeting. All the good things that are more secure are more pleasant than those that are less secure. In effect, since health is more secure than beauty, it is more pleasant to have health than to have beauty. The only reason for pleasant or more pleasant things to belong to us in this manner is one of two points: either we get used to the thing for so long that it becomes enjoyable by habit, as in the case of pleasure derived from knowledge, or [it is the case] that these things are so pleasant for us by instinct and desire. Things only become more pleasant either by lasting a long time or by desire agreement reached by instinct. All things that suit our desire more are useful for us only because they are stable and secure.

1.7.30. Premises of the more useful and the better type are often taken from like terms and derivations, so that if bravery is better than temperance, a brave man is better than a temperate man.

1.7.31. [Aristotle] said: The thing that is chosen by all people is better than what is not chosen by all people. Also, the thing that is chosen by many people is better than what is chosen by a few people. Good, as it has been said, is what all people desire.

1.7.32. Also, what the first judges have chosen, I mean those that do not take judgments from someone else—and they are the legislators—is better than what they have not chosen. Similarly, what those that receive judgments from [the first judges] have chosen is better than what [the first judges] do not choose. Those who receive judgments from the first judges—and they are those from whom the fundamentals of judgments are taken—are of two kinds: either a listener who only transmits [what he hears] or a knowledgeable listener—that is, someone who is able to discover from those fundamentals judgments that the first judges have not declared. And [those of the latter kind] are of two kinds: those who are authorized by the first judges, and they are [the magistrates] and their like, or those who are not authorized, and they are the jurists. It belongs to all types of people receiving judgments from the first judges to speak of some of these things, and that is what they have heard or witnessed from the first judge. Some other things are proper to men of science, among these types, and that is what is said of things discovered from the first judgments that the first judge has declared. Listeners without knowledge are not permitted to speak of these things. As to what is proper for the first judges to speak of, they are the fundamentals that are of the rank of principles for all things that knowledgeable listeners judge. I mean authorized judges and jurists. And these fundamentals are the things that Aristotle calls the greatest matters.

1.7.33. Excellent and pious men from whom all or most people ordinarily learn have better judgment. In effect, the fact that one does not learn from an excellent and pious man sometimes makes one imagine that he has something disgraceful and faulty and one accepts little of what he says. In fact, the words of these excellent and pious men may be acceptable, although nobody from the public learns anything at all from them, or [the public] learns only very little. That is, the words of these men are believed to be acceptable from another standpoint, since the man that the public finds satisfactory may not be satisfactory himself, and [men of discernment are a small minority]. Again, excellent men who conceal their excellent qualities from the public are praised more, and they are fewer in number and more cherished, for they have concealed their excellences from the public only for fear [that] honors and positions of leadership might fall upon them. In effect, one fears that such honors and positions of leadership, once received by a person, might be the cause that these things that come along with excellences are indeed what they seek to obtain through these excellences. For this reason, the words of this type of men become acceptable, in the same way the words of the first type, which is contrary to this type, are acceptable. And they are the men from whom the public learns.

1.7.34. **[Aristotle] said:** Given the fact that honor is a reward earned for excellence, of the type of men whose words are very well received, there are men whose honor is greater, since it is believed that a man's excellence is greater every time the honor he receives is greater.

1.7.35. The words of the type of men who have suffered enormous damage and great misery because of their excellent qualities are also well received, as in the case of Socrates and others. And the type of men that these two types of men—namely, those whose honor is greater and those who have suffered enormous damage because of their excellent qualities—consider that they are excellent and recognize that they are excellent are also better and greater.

1.7.36. These are then the types of men who, when they choose something and others choose something else, choose something better and desirable.

1.7.37. **[Aristotle] said:** The division of the thing into its particular elements makes one imagine that the thing is greater. Thus when Homer, the poet, wanted to make the evil that the city suffered look greater, he took instead its particular elements. He mentioned the massacre of children, the wailing [of women], the burning of the city, and other kinds of evil that it suffered.

1.7.38. **[Aristotle] said:** Similarly, combination often makes the impression that the thing is greater. And this is contrary to what has been previously said. I mean as a substitute for the parts, we take what is common to them all.

1.7.39. The reason for persuasion in these two types [of discourse] is change and substitution.

1.7.40. And since things are believed to be better when they are harder and rare, the things that are plentiful and easy to get are considered great when they exist in places where they are rare; or also in the times when they are rare; or in the ages where they are rare, as when someone is an orator in his youth; or in the spaces of time where they normally are not found, as in the case of someone who accomplishes in a short amount of time something that naturally takes a long period of time to accomplish; or when these things come from powers from which things rarely come, as when a weak person accomplishes the act of a strong person and a sick person accomplishes the act of a healthy person. All these things and the likes of them make the matter that is not great become great and extraordinary.

1.7.41. Again, the best part is from things that are greater, as the heart and the brain are the best parts in a living being,[23] or the spring season is the best part of the year, and youth is the best part in the city.

1.7.42. Again, a useful thing for which the need is more is more useful; the harmful in it is more harmful. For example, in the case of health and sickness in old age, health in old age is better than health in youth, but sickness in old age is more harmful.

1.7.43. Again, of two things, that which is closer to the goal is better.

1.7.44. Again, what is achieved at the end of life is better, since the things that suitably belong to people at the end of their lives are better, such as wisdom, knowledge, and other excellences that come to perfection with age.

1.7.45. Again, the things whose act, when they are done or received, is their truth are greater than those things whose act, when they are done, is absolutely not the truth. Aristotle calls the things whose act, when they are done, is their truth the things by which we intend the truth. And he calls the other ones the things by which we intend praise. I mean the ones whose act is not their truth.

1.7.46. [Aristotle] said: The definition of things by which we intend praise is that those things, when done through ignorance and error, are not praised at all. And those things by which we intend the truth are the ones that, however they are done, are perfectly achieved.

1.7.47. [Aristotle] said: This is why the good of receiving a beautiful thing is more desirable than the act of doing a beautiful thing, since the act of doing a beautiful thing, when done through error and ignorance, is not well received and the doer is not praised. As to the good of feeling and receiving, no matter how it happens, the person who receives it draws good benefit from it.

---

23. The term *ḥayawān* in the context used here by Averroes refers to its synonym *ḥayy*, which I have rendered as "living being."

1.7.48. Again, that the act of which is desirable because of itself, although nobody knows anything about it, is more desirable than what has been chosen only from the standpoint of what is known, as in the case of health and beauty, since health is desirable because of itself, whereas beauty is desirable because of someone else.

1.7.49. Again, what is useful in many things is more useful, like what is useful in a long life, in a good life—that is, a prosperous life—in pleasures, and in benevolence. This is why health and wealth are considered great, since they bring together freedom from sadness and the act accompanied with pleasure; that is, health is the cause of the act accompanied with pleasure and wealth is the cause of freedom from sadness—that each one of these two is on its own excellent and chosen for itself; that is, freedom from sadness and pleasant acts—that when they come together for a person, they make him greater than everything, whether he who knows that knows or whether he who does not know does not, since these are good things truly acquired and not drawn from good things by which praise is intended. Given the fact that wealth is the cause for driving away sadness, some people believe it is happiness, while others consider that happiness in joining together wealth with something else. And that is something necessary, since it is more appropriate that happiness is stable and secure. In effect, the injury inflicted on a man who loses one of his eyes is not the same as the injury inflicted on a one-eyed man when he loses his eye, since the one-eyed man has been robbed of something he dearly loved compared with what a man with two eyes has lost. Similarly, if happiness is in wealth together with something else, injury inflicted by the loss of wealth is not the same as injury inflicted by the loss of wealth if wealth alone has been the source of happiness.

1.7.50. The discourse on all these things here is not so much about making sure things are sound as it is about the amount of knowledge that the orator needs. When the orator advances conclusions drawn from premises such as these, he will always need to support them with examples taken from the people who have done those things and have gained benefit or have suffered injury. Therefore, the orator must have a good memory of stories and accounts.

1.7.51. **[Aristotle] said:** These are the things by which we establish that something is more useful or more harmful. As to the things by which there is permission and interdiction, enough has been said about them earlier.

8

1.8.1. However, the most important and greatest thing concerning these is the discourse on the things by which one is able to produce excellent persuasion in the subject matter of laws and also by which one is able to give counsel regarding laws more useful than [that] which does not exist. Therefore, we must speak of them thoroughly here. Then we say, counsel regarding useful laws and perfect persuasion concerning them are achieved by the knowledge of the types of political regimes and of the morals and laws proper to each political regime. In effect, for each political regime, there are laws that are useful to it, and they are the laws by which the city achieves its freedom and sustenance. Valuable and significant laws are just laws—that is, laws instituted on the basis of justice—laid down by the head of the city-state or by the person authorized by the head. These valuable laws—that is, just laws—differ from one political regime to another, depending on their ends, [and] their number depends on the number of the political regimes. For example, the justice system in a despotic political regime does not hold the head of state accountable for anything when he strikes a subject, whereas in a free political regime, the head of state receives the same blow he aims at the subject.

1.8.2. In general, there are four political regimes: the collective political regime [democracy]; the vile political regime [oligarchy]; the political regime of excellent authority [aristocracy]; and the political regime of a single [governing] power, which is the regime of nobility [monarchy]. What the laws instituted for these forms of government aim for is the city and the community, not the individual.

1.8.3. The [democratic] city is one in which government is achieved by luck and good fortune, not by merit, since in this city, nobody is superior to anybody else.

1.8.4. The vile government is one in which those who are authorized to rule govern the citizens by forcing them to pay taxes and fines, not as a way to cover expenses for the pay of guards or to accumulate reserves for the city, as in the case of other forms of government, but as a way to acquire wealth to the benefit of the head of state. If the head gives the citizens part of the riches, that is a government of riches; and if he does not give them part of the riches, that is a despotic government, and the citizens are then similar to slaves in their relation to the head of state, and the protection he provides for them is similar to the protection a man provides for his slaves.

1.8.5. The government of excellent authority is achieved through education and conformity to what the law requires. Those who give advice to what the law requires are authorized to govern by excellent authority. This is the authority by which a good condition and happiness for people in the city are obtained. Therefore, these counselors have excellences and the ability to do acts that make the condition of the city better, and they are men of determination and caution against what may corrupt the city from outside or from inside. For this reason, the city has been called by this name.

1.8.6. This power that [Aristotle] has mentioned is of two kinds: the first kind is the monarchy, and that is the city whose views and actions are achieved according to what theoretical sciences require. The second kind is government by the best, and that is the government whose actions alone are excellent. This kind of government is known as the government of the *imāma*,[24] and as Abū Naṣr [al-Fārābī] has reported, it is said that it existed during the times of the first Persians.

1.8.7. **[Aristotle] said:** As to exclusive authority, it is the form of government in which the king wants to hold the exclusive honor to rule, and he does not want anything to be missing from this honor so that he will not share the power with anybody else, and that is contrary to what happens in the city of the best.

1.8.8. Perhaps the laws instituted in these cities were definite, invariable, and permanent, as in the case of our Islamic law. And perhaps these cities did not have definite laws, but the matter was delegated to those who held the power, depending on what was more useful at each moment, as in the case of Byzantine laws.

1.8.9. From the definitions we have outlined of these forms of government, we must be aware of the end of each one of them, because when we know the end, we also know the things chosen for that end. The end of collective government [democracy] is freedom; of corrupt government [oligarchy], wealth; of excellent authority [aristocracy], excellence and conformity to the law; of exclusive government [tyranny], honor. The end pursued by those who institute governments in which no invariable laws are instituted is the protection of the law from disturbance caused by change of times and places.

24. This term carries the meaning of a position of leadership, especially in the Shīʿa doctrine.

1.8.10. You must know that these forms of government that Aristotle has mentioned are not found [to be] simple; they are in most cases complex, as in the case of the existing government. If we examine it carefully, we will find it composed of excellence, honor, freedom, and tyranny.

1.8.11. **[Aristotle] said:** Clearly, now that we know the types of government, we can also understand the moral qualities and the laws that lead to the end of each one of them. I mean the moral qualities and the laws useful for this end. We can also take these moral qualities and adhere to the type of laws in which we intend to effect persuasion—since the arguments by which counselors urge people to choose laws are persuasive only when counselors themselves are of good character and good action—so that these things mentioned here are known to us and belong to us. So when we have the moral qualities that we urge people to take, our argument in urging people to take them is more persuasive. Therefore, we must give counsel only by what we have and what we are determined to have. It is a known fact that knowledge of the laws that are useful for the end is only discovered, by way of analysis, from an examination of the end.

1.8.12. Now we have explained, in a sufficient measure in this art, where persuasive arguments come from, with respect to what is useful in the laws peculiar to each form of government, how many types of government there are, and the laws followed by these governments. As to the discourse on these things exactly, that belongs to politics.

9

1.9.1. On Praise and Blame

1.9.2. **[Aristotle] said:** After this, we now speak of excellence and deficiency, the beautiful and the mean, since these are the objects of praise and blame. After we have defined these things, we shall proceed with the definition of the things by which a man establishes the excellence of his own character, since that is the second of the three methods of persuasion, as we have mentioned earlier. In effect, the second method of persuasion is a type of praise; that is, the things by which we are able to praise someone else are also the things by which we are able to praise ourselves, even if that does not agree with all the things by which we praise someone else, but that happens by excellence only; and these are the things that are related to choice.

1.9.3. [Aristotle] said: Because it happens very often that human and spiritual beings are praised because of excellence and things other than excellence, and that this happens not only in the praise of these beings but also in the praise of animate and inanimate things—I mean that they are praised because of things external to excellence—we must speak here of the things from which premises are taken for praise because of excellence and because of nonexcellence, so that our discourse on this subject is general.

1.9.4. Then we say:

1.9.5. The beautiful is chosen for its own sake, and it is worthy of praise, good and pleasant because it is good.

1.9.6. If this is a true definition of the beautiful, excellence is undoubtedly beautiful, since it is good and worthy of praise. Excellence is a faculty determining every act that is good based on that determination, or because one has the opinion it is good—I mean the faculty preserving this determination and being the efficient cause for it. This is why excellence makes every act by which an end is aimed for to exist, as this act is of considerable value and favorable nature for this end to result from it.

1.9.7. The constituents of excellence are righteousness—or justice in general—courage, chivalry, temperance, magnanimity, clemency, liberality, intellect, and wisdom.

1.9.8. Of these excellences, some are peculiar to the excellent man only; others are excellences in the sense that they act upon others. These excellences that act upon others are greater for some than for others, and they are also greater in some circumstances than in others. For example, courage is better in times of war than in times of peace. As to justice, it is better both in times of peace and in times of war. The excellence of liberality and chivalry is appreciated by those who are in need more than by those who are not in need.

1.9.9. Chivalry is distinguished from liberality only by more or less, because the action of both is concerned with money. But the act of chivalry is more than the act of liberality.

1.9.10. As to righteousness, it is the virtue of justice by which the excellent man gives to every human being what he deserves in accordance with the law. Injustice is the character by which a man takes the things that do not belong to him and that he should not take in accordance with the law.

1.9.11. Courage is the virtue that disposes a man to do good deeds that are useful in times of a holy war, in accordance with the law, so that through his act he becomes a servant of the law; cowardice is the opposite.

1.9.12. Temperance is the virtue that disposes a man to control physical pleasures in accordance with the law; licentiousness is the opposite.

1.9.13. Liberality is the virtue that disposes a man to do good favors known in situations involving money; meanness is the opposite.

1.9.14. Magnificence is the virtue productive of excellence in matters of great deeds; smallness of spirit and meanness are the opposite.

1.9.15. Understanding is the virtue of reason by which good deliberation and reflection are achieved, with moral excellences related to a good condition.

1.9.16. **[Aristotle] said:** This has been an account of virtue and its constituents, according to what we need in this art.

1.9.17. As to all the other things, excepting virtue, that constitute an object of praise, they are not hard to understand. It is evident that things productive of virtue, such as civility and practice of things by which virtues are obtained, are beautiful things and are praiseworthy.

1.9.18. We now speak of the things that exist in the virtues themselves—that is, the signs that exist in them—and the things that exist following these virtues, for they are the signs of virtues.

1.9.19. The signs of virtues that are attached to virtues and their acts are praiseworthy only when they are good and laudable. Several virtuous acts are not worthy of praise, and the same is true of several signs [of virtue]. As examples of acts and signs of virtue, we mention the acts of courageous men during the war or those who have done the deeds of courageous men during the war even if they lacked the faculty of courage. Similarly, the signs attached to courageous men are worthy of praise. As examples of the acts that are not worthy of praise at a certain time, we have the donation of money. In effect, it is one of the acts of liberality. However, this act may have been done by way of wastefulness. As examples of the signs that are not praiseworthy, we have the emotional reaction of suffering from justice and the fact of accepting it. In effect, to do an act of justice is praiseworthy, but an emotional reaction of suffering from it is not, since one believes that it is shameful and unjust. In general, virtuous acts are praiseworthy only when they are determined praiseworthy by justice.

1.9.20. Among the things worthy of praise are the greatest, toilsome acts for which the reward is honor only, since the acts for which the reward is honor are better than the acts for which the reward is money. That is why when the reward for an act is in both ways at once, and the person does the act for the sake of honor only, he is worthy of praise for that act.

1.9.21. A man is worthy of praise for every act of virtue that is not done for his own sake. Similarly, to do things that are absolutely good is also worthy of praise. Things that are naturally good, even when they are harmful to the man doing them, are also worthy of praise, like doing a just act, for the just man most often suffers harm from doing it. Acts proper to honoring the dead are worthy of praise, since acts done for the sake of the living are acts by which a man seeks only, in most cases, his own interest. In general, every act [in which] a man aims for someone else's sake and not for his own interest, or from which he suffers harm, is worthy of praise. A service done to benefactors is also worthy of praise, for it is a just act, since the man doing it does not draw benefit from it.

1.9.22. One of the signs that a man is virtuous is not to do acts by which men doing shameful things are shamed and to educate those men with words and deeds.

1.9.23. The same is true with assisting virtuous men and praising them for what is worthy of praise.

1.9.24. A feeling of shame at the mention of vile things may be a sign of virtue, because one believes that shyness restrains a man from doing those vile things. Shamelessness at the mention of vile things may also be a sign of virtue that is worthy of praise. In effect, sometimes one thinks that a man feels ashamed at the mention of shameful things only when he has done them, or has received them, or that he intends to do them, as in the story that Aristotle has told of what happened to a woman famous for wisdom among [the Greeks]. A famous man, insinuating that she did a shameful thing, said to her, "I want to say something. Only shame restrains me from saying it."[25] The woman, reflecting gently on what he said, did not answer with shameful words, and so she did not suffer any pain or any other bad emotion from it, since, given her noble character, she considered that nobody could insinuate anything at all against her, whether by example or by words, for these are two types of

25. The woman is Sappho and the man is Alcaeus in Aristotle's treatise (Book I, chapter 9, 1367a).

insinuation. But in that case, she began to compose verses on the virtues, praise virtuous people, show solidarity with them, and defend them. Also, those who were with her did not feel bothered by what the man said or by what he insinuated, knowing that [such a virtuous woman] as herself could not be accused of such a shameful thing.[26]

1.9.25. **[Aristotle] said:** This is why ardent zeal for things that bring glory and the defense of those things put the zealous person and defender of those things in the category of those people who possess virtues that are gained only through a great struggle against nature, such as temperance, courage, and other virtues. The same is [true] when a person acquires a faculty by repeatedly doing these things and showing ardent zeal for them and defending them, as in the case of this woman [Sappho] whose story with this man we have told. In effect, acts such as these put a person in the category of those people who possess virtues gained only through great struggle.

1.9.26. **[Aristotle] said:** An act of benefaction, when the benefactor does not draw any profit from it at all, is worthy of praise. Justice and righteousness are worthy of praise because they are useful. In the same way, they are worthy of praise because they are beautiful.

1.9.27. To avenge oneself on one's enemies and not to be pleased with them at all is also worthy of praise, for revenge is requital, and requital is just, and justice is beautiful.

1.9.28. Love of victory and love of honor are also worthy of praise, since both are signs indicating that we prefer virtues [for their own sake], not for the sake of money. Love of victory indicates that we prefer courage; love of honor indicates that we prefer all the virtues. That is why the virtues that we prefer and choose are the ones by which those who possess them do not seek wealth at all, which is a sign of eminence of virtue.

1.9.29. Of the acts that are worthy of praise are the ones that are forever remembered by people.

1.9.30. Of the things that are worthy of praise are the laudable dispositions of a particular people, who make these dispositions signs by which to recognize noble men, like long hair for the Greeks, since it is a mark of nobility, as it is not easy for everyone to have long hair; for men with

26. Aristotle gives only Sappho's reply; Averroes seems to relate this story from his own perspective.

long hair, and who also do not have any kind of trade, do not perform tasks performed by men who do not have long hair. The clothes that our people used to wear are of this type mentioned by Aristotle.[27]

1.9.31. [Aristotle] said: It is noble for a man not to need other people, but to be self-sufficient.

1.9.32. [Aristotle] said: In praise and blame, we must take the things that are close to virtues and imperfections. Imperfections are those [characteristics] from which virtuous acts are derived; virtues are those [characteristics] from which imperfect acts are derived. Imperfections from which we derive virtuous acts are praised, and that happens when they are made to appear as virtues, so that acts derived from those [imperfections] are made to appear as if they have been derived from virtuous acts.

Similarly, virtues are made to appear as imperfections so that imperfect acts are by accident derived from them. As examples of imperfections from which virtuous acts are derived and which are assumed to be virtues, we have the feeble man from whom acts of gentleness originate, for by these acts he is assumed to be gentle; the simple-minded man from whom acts typical of good-mannered people originate, for by these acts he is assumed to be good-mannered; the insensitive man who is assumed to be temperate, since by accident he happens to do acts typical of temperate people; also the impetuous man who is assumed to be brave; and the impudent man who is assumed to be noble-minded. As an example of acts that are assumed to be imperfections when they are not imperfections, we have [the case] when a high-minded person accidentally shuns small things and is assumed to go wrong and allow himself to be deceived. A high-minded person acts that way only in small matters from which nothing immensely fearful or seriously harmful will happen to him and also in a situation where it is better to pretend not to see those matters. This situation also makes one assume the opposite, which is to say about the man who is deceived that he is indeed a high-minded man.

1.9.33. That a man gives to his friends and to those who are not his friends, that he gives to those he knows and to those he does not know, is worthy of praise, since one thinks that the noble virtue of liberality is to give money to everybody.

---

27. Averroes seems to be indicating that wearing fine clothes is a laudable disposition among Arabs that is of similar significance to having long hair for the Greeks.

1.9.34. [Aristotle] said: The speech of praise must be given in front of an audience that likes the man being praised, for as Socrates said, "It is easy to praise Athenians in Athens."[28] Every man must be praised according to what is worthy of praise among his countrymen, for making a speech of praise varies depending on the audience.

1.9.35. [Aristotle] said: Of praise for external things, we have to praise ancestors and mention their past exploits; to praise a man for high-aspiring ambition and for not being content with what he has already acquired. A high-minded man whose ambition is not limited to the position he has already achieved is worthy of praise for these two external things—that is, the excellence of his ancestors and what he aspires for, as when we say, "From what exploits [left] by his ancestors he has started and at what exploits through his own ambition he has arrived." As to the man who does not aspire for more than what he has achieved, with respect to the two external things, he is worthy of praise only for the exploits that he has inherited from his ancestors. Here [Aristotle] seems to consider that praise should not be limited to the exploits of ancestors and that it should also include the excellence of the man, as the poet has said:

Although our ancestors were once of noble birth,
We do not count even for one day on noble birth.
We build as our ancestors once built,
And we act as they once acted.

[Aristotle] also seems to consider that praise could be limited to excellence, without the mention of ancestors, as [the poet] has said, "The spirit of ᶜIsām has made ᶜIsām a master."

1.9.36. [Aristotle] said: Praise is, in truth, for acts that are intentional and chosen. An act that is done through deliberate intention and by choice is an excellent act. What is worthy of praise for things that happen by chance or by accident, because they embellish and amplify excellences when they are joined with them, is of the rank of noble birth that is joined with excellence and good luck that is joined with excellent acts. The acts that occur by chance and the accidents that are fortuitously

28. The Arabic text shows these words put in a direct quotation. Aristotle reports what Socrates said: "[F]or, as Socrates used to say, it is not difficult to praise the Athenians to an Athenian audience" (Book I, chapter 9, 1367b). The source for this quotation in Roberts's English translation of Aristotle's treatise is Cp. Plato, *Menexenus*, 235D.

joined with intentional acts are considered praiseworthy only when the chance and the accidents repeatedly occur several times and in the same manner to the point that they are assumed to be so. In effect, when that happens accidentally to them, those acts are assumed to be a sign of excellence, as when a man is timid by chance several times in situations where timidity is praised. These things are considered praiseworthy only because praise is an expression describing the greatness of virtue and because they are the things by which virtue is celebrated. When these things are used in praise, they must be used as if they were the product of deliberate reflection. Of the things that happen by chance, there are things that are not caused by man, neither in essence nor by accident, such as noble birth and excellent education; there are other things that accidentally happen from acts that are the product of deliberate reflection. As to good coincidences that accidentally happen from acts, they are taken as a sign of excellences. As to coincidences that surpass man, they are taken to confirm and establish excellence, as the things we say in praise, "The best is born among the best," and in blame, "The serpent begets the serpent." In general, the acts are the things for which a man is praised. As to the traces of acts, they are signs of the act, and they are used in praise only when we establish the act from which they come.

1.9.37. **[Aristotle] said:** Good fortune, which we have previously said is happiness, according to the point of view of the people, is, together with the fortuitous things that constitute praise, one with regard to genre, and it is not, together with excellences, one with regard to genre. Rather, as a good condition is a genre belonging to excellence—that is, enclosing it—in the same way, what happens by chance is a genre that encloses happiness.

1.9.38. These two genres—that is, the virtues and what happens by chance—are included in the chapter on praise and the chapter on deliberation, but from two different standpoints. Things are such only because when we know the things that we must do, we know the things for which a man is worthy of praise when they are done. Therefore, when these things are mentioned in an absolute manner, it is possible to include them in the category of deliberation and in the category of praise, and we do that by adding the mode by which they are included in the category of deliberation or the mode by which they are included in the category of praise. And this is similar to when someone says, "We must not necessarily bestow greatness and excellence on a man for things that happen to him by chance, but for the things that happen through deliberate reflection and by choice." When we add to this, "Therefore, we must not bestow praise on those people whose happiness happens by chance; rather we must bestow praise on people whose happiness is achieved through deliberate reflection and by choice, as so and so," this is included in the chapter on praise. And when we add to this, "Therefore, we must not seek the things that happen by chance, but the things that are the product of deliberate reflection," that is included in the category of deliberation.

1.9.39. Fortuitous things may be used sometimes in praise and sometimes in blame. People's opinions about them vary. Some people believe that good things that occur by chance must not be used in praise, since they are neither acquired nor earned by a man. Other people think that they must be used in praise, for they are the sign of divine providence in favor of the man to whom it happens by accident. As to the things that come by choice, what is praiseworthy among them is always praised and what is blameworthy is always blamed.

1.9.40. **[Aristotle] said:** In praise we must use the things by which something is extolled and amplified. And that means to imagine something forcefully becoming several things, for instance by saying, "He is the first one to have done this," as what has been said in the story of Abel and Cain; or "He is the only one to have done this"; or "He has done in a small amount of time what is normally done in a great amount of time"; or "He has done something whose effects are numerous." All these things point to the greatness of an act. The same is when we say, "This was done at a time when it was difficult to do it," and that is when we consider this act according to what is suitable to each particular man. Also, if the man doing the act very often serves as a good example by his acts and his words, his act is indeed great, as when we say, "Oh, you group of men, you are [religious leaders] that indeed serve as a good example." The acts that serve as a good example are not the acts that happen by chance; they are the acts that happen through willpower and deliberate reflection.

1.9.41. We may include these things in the category of deliberation—that is, the things that amplify the thing—as when we advise someone to act in a manner similar to the manner of the first man worthy of praise in that type or to resemble him in praise; or when we advise this man to be one of the men worthy of praise, whose praise nobody disputes, as the men praised in the marketplaces, or to resemble them in praise.

1.9.42. What makes men worthy of praise great is when they are compared with people whose acts are the opposite, and that is when their excellent acts are mentioned.

1.9.43. [Aristotle] said: Those who naturally act in the fashion of men worthy of praise to the maximum and continuously compare themselves with these men must be compared with these men and treated in the same way in praise, and even if they have not reached the levels of these men, their excellences are continuously increasing. The comparison a man makes of himself with someone else is correct only when it comes from an excellent man. Because of the love that a man has for himself, he thinks that his flaws are less serious than everybody else's flaws, even when they are more serious, and he believes that his excellences are greater, even when they are smaller. For this reason, nobody is able to compare himself with other people. Only excellent men are able to do that, as when Aristotle said of Socrates that he compared himself with other men and judged his moral character himself; that is, he examined himself in comparison with other men, and if he found a virtue in himself, he would reward himself for it, but if he found a flaw in himself, he would reprimand himself for it. Useful comparison for a man who wants to increase his virtues must be made only with people very much worthy of praise. What constitutes a sign that such people are worthy of praise—that is, those whose excellences are continuously increasing—is that those who have made an effort to reach the level of excellent men and have failed are worthy of praise in the eyes of people.

1.9.44. It is plain that to amplify something is in the category of praise, since to amplify something is to make it noble, and the noble belongs to the things for which there is praise.

1.9.45. When we want to amplify something through comparison, that thing must be compared with several praiseworthy things, since this act is a way to make the praiseworthy noble and to provide a sign of its excellence for people to see.

1.9.46. Generally, we say of the kinds common to the three modes that amplification, even when it is common to the three rhetorical modes, is more proper to praise and blame, since a man is only praised or blamed for existing things, whose existence is recognized; that to amplify something is more proper to something that exists than to something that does not exist; and therefore, the man who gives praise must describe the magnificence of the thing, its splendor, and its embellishing aspects.

As to the use of symbols and examples, it is more proper to deliberative oratory, since from past things, we conjecture future things, for to give the reason and the cause based on past things is more acceptable to us, and we celebrate it since it has ceased to exist. As to knowledge of justice and injustice, that is proper to forensic oratory.

1.9.47. In general, all praise and blame are done only through comparison with past praiseworthy and blameworthy people.

1.9.48. To praise or to blame, the speaker must understand the audience in front of which he praises or blames. I mean, he praises in front of the friends of the people he praises, and he blames in front of the enemies of the people he blames. Also, he must know the places from which to draw praise and blame, and these are the places we have previously mentioned, and they are the excellences, their agents, their signs, and their accidents.

1.9.49. It is clear from what we have said of the definitions of these things that we know their opposites, since the opposite is known to us from its opposite. Since we know these things from their opposites, and blame is realized only with the opposite of those things, it is plain that we know from these words not only the things by which there is praise but also the things by which there is blame.

10

1.10.1. On Accusation and Defense

1.10.2. **[Aristotle] said:** Since we have spoken of deliberative oratory and of praise and blame, we must speak of the third kind of topics of this art, which is accusation and defense. We shall do that by enumerating the types of premises that make up the syllogisms used according to the method of accusation and the method of defense and also by describing the nature of each one of these types.

1.10.3. The types of premises from which arguments concerning accusation are made are generally three: the first one consists of premises taken from the doer—that is, the wrongdoer; the second type consists of premises taken from the person who has suffered the act of wrongdoing—that is, the person who is wronged; the third type consists of premises taken from the act of wrongdoing itself. As to the premises taken from the doer, we know them by enumerating the things that, when they exist in a person, make us think that he has done wrong and also by describing the nature of those things. As to the premises taken from the person who has suffered the act of wrongdoing, we know them by also enumerating the things that, when existing in a person, indicate that he was susceptible to suffer an act of wrongdoing. As to the premises taken from the act of wrongdoing, we know them by describing the nature of the acts by which men become wrongdoers, the conditions of the acts when wrong is done, and how the acts of wrongdoing become easy for these men.

1.10.4. **[Aristotle] said:** First, we must define the act of wrongdoing, and then speak of each one of these three things.

1.10.5. **Then we say:** An act of wrongdoing is injury inflicted voluntarily by way of transgression of the law.

1.10.6. The law is of two kinds: it is either special or general. Special laws are written laws that one fears will be forgotten if they are not written, and they are proper to each particular community of people and each particular nation. As to general laws, they are unwritten laws recognized by all, like reverence toward parents and gratitude toward the benefactor.

1.10.7. An act is voluntary when it is done consciously, without any constraint or any other thing that we shall mention afterward. In addition, the act is motivated by the doer's wishes and desires. Of voluntary acts, some are deliberate and some are not deliberate, but they come from poor reflection because of a bad character or a bad habit. It is evident that people who do things deliberately do them knowingly.

1.10.8. Since that is the case, it is evident that people who deliberately or from poor judgment do harmful or deceitful things, that is, things mixed of harm and utility, by which they transgress the law, are unjust. And it is evident that those things are evil or come from poor judgment, and that a person who possesses one of the things that cause poor judgment and was the cause of the existence of that thing in him is ignorant, wicked, and unjust. Some examples include injustice done about money and caused by the desire for money; injustice done about matters of physical pleasure and caused by excessive lust and greed; idleness that is the cause of injustice about several things; and so with cowardice. This is why the coward deserts his companions and betrays them at the slightest misfortune that falls upon [them]; and so with the lover of honor who abandons his companions for the sake of honor; and so with the lovers of victory who abandon their companions for the sake of victory. The quick-tempered, the hot-tempered and disdainful man harms his friends because of dishonor that falls on him. As to the foolish, ignorant man, he commits acts of injustice because he confuses justice with injustice. As to the impudent man, he commits acts of injustice because of a lack of desire for thankfulness. And so with other similar conditions that are the cause of acts of injustice not done deliberately.

1.10.9. We understand these conditions from what has been said earlier of the virtues and from what we are going to say about the emotions. In general, these conditions are either a vile character trait or a vile emotion. From what has been said earlier, we know the meaning of "vile characters"—that is, from what we know of their opposites, which are the virtues. We shall discuss the emotions in Book II.

1.10.10. [Aristotle] said: Since we established this matter, our discussion has come to the point where we must explain the motives behind the acts of wrongdoing committed by wrongdoers, the states of mind of wrongdoers when they do wrong, and the things about which they do wrong. However, we must first explain the things about which wrongdoers do wrong—that is, the things about which they do wrong when they desire them or do wrong as well when they hate them.

1.10.11. It is evident that we must first speak of accusation before we speak of defense, since the accuser must know the things about which there is accusation, how many they are, and which ones they are. The places of defense are not as defined as the places of accusation; they are defined according to the places of accusation. Accusation is a firmly established matter in human society. This is why you see many people harm their neighbors and their [fellow members], when they are not accusing someone.

1.10.12. Every person committing an unjust act either must commit it for his own sake and by his own will and choice or he does not commit it for his own sake and by his own choice.

1.10.13. The latter commits an unjust act either by chance—and that is called a slip—or by necessity. The act that he commits by necessity is sometimes due to his natural disposition, such as when he naturally has a bad character trait, and sometimes it is due to external pressure; that is, the act, in principle, is not done voluntarily but is due to intimidation or a threat and other similar things coming from outside.

1.10.14. The act that he does of his own accord is the thing that is due to him and of which he alone is the cause, and nothing from outside is associated with it. The act that he does of his own accord is sometimes due to a bad habit or a bad character; sometimes it is due to an appetite and craving. Sometimes the act is due to craving that is presumed rational; sometimes it is due to craving that is imaginary. Sometimes the act due to craving is due to choleric craving; sometimes it is due to appetite.

1.10.15. Thus the acts done by wrongdoers are undoubtedly due to one or another of seven causes: one of them is chance; the second, nature; the third, compulsion; the fourth, habit and character; the fifth, reasoning; the sixth, anger; the seventh, appetite. All, except the one coming from reasoning, are the divisions of poor judgment that we have mentioned earlier.

1.10.16. **[Aristotle] said:** The division of unjust acts according to the doers' ages, ambitions, and good fortunes is not an essential one. In effect, although the wrong that young men do is greater, it is not essentially due to the fact that they are young; it is due to the fact that they have hot tempers and strong appetites. Similarly, it so happens that the poor have a strong appetite for money more than the rich do because of their indigence, as it so happens that the rich have a strong appetite for money more than the poor do because of unnecessary pleasures, so that when any type of wrongdoing is linked to the rich or the poor, the immediate cause of that is not wealth or poverty, but appetite and character that the soul acquires from poverty and wealth. And so with ambitions—that is, if something of them is linked to wrongdoing, that is not essentially and primarily so, but it is due to the fact that ambitions constitute one or more than one of those seven causes, which are primarily and essentially the causes of wrongdoing. This is why righteous men, foolish men, and all the other men who are said to act according to their ambitions only do so either according to one or more than one of the seven causes previously mentioned or according to their opposites. And they are the men of good ambitions; that is, foolish men act according to those causes, and righteous men according to their opposites. For example, excellent appetites are associated with the temperate man, and vile appetites are associated with the foolish man. This is why we must ignore this type of division here and mention these things in the end as the causes of these seven causes, not as the primary causes of acts of wrongdoing.

1.10.17. As to the things that are causes by accident, we must avoid mentioning them here at all, such as the fact that a man is dark or fair, or large or thin, since these may by accident be followed by different characters and appetites. We must only mention here among the causes of these things—that is, the seven causes that we have previously mentioned—the accidents that produce a change in the character itself, whether it is psychological or physical or external, such as old age, youth, poverty, or wealth. For when a man becomes poor, he will think of himself as a man of small value, and he will feel ashamed of everything he does; and when he becomes rich, he will think of himself as a man of great value, and he will not feel ashamed of anything. But we shall speak of these accidents later.

1.10.18. Here let us go back to what we have been discussing and say, when the efficient causes of wrongdoing are made clear, the end causes of each one of them are also made clear.

1.10.19. Those who do wrong by chance do not have a definite purpose in view. Therefore, their wrongdoing is neither permanent nor frequent, nor does it come from a fixed faculty or disposition. We know this from things that happen by chance, for chance becomes the cause of things only less frequently, according to what has been discussed in *Kitāb al-Burhān* (*Book of Demonstration*).

1.10.20. Wrongdoing due to the natural disposition and instinct of the wrongdoer is due to a fixed disposition. The acts due to this natural disposition have the same quality either permanently or more frequently. Their end is the end vile emotions that we shall discuss later.

1.10.21. As to wrongdoing that is due to a condition outside of a natural disposition, such as insanity and other evils that do not follow a natural course, it seems to be attributed to chance and not to something essentially.

1.10.22. As to acts due to compulsion—that is, those that are due to choice but begin with compulsion—their end is the end of unjust acts that are due to choice, since compulsion happens accidentally to acts due to choice.

1.10.23. The end of wrongdoing that is due to deliberate reflection and thought is either the things that are believed to be useful—and they are the things that have been mentioned in the chapter on deliberative oratory, which is about the thing that is believed to be good either because it is believed to be a useful end or because it is believed to be useful to a useful end—or the things that are believed to be pleasant. This is why foolish men often do useful things for the sake of pleasure.

1.10.24. The end of wrongdoing that is due to anger is revenge. Revenge is something other than punishment, for punishment is inflicted for the sake of the person punished, either for his own good or for the good of the city, or it is inflicted for the pleasure felt because of the punishment itself. And this is a ferocious form of punishment. As to revenge, the aim is to establish equality with the crime committed; that is, the wrongdoer suffers a wrong that is equal to the wrong he has inflicted. This is the end of revenge, which is imposed by the person taking revenge. As to understanding the definition of anger, what it is, and its consequences, we shall speak of all this later, when we discuss the emotions.

1.10.25. Wrongdoing due to character or habit is committed only for the sake of pleasure and so with what is due to appetite. This is why all the things that are believed to be pleasant are done only because of one of these four causes, by which a man acts of his own accord, and which are deliberate reflection, anger, character and habit, and appetite. Pleasures due to character and habit come in many aspects; that is, some of them are natural and some are unnatural, for they are felt only by habit.

1.10.26. In general, all those who commit acts of wrongdoing of their own accord only do so either because of things that are in truth good or are assumed to be good, or because of things that are in truth pleasant, or because of things that are assumed to be pleasant, since people who do things of their own accord do so only for the sake of good that will come sooner or later. This is why they sometimes act because of an evil that they suffer when they believe that they will obtain by it a greater good than the good that they have lost because of that evil, or when they believe that by that evil, a greater evil is pushed away, and that what follows the first is minimal. This is why we also choose to precipitate sad and painful things when we believe that we will soon obtain by them a greater good or a lesser evil than is expected to happen if we do not do so. This type of intention is used in different ways.

1.10.27. Since we have explained that what the wrongdoer desires is either useful or pleasant, we must examine the things that are useful and the things that are pleasant—that is, their number and their nature. The things that are useful have been previously discussed in the chapter on deliberative oratory. What remains to be discussed separately here is the subject of pleasant things. We shall discuss these things and give full definitions of them only according to what is sufficient in this art, and these are well-known definitions, although they may not be true.

11

1.11.1. **We now say:** Pleasure is a change into a disposition that suddenly occurs from a natural sensation—that is, when the sensation is naturally experienced by a person. Grief and pain are contrary to this [change].

I mean the change [they represent] is a change into a disposition that suddenly occurs from an unnatural sensation. Since pleasure has this characteristic, it is clear that pleasure consists of sensations that produce this disposition in the soul and that painful things are contrary to these sensations—that is, the things that corrupt these and produce the opposite of this disposition in the sensitive soul.

1.11.2. Since pleasant things are these sensations, the things among them that naturally have this characteristic must be more pleasant, especially when this disposition is an emotion and not an act. Character and habit become pleasant only because the thing that one takes as a character trait or has become habitual becomes like the thing that is naturally pleasant in a permanent manner, for habit is like nature. What happens very frequently is close to what happens naturally, and that is what happens permanently. Habit occurs very frequently; it is, therefore, close to what happens naturally.

1.11.3. A natural thing happens without compulsion. This is why compulsion is painful and grievous; as the Greek poets have said, "All that is done on compulsion is painful and grievous."

1.11.4. **[Aristotle] said:** Acts of concentration, serious effort, and strains are painful, since they involve constraint and compulsion if one is not accustomed to them. As to their opposites, they are pleasant. Hence laziness, flabbiness, disrespect for decrees imposed by the laws controlling acts, rest, and sleep are among pleasant things, since none of them is done on compulsion.

1.11.5. Where there is desire, there is also pleasure, since desire involves craving for pleasure. Some desires are natural; others are irrational. By irrational, I mean everything that is desired, but not from deliberate reflection and thought. These are called desires, like the desires related to the body, such as the desire for nourishment, called hunger; the desire for water, called thirst; the kinds of desires answering to each type of taste; and, in general, everything related to the sense of touch and the sense of smell, such as sexual intercourse, food, drink, and pleasant fragrances. As to the desires of hearing and vision, they are associated with a certain amount of reason. I mean they do not arise stripped of reason at the beginning, as in the case of the desire for the food we eat and the person with whom we engage in sexual intercourse. The reason for this is that these two senses are more associated with reason than the other ones. In effect, hearing is associated with reason with respect to words, and vision is associated with reason with respect to writing and sign used in communication. Hearing is more associated with reason than vision is. This is why a person very much desires to see what he has heard and he does not desire to hear what he has seen, since pleasure based on the senses is more like a type of bodily sensation.

1.11.6. **[Aristotle] said:** Imagination is a feeble sensation that produces either memory or expectation. When it is devoid of memory, it is also devoid of expectation. Expectation is a possible future composition of past sensations, which is memory, so that every time memory is removed, expectation is necessarily removed. And since imagination is a sort of sensation, it is plain that pleasure exists only in memory and expectation, because the two are part of sensation to the point that all pleasant things only exist necessarily in sensation. In effect, when sensations are actually present, the pleasure is felt in the direct practice of them and the sensation drawn from them. When they are past sensations, the pleasure is felt in remembering them. When they are future sensations, the pleasure is felt in expecting them, for sensation is proper to present things, memory to past things, and expectation to future things.

1.11.7. Pleasant realizations are not only those that are close to the present time. But certain things sometimes become unpleasant the closer they get to the present, and when they are far away in time, they become pleasant, since what is close becomes dull and what is distant becomes to the person remembering it more beautiful and better because of the distance in time, so that it becomes like expectation.

1.11.8. The memory a man has of past toil and strain and from which he has freed himself is pleasant. In effect, a hardworking and eager man enjoys remembering toil and exertion when he succeeds in his endeavor or has been saved from evil because of them, since to be saved from evil is also reason for pleasure.

1.11.9. As to pleasant things that are expected, they are the ones that bring joy or are useful, when they are close, and that is when they are thought to be great or useful when they are great when their usefulness is not affected by pain. In general, expected things that are pleasant are close to the present time and exist easily. This is why anger is pleasant, since anger exists only when a person expects to inflict evil on someone he is angry with and it is possible to inflict evil on him. Thus Homer said of anger, "Sweeter it is than the drops of honey." As anger exists only when revenge is possible, not present and not impossible, no one grows angry with a feeble person on whom evil has fallen or with a person on whom there is no prospect of seeing evil fall on him, and it is the one whose rank is not related to the rank of the person who is angry with him, like the subjects and the monarchs. In the same way, the man who grows angry does not grow angry with the person who, having very little value, does not have any kind of relationship with him.

1.11.10. Several appetites are not associated with pleasure while they are actually present—that is, while they are felt; they are associated with pleasure while they are imagined. Therefore, those who remember the thing they desire, no matter how they remember it, find a certain pleasure in it. Similarly, those who expect to obtain something find some pleasure when they obtain it. This is why persons down with a fever and whom doctors do not allow to drink water enjoy the memory of drinking water and look forward to feeling better and drinking water. And those who ask people what is good for them or write about it, or pursue it, they enjoy the request and pursuit—since they hope to obtain the things they have requested—while waiting to obtain these things so that they actually enjoy them.

1.11.11. The things that all men truly love are three: one of them is when the pleasant thing is present; the second, when they imagine it, when not present, by either remembering it or expecting it; the third, when they get a quick consolation from grief and sorrow. This is why they hate to see those in grief and do not attend funerals or hear lamentations, because these things increase feelings of sadness.

1.11.12. Some desires have both grief and pleasure in them, such as remembering a loved one who is absent or who has passed away, when we think of the person he was and of his deeds. This is why those who produce elegies feel both pleasure and grief.

1.11.13. **[Aristotle] said:** Homer spoke well about this point when he said, "When the orator delivered his funeral oration, the audience uttered a shout mixed with grief and pleasure."

1.11.14. It seems that revenge belongs to this chapter, since it is both pleasant and sorrowful; and it seems that it belongs to pleasant things only.

1.11.15. That the enemy does not succeed is pleasant.

1.11.16. When the person who grows angry does not reach the punishment he hopes to inflict on someone, he feels both pleasure and grief. He feels grief because he does not achieve the punishment he wants to inflict on someone; as to the pleasure that he feels, it comes from the hope to achieve the punishment he wants to inflict on someone.

1.11.17. [Aristotle] said: Victory is pleasant not only to those who love it but also to everyone, for victory is a sort of appetite for nobility. I mean some sort of superiority known to people. All people desire nobility, even if they more or less differ in that regard.

1.11.18. Given that victory is pleasant, cultural contests and combative sports are also pleasant because they are useful in obtaining pleasure, since in most cases victory happens by these. And that is like ball [games], swordsmanship, chess, dice, and skill in all cultural activities ensuring a good education—that is, sports by which we aim to obtain a certain faculty.

1.11.19. These cultural activities ensuring a good education are of two kinds. Some are not pleasant from the first, until a person gets accustomed to them, and then they become pleasant from habit; and they are the cultural activities that are not associated with pleasure that is associated with the faculty obtained in the end by these cultural activities, but are associated from the first with exertion only, like being educated by wisdom. Other cultural activities are pleasant from the first, such as hunting and playing chess. The beginner in these activities enters into partnership with the one who is skilled in them—I mean he enters into partnership to achieve the end for which he aims, which is victory—and enjoys them from the first, the same way a perfectly skilled man does.

1.11.20. Victory by justice is pleasant. Victory by means of discord and distortion of facts is pleasant for the sophists, who are accustomed to achieve by such means their goals and aspirations—that is, external goods, like wealth and honor.

1.11.21. Honor and majesty are pleasant things, since honor makes the man being honored imagine himself to be an excellent man or one of those who are trying hard to obtain excellence when honor comes from a person whose nature is to produce, by the honor he bestows, in the person being honored a similar opinion of himself and a similar impression. I mean the man being honored imagines himself to be an excellent man.

1.11.22. Among those who bestow honor, those who are present are more appropriate to this act than those who are absent, since those who are present see in the person being honored what those who are absent do not see, so that when they bestow honor on someone, he has the impression that they have bestowed honor on him because of a virtue that they have known in him. For this same reason, honor bestowed by someone who knows the person being honored is more appropriate than honor bestowed by someone who does not know the person being honored. His fellow countrymen are more appropriate to that act than strangers. Those who are present are more appropriate to that act than those who come afterward. I mean those who bestow honor on someone during his lifetime are more appropriate to that act, in this sense, than those who bestow honor on him after his death. Honor bestowed by a greater number of people is more appropriate, in this sense, than honor bestowed by a smaller number of people. These kinds of men are more appropriate to have their words believed when they are spoken about a man of reason and intellect, and their testimony about him is more useful than the words and testimony of the types of men who are of the rank of children and animals, and they are the ignorant and common men. This is why nobody makes a great case for the honor bestowed by such men on anyone, and nobody is glorified by that, except when one believes that they do that because they obey him very much or fear him.

1.11.23. Loved ones also belong to the class of pleasant things, because it is pleasant to love, and everyone who loves something draws pleasure from it. This is why someone who does not like wine does not find it pleasant, the reason being that the loved one, for the one who loves, belongs to the class of all the good things that all people desire. By all [people], I mean those with feelings and imagination. That a man is loved and considered close for his own sake, and not for the sake of someone else, is pleasant to the man who is loved. I mean that a man is loved for his own sake.

1.11.24. Similarly, for a man to be considered admirable by others—that is, to be admired by others—is also for this same reason—that is, for the sake of good that all people desire—because one admires a man only when he is distinguished by a good quality that does not exist in a majority of people. In effect, the thing by which a man excels in comparison with the majority of people is pleasant. Those who seek to be admired resemble those who bring people together so that they see the effort they have made in order to attain wonderful and excellent things.

1.11.25. **[Aristotle] said:** Flattery is also pleasant, for the flatterer makes you imagine that he admires you and that he is one of those who love you, for the flatterer is an insincere lover or one who exalts people in an insincere manner.

1.11.26. Repetition of the same thing is pleasant, for by repetition, the thing dominates the soul, and anything habitual is pleasant.

1.11.27. Change from one condition to another is naturally pleasant, since it means a new sensation of a new thing. This is why the things that happen in the world naturally at intervals are pleasant, like the change of seasons, the change of countries, and in general, the changes that happen to people and change people. The reason for this is that the soul has satisfied itself from the present thing to a certain extent, and that there is nothing left in that thing that will satisfy it, especially when the thing has lasted longer so that the soul seeks to take a break from it and move on to something new from which it will obtain what it does not have. The less frequently a thing occurs in time, the more pleasant it becomes.

1.11.28. [Aristotle] said: Learning is also pleasant in most cases. The desire to learn happens only because man desires to become admirable himself or to become such that he is admired, these two things themselves being pleasant. Also, since learning, which is a genre of comprehension, naturally goes from power to the deed and then to perfection, it is also considered pleasant.

1.11.29. In general, a good deed and a good passion are also pleasant things. One does not enjoy a good passion for itself, but one enjoys it only because of the desire for perfection that is happening or that one believes is going to happen from that passion. As to a good deed, man enjoys it for its own sake and for the sake of something else, which is the thing by which a good deed happens.

1.11.30. To educate relatives is pleasant.

1.11.31. To give enough and supply what people need is pleasant.

1.11.32. [Aristotle] said: Since learning is pleasant and also the fact that a man is admirable or admired, it follows that acts of imagination and imitation, being similar to learning, are also pleasant; and that is like imitation by painting, sculpture, and all the acts by which one aims to imitate the first models—I mean existing objects, not the acts by which one imitates objects that do not exist. In effect, the pleasure we draw from acts of imitation of existing objects does not come from resembling images being attractive or unattractive, but from the fact that these acts contain some type of syllogistic activity. The definition of what is more hidden, which is the absent object that is compared, by what is more apparent, which is the example put in its place, has in it, in a certain manner, one of the types of learning by syllogism, for the image of an object is of the rank of a premise, and the object that one aims to imagine and explain is of the rank of a conclusion; and because of the similarity that exists between imagination and learning, imagination is pleasant.

1.11.33. [Aristotle] said: It is also pleasant to devise tricks by which to dodge perils and to escape from them.

1.11.34. Imitation and learning have become pleasant because they happen only by grasping the relationships between the objects; and to know the relationships between existing things is naturally desirable. This is why similarities and proverbs are pleasant. In effect, a human being enjoys another human being, a horse enjoys another horse, a young man enjoys another young man. From here we draw proverbs. For example, we say, "The boy rejoices at the boy; the thief knows the thief; the bird chases the bird; the animal of prey does not attack the animal of prey;" and other, similar proverbs.

1.11.35. In general, things related to one another and things akin to each other are all pleasant in themselves; what each individual finds pleasant in what is similar is a known matter. Mutual hatred between those who resemble each other happens only by accident. Pleasure is found only in understanding the relationship between two of the things existing in the world.

1.11.36. Every man is fond of himself, but some men excel in this act more than others, so that every man whose love for his own being is stronger draws more pleasure and has more love for men akin to him.

1.11.37. Because a human being is fond of himself, his state of being is most certainly pleasant for him—that is, his deeds and words. This is why most people—and they are the public—love good deeds, honor, and children only because they are fond of themselves, since children constitute one of their vestiges. To supply what is needed is pleasant from this standpoint, since it is one of a human being's deeds. The same thing goes with power over others. For a man to be thought wise is pleasant because of the fondness he has of himself. Also, the love of honor is pleasant in this sense. To be useful to relatives, in this sense, is pleasant, and also, it is pleasant to have power over them. For a man to practice the things by which he obtains excellence is pleasant and honorable, since he imagines that he has gained those virtues that he has practiced. Hence Homer praised a man who divided his day into segments so that he could do in each segment a deed by which he could accomplish some sort of excellence, and therefore he gained those excellences when he divided his day into those segments, and by those excellences he became a perfectly excellent man.

1.11.38. [Aristotle] said: Comical things that make a person laugh are pleasant. Original comical things in deeds and words are most certainly pleasant. In the treatise *Art of Poetry*, we have discussed the things from which comical things and anecdotes are produced and how they are used.

1.11.39. Since it is plain from these words what things are pleasant, it is also plain what things are painful and grievous, for they are the opposite of those; and when we know one of the opposites, we know the other.

12

1.12.1. Since it has been made clear from these words the things for which and by which the wrongdoer does wrong, we must now move on to the discussion of the particular circumstances and conditions that make it easy for wrongdoers to do wrong, their motives for doing wrong, and the states of mind they are in when they do wrong.

1.12.2. We then say: Wrongdoing may come from wrongdoers when they think that the act can be done, that it is possible for them to do it, that it is not found out and known about, or that it is forgotten in a little amount of time if it is found out; and if the act is of the kind that is found out and not forgotten, it is then of the kind from which absolutely no evil falls upon the wrongdoer in committing it—neither upon him nor upon those he cares about, since he considers the latter like himself—or the evil coming from this act is less than the benefit or the pleasure that he gains by doing wrong, either for himself or for those he cares about.

1.12.3. As to the mention of the things by which the act of wrongdoing becomes possible, we shall discuss that later in Book II, since the discussion of that subject is common to all three kinds of speaking. As to the conditions in which absolutely no evil falls upon the wrongdoer or in which something below the good he hopes for happens to him, or in which the act is of the kind that is not found out or that is forgotten in a little amount of time, we shall speak of these things here, since it is proper to discuss them in this context.

1.12.4. [Aristotle] said: It may be believed that the sort of people who think they have more power over others and that they are safe from evil, either in themselves or in those they care about, when they do wrong, are more capable of doing wrong than others. These people belong to one of these two types: either the type of people who do wrong because they have more power or the type of people who do wrong because they have experience and deliberate reflection to the point that they carefully think about the manner in which they will escape from evil, and that is due to a lengthy experience and earlier practice.

1.12.5. Wrongdoers escape from punishment when they have many friends or their friends are wealthy, especially when they are participants in the business of wrongdoing—I mean they obtain from the act of wrongdoing a benefit or pleasure—for the wrongdoer becomes more capable of wrongdoing. The same thing happens if those who participate in the business of wrongdoing are friends of friends, or servants of friends, or hired hands of friends, or those devoted to them, or their associates, for when wrongdoers have this characteristic, they are capable of doing wrong and of abstaining from paying a penalty or the price for retribution. And it may happen that their acts are not found out or are forgotten. As to the acts not being found out, that comes from their associates; as to the acts being forgotten, that comes from the fact that these do not begin from the first to complain about the act of wrongdoing committed by the wrongdoer.

1.12.6. **[Aristotle] said:** What makes the act of wrongdoing easy is when the wrongdoers are on friendly terms with those to whom they do wrong or with the judges. As to being friends with those to whom they do wrong, that happens for two reasons: one of them is that the friend is not on his guard against his friend, so that he ends up being easily wronged; the second is that the wrongdoer gives the friend being wronged the smallest compensation [to appease him] before they go to court, because a friend dupes himself in favor of his friend. As to the judges being friendly, that happens because they rule in favor of those they like, either by letting them off without paying anything altogether or by imposing a lighter fine.

1.12.7. And here we have conditions that are contrary to these conditions related to power, so that when they exist in the wrongdoer, they cause him to do wrong, such as sickness, weakness, and poverty, for the weakling and the sick are assumed not to do wrong, since they will not tolerate corporal punishment; as to the poor man, it is because he has nothing with which to pay a fine.

1.12.8. The act of wrongdoing, when it is committed in public to a highest degree, is concealed by the wrongdoer, who gives people the illusion that it is not an act of wrongdoing, for when the act committed by the wrongdoer resembles an act committed by a crafty man or a joker, that leads to error of judgment to the point that one thinks it is not an act of wrongdoing. Again, nobody takes precaution against an act of wrongdoing committed in public, because that rarely happens. One takes precaution against an act of wrongdoing only from the point where it habitually happens, which is concealment. This is why one does not take precaution against someone of no value or against friends and children.

1.12.9. There are people who do not pay attention to their acts so as to make other people assume that they do not know what they do or forget what they do. And perhaps they pretend not to see what happens to them so that other people do not assume, against them, that they ever start the act of wrongdoing.

1.12.10. Of the things that help the wrongdoer in committing acts of wrongdoing, there is the ability to conceal his acts, and that is because of secret places that he has for his convenience or because of conditions in him that help him conceal his acts, such as when his appearance is the appearance of someone whom one does not suspect of committing bad acts.

1.12.11. Those who are found out and whose acts of wrongdoing are found out are sometimes able to commit acts of wrongdoing when the judges are unjust in one of two ways: either by bending the law or by deferring the victim's right so that the victim gets tired and drops the charge. This is why when the wrongdoer is capable of evading or stalling the payment of the fine or when he is destitute, the act of wrongdoing becomes easy for him.

1.12.12. As to those for whom the benefits gained from acts of wrongdoing are clear and evident or great, or near and present, and for whom the damages resulting from the act of wrongdoing are either small or unknown, or distant, or slow coming in time, the act of wrongdoing is easy for them. In effect, they do not abandon something certainly beneficial for an unknown damage, and also, they do not abandon something immediately beneficial for a future inconvenience or numerous benefits for a small inconvenience.

1.12.13. What makes wrongdoing easy is when it is an act for which the wrongdoer is praised and remembered, such as what happens to someone who takes revenge on a person who has done wrong to him, to his father and mother, or what happens to someone who, seeking revenge on one person in a city, kills all the people in that city, especially when the harm inflicted on these men seeking revenge amounts to loss of money and banishment, for this kind of act is most often a subject of praise, as the poet has said:

> *Take my home and destroy it, for it is*
> *A heritage left by a noble man who does not fear*
> *consequences of his actions.*

1.12.14. These people are unjust in what they take and what they refuse; that is, they take what does not belong to them and refuse to give what they must give.

1.12.15. These, then, are the things that make wrongdoing easy for men of great aspirations and deliberate reflection. As to the opposite of these men in character and judgment, who are men of poor judgment and character, they are motivated to do wrong by a small unknown benefit that they expect; I mean something they are not sure they will or will not get. They may be motivated by the fear of a small loss they may incur and not by the prospect of gaining, from their act of wrongdoing, some benefit, if only to avoid the loss of a few of the many things that they possess.

1.12.16. What may motivate this type of people to do wrong is to do wrong and miss their goal and not attain the wrongdoing they aimed for, which prompts them to do wrong one time after another, such as what happens to many people who have been defeated and they relentlessly go back to fighting after they have been defeated once and then twice.

1.12.17. Those who are led to do wrong by pleasure in the first place, despite the pain that follows in the end, or who precipitate utility first, despite the damage that happens to them in the end, are also of this type, for people of poor judgment are sometimes in this situation every time they desire something.

1.12.18. The opposite of these people are those who are motivated to do wrong when the painful and harmful thing comes to them first and the pleasant and beneficial thing comes later after a certain amount of time. These are highly self-controlled and sensible people, and they are extremely vicious, for one assumes that they have not attained those subsequent benefits and pleasures by their act of wrongdoing, and that what they have attained by doing wrong is the damage or the pain that they have precipitated, so that one thinks that they have not done wrong at all.

1.12.19. What motivates sly and cunning people to do wrong is that they present the act of wrongdoing in such a manner as to make other people believe it is not a wrongful act. That happens in several ways, one of which is that one assumes that the act happened by chance; or that it happened on compulsion; or that it happened naturally; or that it happened by accident and through ignorance and not through premeditation; or that it happened through a habit that the wrongdoer had in the past; or that the act is such that the profit to be gained from doing it is not in the present but in the future. The act from which there is no profit to be gained in the present may be believed not to be aimed by anyone and that there is no need for it, for one does wrong only because there is need for something in it.

1.12.20. Those in need are of two kinds: those in need through necessity, like the poor, or those in need through greed, like the rich. Wrongdoing through necessity is excused more than wrongdoing through greed. This is why people blame the latter very much, although they very often succeed in doing wrong.

1.12.21. When a man of reason and determination appropriates something for which he does wrong, he appears to other people as though he does not appreciate or enjoy that thing. As to people of poor judgment, they manifest their joy at obtaining something unjustly.

1.12.22. The opinions of those who do wrong for one of these reasons that help conceal wrongdoing or make it easy to do wrong become convincing when they seize what they hoped to get.

1.12.23. In sum, this is what [Aristotle] has said of the things that make wrongdoing easy for wrongdoers and incite them to do wrong.

1.12.24. As to those who are harmed by wrongdoers, and they are naturally the victims—that is, victims of the greed of evil people—they are those who do not know what is done to them, for they do not realize that it is an act of wrongdoing; or they are those who quickly forget the wrong that has been done to them even when they find out about it; and those who resemble these people among those who have no friends or have friends that are poor.

1.12.25. Wrongdoing caused [by a desire] for money happens to a person who has money only when in that money the wrongdoer finds what he needs, and that is either through necessity, if he is poor, or through greed, if he is a wealthy man whose goal is to accumulate money only or to take pleasure in life if his goal is to spend money and enjoy it.

1.12.26. Those who suspend their rightful claims are often victims of wrongdoing. The same is true with relatives and friends, because a person does not guard against his friend, and when his friend does wrong to him, the victim does not find out that his friend has wronged him. All these types do not take their revenge on the wrongdoer either because they lack support, as when they are poor, or because they lack friends, or because they put off their vengeance until later. This is why people who rob their relatives often succeed, when their relatives do not find out about being wronged from the first until the moment when the act of wrongdoing is erased [from memory] and forgotten.

1.12.27. The type of people who protect themselves from evil and stay away from it—that is, those who keep themselves from being degraded in disputes—are often victims of wrongdoing. The same thing happens to people against whose evil one does not necessarily have to protect oneself, whose conduct is correct, who are trusted and fair—I mean such people that wrongdoers have an avid desire to do wrong to. And it is sometimes possible that one does not know the conditions these people are in, and therefore nobody sets out to do them wrong.

1.12.28. Wrongdoers have an avid desire to do wrong to lazy, nonchalant people. The same is true with those who do not know what is unjust and what is just and, in general, what the judge decides, for only a man with penetrating insight can deduce rights from the judges' decisions. I mean the man who knows the rules by which judges reach their decisions.

1.12.29. Of those who are victims of wrongdoing, there is the kind of men who get overwhelmed by shyness, since they do not proceed with clamor or deceit in claiming their benefits.

1.12.30. Also, those who have been wronged by many people are victims of wrongdoing because they have been humiliated and rendered inoffensive.

1.12.31. People in whose favor judgments have not been pronounced when they appear in court in front of judges and sultans because they have no [social] value are victims of wrongdoing. In effect, they are, as it has been said, always being pushed aside. Again, those who attempt to obtain their rights several times and obtain nothing are victims of wrongdoing. In effect, both types are discredited to the point that one does not guard against them either absolutely or at a certain time, because these people are blamed, and one does not guard against those who are blamed, since they have no support. Things are such because these people do not put in action their will or their points of view, because they are afraid of speaking and they are incapable of granting permission or imposing prohibition. In effect, none of these people fail to be surpassed in court or humiliated or rejected.

1.12.32. Those who are responsible, in the eyes of certain people, for a crime committed in the past or for a bad misfortune either by their ancestors or by their fathers, or by themselves, or by their friends are predisposed to suffer more acts of wrongdoing from the part of those people than the acts of wrongdoing committed in the past. The same is true if they treated with disdain those people, or their fathers, or those they care about. As the proverb says, "A little amount of evil excites more evil." And "Evil starts first with its little ones." If those who have committed an old crime are friends and this crime is small, to speak ill of them and to listen to evil things said about them is easy, and it is not despicable to those who are spoken about. If the crime is a serious one, those who have been victims enjoy speaking ill of them or listening to evil things said about them. If they are enemies, to speak ill of them and to listen to evil things said about them are accompanied with disdain for them, and they are considered to be of no value. As to those who listen, either they do not speak ill of them at all, or they disapprove of what the speakers say, or they take sides with those speaking ill of people and even add to what they say.

1.12.33. And here we have a type of people who are victims of wrongdoing and are subjected to harm and vengeance, not for the wrongdoer's benefit, but for his pleasure. These people are foreign to the city, or to the race, or to the moral values, or to the language, or to the religious community. In effect, human beings find pleasure in doing wrong to foreigners in these five ways. Wrongdoing inflicted on these people is negligence, for wrongdoing happens in the areas of wealth, honor, and security. Also, heedless people are victims of wrongdoing. People enjoy doing wrong to foreigners only because the latter do not understand what is humiliating and degrading in the eyes of the people in that city or that race. The same is true with heedless people, whom we have just mentioned.

1.12.34. Among those one enjoys doing wrong to are the kind of people who worry about and get distressed by small matters. And that is evident in the actions of players at a game, as far as this kind of people is concerned.

1.12.35. **[Aristotle] said:** One enjoys doing wrong, without looking for benefit in the act, to those who have often done wrong to people, and one assumes that doing wrong to such wrongdoers is nearly not an act of wrongdoing. And that is like when someone strikes a person who has been accustomed to insulting and degrading people to the point that he bashes him in or injures him. Wrongdoing is pleasant and good in the eyes of people when it is inflicted on those who have, intentionally or unintentionally, committed something bad and indecent in the eyes of people. The doer of such act is not considered a wrongdoer.

1.12.36. Also, people find pleasure in doing wrong to those who rejoice at the acts of wrongdoers, or who are friends of wrongdoers, or who admire the acts of wrongdoers, and in general, those who rejoice at the act of someone who has done wrong. The same is true, in general, with those who are attached to or live with someone who has committed a wrongful act.

1.12.37. People find pleasure in doing wrong to those who do wrong to people who patiently endure wrongful acts done to them and overlook the truth [of that wrongful act].

1.12.38. Injustice inflicted on those who are first to begin with an act of injustice is nearly not act of injustice. This is why it has been said, "He who starts an act of injustice is more unjust." And this is like when a man kills someone who seeks to kill him.

1.12.39. People rush to commit wrongful acts against those who are on the brink of destruction, since nobody knows that they were behind those acts. One finds pleasure in doing wrong to the group of people who commit wrongful acts against those who are on the brink of destruction, especially when these have had the power to push back the group of wrongdoers but have done wrong to one another in favor of this group, have forgiven this group, and have refused to harm them; and when we know, in addition to this, that if these victims had not reached this state by the wrong that they had done to one another and by the forgiveness that they had granted to the group of wrongdoers that had led them to this state of imminent destruction, the group [of wrongdoers] would not have dared to commit wrongful acts against them. It is like what [Aristotle] has said about what happened to [the people] of an island known to [the Greeks]. In effect, there were people who forcibly and unjustly insulted the inhabitants on this island because they found them on the brink of destruction because of a previous act of aggression from another people. The inhabitants of this island could have pushed away the wrongful act done to them by those who put them in that state [of near destruction], but they did not do anything about it. Instead, they did wrong to one another and forgave those who did wrong to them, which led them to the state where it was possible for the latter group to insult them forcibly and unjustly.

1.12.40. Such are the things that, when existing in a man, incite the wrongdoer to commit wrongful acts against this man. This is, of course, about victims of wrongful acts.

1.12.41. As to the things in which wrongdoing is easy, so that all or most people commit acts of wrongdoing in them, they are the things in which there is forgiveness and the things that can be covered and hidden. The things in which there is forgiveness are small, petty things. The things that can be covered and hidden are the things that can rapidly be spoiled, like foods; or the things that can be easily changed in shape or in color; or the things that can be changed through combining and mixing [of ingredients]. The things that generally can be changed in shape in several places are easier to hide, especially when the change occurs in small places. The more it is possible for something to change, and also, the easier it is for it to change, the easier it is for it to be hidden. Similarly, things are hidden when we know that the wrongdoer possesses things that resemble them or things that do not resemble them, but he includes them in the sum of things that resemble them, or he changes them into things that do not resemble them among those that one knows he possesses. This is why many of those who want to do wrong first acquire the type of thing in which they want to do wrong or the type of thing into which they want to change the first type. Everything that the victim is ashamed to mention is the type that gets hidden, such as a wrongful act done on women, since to reveal that act is, for the victims, a scandal and a disgrace with respect to their children. These things and the things that resemble them are the things in which wrongdoing is easy to commit since they involve forgiveness or concealment.

1.12.42. The above is an explanation of the things for which the wrongdoer does wrong; and the circumstances that, when they exist in a man, make an act of wrongdoing against him easy to commit; and the circumstances that make wrongdoers desire to do wrong to others. What remains to be discussed is the third type of the three things from which we draw premises by which we demonstrate that the wrongdoer has done wrong. That means knowledge of the acts, which, when we demonstrate that the wrongdoers have committed them, we also know that they have done wrong, and also knowledge of the circumstances under which the act of wrongdoing has been done, which, when they exist in the act, we also know that the act was a wrongful act.

13

1.13.1. We must first introduce the types of unjust acts and the types of obligations—that is, the acts that are not unjust. We have previously said that the types of unjust acts are geared toward two things—either toward what is pleasant or toward what is beneficial—and they are found in the class of people in which they exist in two ways, either to ward off harm or to attract a benefit.

1.13.2. The laws that define what is unjust and what is not unjust are those that are specific to a particular group of inhabitants in the city and those that are common to all inhabitants in the city. Of these two types, there are written laws and there are unwritten laws. By unwritten laws, I mean those that naturally exist in all people. They are the ones in which everyone naturally sees what is just and what is unjust, even if there does not exist between one person and another any agreement or contract. These laws are also generally called universal laws in this respect. Nobody knows when these laws were laid down and who laid them down. They are often contrary to written laws, and they are used for persuasion to demonstrate that what one believes to be unjust according to written laws is not unjust. This is like what Aristotle has said about a man famous among [the Greeks]. When it was reported that this man was not properly buried according to the law of his country, the excuse given about the manner of his burial was that he was buried according to universal law, which is the law of nature, and therefore the manner of his burial was just and not unjust.[29] As to written laws proper to each particular people, they are like the laws according to which some people consider that one should not kill animate beings—that is, animals—for that is unjust. In effect, this is not an obligation among all people, nor is it an obligation by nature.

1.13.3. Since the laws that inform people about what is just and what is not just are, [in the case of] some, turned toward common people and

29. The reference here is to the burial of Polyneices, which Aristotle took from Sophocles's *Antigone*.

the whole community in the city, and others toward each one of its members—I mean that among them there are laws that inform people what they ought to do and what they ought not to do with respect to the whole community and laws that inform people, in this sense, about what they ought to do and what they ought not to do with respect to each one of the members of the community—it is evident that the types of injustice and obligation—that is, what is not unjust—are limited to these two types. I mean that injustice and the act consisting of what is obligatory are geared either toward someone in particular or toward everyone. For example, the person who commits adultery or assault does wrong to some definite person; and the person who refuses to serve in the police force, which, according to Aristotle, is about the protection of the community from one another in the city, does wrong to the community. The same is true with the man who refuses to go on duty as a guard of the city—and that is the duty of the man who defends the city against what comes from outside and does not, in his duty, transgress the frontiers of the city—and the man who refuses to take the duty of military command, and that is the duty of the man who leads the armies and defending forces of the city against a foreign people to seize their individual members, or their wealth, or their city. A general injustice and large-scale damage are inflicted on the city by each one of these individuals when they do not do what they ought to do. This division applies to all the types of injustice. I mean some types revolve around the community and others around a definite member of the community.

1.13.4. Since we have described the types of injustice, we must describe what "being wronged" means—that is, the meaning of that which, when it falls upon a man and he reacts to it, is called "being wronged." We, then, say that "being wronged" means that a man suffers a voluntary and intentional act of wrongdoing from the part of another man. In effect, wrongdoing, as it has been said earlier, means to cause harm voluntarily, so "being wronged" means to suffer harm being inflicted voluntarily by the wrongdoer. The classification of harmful things, in this regard, is necessary, but they have already been explained in the chapter on deliberative oratory, since when good things were explained in that part, their opposites were made evident. These things are also explained in the chapter on blame. And similarly, the types of things that happen voluntarily have also been discussed in an earlier part.

1.13.5. In general, accusations, general ones and particular ones, are limited to four types: one of them is when the doer does not know what he is doing and the act happens by chance; the second is when the doer knows what he is doing and the act is not done voluntarily, and that is the act that happens on compulsion; the third is when the act is done intentionally and through deliberate reflection; the fourth is when the act is driven by a passion and most often it is driven by anger. As to anger and what comes from it, they will be discussed later. As to the acts that are premeditated and deliberate, they have already been discussed in the previous sections.

1.13.6. It is not only the accuser who needs to understand the types of "being wronged" and wrongful acts or the conditions by which an act becomes wrongful and unjust. The man who evades responsibility for his acts and the one who seeks an excuse for his acts also need to understand these things, since the accused often admits committing the act of which he is accused, but he denies the condition by which that act becomes unjust. For example, he will admit that he took a thing but not that he stole it; that he insulted someone but not that he committed a slanderous act; that he had sexual intercourse with a woman but not that he committed adultery. This is why the accuser and the one denying the act must understand what is theft, what is slander, and what is adultery according to the general law and the law that is proper to the people they come from. By understanding these things, the accuser is able to establish that the act is unjust and wrongful, and the man seeking to evade responsibility is able to establish that the act is not unjust. In effect, the contention is about whether someone is guilty or not guilty of a wrongful act. And the truly wrongful act for which there is no excuse is a premeditated and intentional act. There are cases of "being wronged" whose names sufficiently signify that they are extremely wrongful acts committed in a premeditated and deliberate manner and do not need to be specified, like theft and adultery, for one cannot imagine that someone steals or commits adultery without deliberate purpose. Therefore, when the accused admits such names, there will be no room for him to defend himself. The person seeking to evade responsibility must be careful and not admit such names, and if he admits them, he must admit only the genre of the act. For example, he admits that he insulted someone and that he did not commit a slanderous act and says, "A slanderous act only consists of insulting the man or insulting his parents by accusing them of adultery." In effect, blaming someone of defects is more or less serious, since sometimes there are defects that do not cause any dishonor to a man even if they are degrading to him, like avarice. And there are defects that are degrading to a man and cause him serious dishonor, like adultery. This is why slander is treated severely in our law. Similarly, [the person seeking to evade responsibility] says that he took a thing and that he did not steal it, since theft happens only when one takes something from a fortified place.

1.13.7. Section

1.13.8. [Aristotle] said: Some wrongful acts and acts that are not wrongful are provided for by laws; others are not. Those for which there are laws are such that some of these laws are written and others are unwritten. Each one of these laws gives a definition of justice and injustice, and of goodness and badness. Goodness, according to unwritten laws, consists of acts the more of which a man indefinitely accumulates, the more glorification and praise, or honor and esteem, he will accumulate, like helping [our] friends and expressing gratitude to [our] benefactors. Badness, according to unwritten laws, consists of acts the more of which a man accumulates, the more blame or the more disgrace he will suffer also indefinitely, like being ungrateful or causing harm to [our] friends. As to the definition of goodness and badness in written laws, it is determined in such a way that one cannot add anything to it or subtract anything from it.

1.13.9. Since this is the case, and the determined law does not apply to every individual person, or to every time, or to every place, it does not sufficiently determine goodness and badness in the conduct of every individual person, so that one needs to add something to its definition or subtract something from it, in accordance to what the written law requires. It is therefore necessary to have in these unwritten laws a written justice and something more, and that means either adding something to the written laws or subtracting something from them. If the addition is to written goodness, it is called beneficence; if the addition is to written badness, it is called a sum [of bad deeds]. In the case of subtraction from written badness, that is called forgiveness and clemency and forbearance and other such names.

1.13.10. In the case of written laws, this happens to legislators, either necessarily or on their part. It happens on their part when they make a mistake and lay down a universal definition, when it is not universal. On the part of the matter itself, it happens because nobody can lay down universal, general laws taking into consideration all the people at all times and in all places, for that is indefinite—that is, the change of what is useful and what is harmful. The goal of the astute legislator in laying down laws is to lay down, in this regard, what is of the degree of more—that is, for the majority of people in all times and in all places. The harder a legislator works to lay down a law that is useful for a longer period of time and for a bigger majority of people, the better the law is. When that is the case, the determined laws are not necessarily true always and ever. I mean in every person and every time. This is why one needs to add things to them and subtract things from them.

1.13.11. You will understand this from an examination of written religious texts in our time. Addition to and subtraction from [the written laws] becomes something more superior when that is followed with praise and honor.

1.13.12. Clemency, in general, consists more of subtracting something from the written [code of law] or removing it in the case where it is followed with praise or honor, like what Aristotle said about the law among [the Greeks] and according to which nobody should lift his hand when he has a ring on his finger, and whoever does that must be punished, for he is guilty of a criminal act. Unwritten law demands that an act like this one should be forgiven. So to forgive someone for an act like this one is just. It seems as though we have something similar to this in the cutting of the impostor's hand, especially when that concerns foods. From this definition of clemency, it is plain what things constitute clemency and what things do not, what sorts of people are clement and what sorts of people are not. A person is clement only in the things where it is good to forgive.

1.13.13. **[Aristotle] said:** Regarding the cases of misdeed and wrongdoing, although they do not constitute one single type but several types, we must not equate what happens among them by mistake, and that is what happens inadvertently, with what does not happen by mistake, and that is what happens through cunning and evil.

1.13.14. **[Aristotle] said:** A misdeed is what does not happen either through ignorance or through wickedness. As to wrongdoing, it is what happens through wickedness and not through ignorance.

1.13.15. The first of the premises by means of which the offender asks for forgiveness for the offense that must be punished according to the written law—that is, those premises that Aristotle discussed in this book—is that the offender says, "Oh punisher, you must not follow the model of this particular rule with regard to the punishment that accordingly must be imposed on me, but you must follow the model of the character of the legislator who laid it down for the purpose of forgiveness and mercy."

1.13.16. The second premise is that [the offender] says, "You must not consider the surface meaning of the words of the legislator for this punishment that he laid down; consider what he intended by those words." And he puts that in the context where the meaning of the words is contrary to what their surface meaning requires for the imposition of the punishment.

1.13.17. The third premise is that [the offender] says, "The punishment must not be inflicted on me based on the act that appears to have been done by me, but it must be based on intention and choice." He says that so that [the judges] think that the act did not happen through his own choice.

1.13.18. The fourth premise is that [the offender] says, "Punishment should not be inflicted for what happened at long intervals and rarely, but for what happened repeatedly from the part of the offender." He says that when the act of wrongdoing has not been committed previously.

1.13.19. The fifth premise is that [the offender] says, "A man should not be punished based on his present condition before his past and future conditions are considered." And he says that when these conditions plead for him.

1.13.20. The sixth premise is that [the offender] reminds the judge who imposes the sentence of the good things rendered from the part of the wrongdoer to the person being wronged.

1.13.21. The seventh premise is that [the offender] reminds the judge who imposes the sentence of the good things that were rendered to the wrongdoer from the part of the person being wronged, since that would encourage him to consider pardon granted to the wrongdoer as part of those good things.

1.13.22. The eighth premise is that [the offender] urges the judge who imposes the sentence to proceed slowly in the case of injustice and says, "A man should not act hurriedly when he suffers an act of wrongdoing from another man and proceed with immediate retribution; he should stop the sentence, since from that a good thing may happen to him in the end."

1.13.23. The ninth premise is that [the offender] says, "A man should be forgiving toward people and allow himself to be persuaded by their kind words, without [having to resort to] action and he should not proceed with strict investigation."

1.13.24. The tenth premise is that [the offender] says, "A man should rise above disputes and punishment."

1.13.25. The eleventh premise is that [the offender] says, "Forbearance and forgiveness constitute a moral excellence. Impetuous men and offenders admit this fact when they compare themselves with clement people, aside from others."

1.13.26. The above has been an account of what is considered grace, clemency, and forgiveness; of what is considered a clement and forgiving person; and of the kinds of premises by means of which a person invokes clemency and forgiveness.

14

1.14.1. Because the victim inflates the act of injustice that falls upon him and the wrongdoer deflates it, we should discuss here the types of grave acts of injustice and small acts of injustice.

1.14.2. Of grave acts of injustice, there is the kind that is inflicted by the strong upon the weak, and there is the kind that is inflicted by the rich upon the poor. This is why injustice in small matters may be grave either because of the gravity of the evil itself in that small matter or because of the gravity of the damage. As to the gravity of the damage in the small matter, it is like when someone robs someone else of his food when there is little of it, and the victim does not have anything else to eat. As to the evil that is grave in itself, although the deed is small, it is like what Aristotle said about a man who cheated the craftsmen called "the close companions" among the Greeks—and they were those who were especially skilled in the construction of *mihrābs* in houses especially designed for the worship of God—by appropriating three consecrated *fels* from money especially designated to houses of worship.[30]

1.14.3. **[Aristotle] said:** The three *fels* are a small thing, as far as injustice committed on money is concerned, [but] taking them when they come from consecrated money that belongs to the "close" craftsmen is a grave evil. In effect, that act signifies the force of evil in taking them, since it is a violation of the sanctity of the house of God and the sanctity of His property. This is why nobody thinks that the man who has committed this act has guarded against anything from injustice, but that he has reached the highest degree in it. However, when one considers the degree

30. A *mihrāb* is a recess in a mosque indicating the direction of prayer toward Mecca; *fels* refers to a small coin.

of damage inflicted by the taking of the three *fels*, there is no injustice that counts. For acts of injustice like these—that is, those that fall upon the houses of God and upon his friends—there is no forgiveness, no clemency, and no forbearance, since forgiveness and clemency for such acts are not required by any kind of interest; but in cases like these, the judge must inevitably carry out the sentence, either for vengeance against the criminal only or for the sake of the general good. This is why the jurists in our tradition have said, "Whoever says that a button on the garment of our Legislator,[31] peace be upon him, is dirty must be put to death."

1.14.4. Of the worst wrong is to bring together on a man the loss of his property and torture.

1.14.5. Of the worst wrong also is that just men, good men, and in general, virtuous men are tortured for their virtues. This is why the injustice that falls upon these men is glory for them and an honor that is not insignificant. This is why you see several unjust kings seeking to humiliate scholars through beatings and other forms of evil, and that becomes glory for those scholars during their lifetime and after they die, like what happened to Mālik and other jurists like him. Also, those among these scholars who get killed receive a great honor, like the honor the companions of Jesus, peace be upon him, received after their death from their followers. In general, every person harmed for something that earns a man honor gains by that harm a greater honor.

1.14.6. Of the worst wrong is the sort of wrong that is newly invented and that nobody else has committed either before or after. Of the things that make wrong worse is when the offender is the first one to have committed the crime, and those offenders who come after him follow him and do what he did, as it has been said about Cain and Abel.

1.14.7. Of the worst wrong is to impose a fine and inflict loss on those who render good services to people, like the wrong that falls upon legislators.

1.14.8. Of the worst wrong is to inflict severe sentences prescribed in written laws, like hurling people to be devoured by the beasts in some nations.

1.14.9. Of the worst wrong is the wrong that is inflicted by a person on his relatives and his private circle of friends; the person does that because he hates them and wants to turn away from them, for only excessive wickedness leads a man to harm his relatives and hate them.

31. "Legislator" refers to Muhammad, prophet of Islam.

1.14.10. Of the worst wrong is a breach of faith, a violation of oaths, breaking of promises, and things similar to those matters reported in written histories. This is why the punishment inflicted on men who commit such offenses is not the same as the punishment imposed on all the other offenders, for in addition to the punishment that they get, they are exposed to shame in public. It is like in the case of punishment inflicted on men who commit perjury. They not only get punished for the act they commit, but they also get their faces blackened with shame in tribunals. This is why in our tradition, impeachment and rejection of testimony have been added to the punishment for committing an act of calumny. Treason and conniving are worse when an act of beneficence has been previously done to the traitor and the conniver. Someone who pretends to do good deeds, while his aim is evil, belongs to this type of offenders.

1.14.11. Wrong that breaks unwritten laws of justice—that is, wrong that violates them—is worse than the wrong that violates written laws. In effect, unwritten laws act like something that constrains the person and become like a natural thing for him to follow, like honoring parents and showing gratitude to the benefactor. As to written laws, they do not necessarily belong to man. And if a man violates the written law and commits a horrific crime, such as killing children and women, he indeed does a greater wrong. To impose a penalty where there is no penalty according to the written law is a greater wrong. This is why this [practice] has been the strongest cause of corruption in governments.

1.14.12. **[Aristotle] said:** This has been an explanation of worse and small wrongs, since a small wrong is the opposite of a greater wrong, for we know something when we know the opposite of that thing.

15

1.15.1. We must speak of means of persuasion that are nontechnical—that is, those that do not originally come from a rhetorical syllogism. Here is the most appropriate place to discuss them, since they are more proper to forensic oratory than to the other two kinds of oratory—namely, deliberative oratory and [epideictic] oratory.[32]

32. For the English equivalent of the term *munāfiriyya* in the Arabic text, we suggest the term *epideictic*. The Arabic term seems to be taken from Avicenna's treatise on logic, *Al-Shifā*, in which Avicenna discusses Aristotle's three kinds of oratory.

1.15.2. These nontechnical means of persuasion are five in number: first, the laws; second, witnesses; third, contracts; fourth, torture; and fifth, oaths. Here we shall speak only of how each one of these is used in accusation and defense.

1.15.3. First, let us speak of the laws and say:

1.15.4. Since there are general laws and written laws, the accuser or defender must, in case the written law is contrary to the thing that he seeks to establish, make his argument, using the general law that is appropriate to it—I mean the law that is contrary to the written law—reinforce it, and falsify the written law.

1.15.5. Of the places that [Aristotle] has mentioned, by which the written law is falsified, is that [the accuser or the defender] says, "It is obligatory to follow unwritten laws, because when a man does only what the written law requires, he will not be beneficent, he will not be clement, and he will not be forgiving." For man, as it has been explained, is characterized by these things only when he follows the general law. In general, praise and honor are made possible only by unwritten laws, since the person who does only what is necessary does not get praised. This is why, according to the written law, a man who gives the necessary amount of money is not called generous.

1.15.6. A second place is that [the accuser or the defender] says, "Only common people, those who lack deliberate reflection, limit themselves to written laws, since those are settled matters. As to following unwritten laws and determining them, that belongs to men of deliberate reflection and to people of distinction."

1.15.7. A third place is that the written laws are tedious, since they limit man to determined things, whereas general laws go well with people's natural dispositions and desires.

1.15.8. A fourth place is that to abandon written laws is often more beneficial, better, and more superior, since a thing that is determined does not go well with every person and at every time. As to unwritten laws, they are determined in such a way that they go well with every person and at every time.

1.15.9. A fifth place is that the unwritten law is permanent and invariable, for it is in people's natural disposition, whereas written laws are variable and change. A story has been told about a woman, well known to [the Greeks], who defended the burial of a man among them in a manner different from what the written law required, saying, "I could not bury him according to a law that exists today and will not exist tomorrow, but according to a law that never expires."[33]

1.15.10. A sixth place is that the written law has the character of opinion, for it is accepted by others, whereas the unwritten law is not accepted by others and is known only by natural instinct.

1.15.11. A useful thing to say about that [point] is [this]: "The general law is that by which the judge does different things according to what is useful for each particular person and at each particular time. The judge is like the man who purifies silver from waste material. This is why the virtuous judge must not limit himself to the written law; he must use both laws at the same time, so that the truth is purified for him and he reaches a decision that is proper to the case he is judging. This is why, whenever he is judging a case and the written law is in contradiction with the unwritten law or there are two laws contradicting each other, the judge must use the old law—I mean the unwritten law—sometimes in one place and discount it in another place. The same is [the case] with the written law. In this way, the apparent contradiction between the two [laws] is negated, and putting them together becomes the correct [thing to do]." What [Aristotle] has said here is made evident by what the jurists do, here in our tradition, in the case of contradictory written laws.

1.15.12. [Aristotle] said: Whenever the manner of bringing [laws] together becomes doubtful for [the judge], he must stop and not apply one of the two laws; instead, he must postpone the judgment until the area of doubt and ambiguity between the two laws becomes clear for him, and then he will apply either the general and useful law or the binding written law.

1.15.13. This is, in general, what has been said here of the rejection of written laws when they are contrary to what we seek to establish.

1.15.14. But when the written law agrees with what we seek to establish and the general law contradicts it, one way of bending the contradictory unwritten law is to say, "The general law is variable as to the subject matter and variable as to time, so that in general, it is undetermined, and it rather needs to be discovered and determined, whereas the written law, it has been dealt with. Then since what is contradictory in the

33. The woman mentioned here is Antigone pleading that in burying her brother, she had broken Creon's law but not the unwritten law.

written law is assumed and not yet known, and what is convenient for us in the written law [is] expressly declared, then we must believe that we should not transgress, in the judgment, the written law."

1.15.15. Another place by which the unwritten law is falsified is that the unwritten law requires a general judgment, such as "Be kind to someone who has been kind to you." The written law requires a special judgment, which is about the amount of kindness and the moment of kindness. Nobody does what is general and universal; only what is particular is done, and what is done must be followed.

1.15.16. Another place that reinforces the written law is that if the institution of the written law is obligatory, its use is obligatory; otherwise, what good is there in instituting something that is not used?

1.15.17. Another strong place in establishing the written law is that the relation of [the legislator] who institutes the law to the public, given his prior knowledge of their interests, is like the relation of the doctor to his patients and, in general, the relation of men of arts to those who do not belong to those arts. And as the patient should not neglect or hesitate to accept the doctor's orders and diagnosis, in the same way [the public] should not neglect or hesitate to accept the words of the legislator who institutes the written law. The harm resulting from disobeying the law instituted by the legislator is worse than the harm resulting from disobeying the doctor's orders, since not following the doctor's orders results in harm done only to one individual person, whereas disobeying the law instituted by the legislator could result in the destruction of all the people in the city.

1.15.18. Another place is that those who are appointed judges in the cities are the only ones who know the written laws, since, as far as unwritten laws are concerned, all people evenly understand them. Since that is the case, the written laws must be followed; otherwise, the use of judges will be absurd and worthless.

1.15.19. The above is an account of what [Aristotle] said about the laws.

1.15.20. On Witnesses

1.15.21. As to witnesses, some are ancient; others are recent and existing. Of those who are recent, some share with the person in whose favor they testify the good that he hopes for or the evil that he fears.

1.15.22. By ancient witnesses, I mean predecessors known to and accepted by all people and whose excellences are well known to all. The testimonies of such individuals on past things are admitted, whether they said or did not say that they witnessed them, since their situation generally carries conviction about what they report.

1.15.23. Testimonies are either a testimony concerned with past things, and they are the things that most people did not see; or a testimony concerned with present things; or a testimony concerned with future things. As to witnesses of past things, they are undoubtedly ancient. Witnesses of things existing in our time are people of our time. Witnesses of future things are of two types: soothsayers, whether their soothsaying is done with art or without art, and those who master the knowledge of current sayings that urge people to do or not to do something, as when we say, "Stay connected with relatives." The Legislator, peace be upon him, said, "Staying connected with relatives makes a person live longer," and something like this.

1.15.24. As to existing witnesses, those who are admitted and whose testimony is valid are the ones who have been put to the test by their acquaintances—that is, their neighbors, or their relatives, or their fellow citizens—and have been found consistent in their testimony. As to witnesses among predecessors, that they are admitted is well established. This is why they do not need to be put to the test. By "their being admitted," I mean their being just if they testify about past things or their having a sound faculty by means of which they give information about future things, if they testify about future things. Of the conditions required in order to admit a testimony given by recent witnesses is that they do not share with the person on whose side they testify a good that he hopes for or an evil that he expects will happen to him, such as being the parents, or the children, or the relatives of the person on whose side they testify. In effect, if he wants them to lie, as Aristotle says, they may do so. As to predecessors, we do not imagine them to do this, since they have already passed away. The testimony of recent witnesses is valid only when they testify that the thing happened or did not happen; their testimony is not valid to the fact that the thing is just or unjust. As to predecessors, their testimony is valid either because they are not suspects, since they do not share anything with the person for whom the testimony is given, or because their statement bears on the fact that the judgment was such in the past.

1.15.25. Sometimes convictions take place through testimonies; other times they take place through a concatenation of similar circumstances and are taken as testimonies. Judgment by means of a concatenation of similar circumstances comes from intelligent and skilled judges. This is why the judge must not make mistakes when dealing with distorted similarities, as the money changer does when dealing with fake silver. Since these circumstances sometimes help the judge understand the true thing itself, with the false testimony being contrary to them, they are even more appropriate to help him understand the true thing where there is no testimony or where the testimony is congruous with them. This is why these circumstances assume, for the judges, the position of witnesses, since there is no difference between using witnesses or similar circumstances that are associated with the speakers. These circumstances are not the enthymemes. This is why they count as testimonies.

1.15.26. Of testimonies, some are concerned with the matter about which there is a dispute; others are concerned with witnesses; and others are concerned with the opponents. Sometimes testimony on witnesses consists in reinforcing witnesses, and sometimes it consists in weakening them. Testimony on the opponents consists in establishing the justice of one and disparaging the other. Testimony on witnesses consists of the witness being a friend, or an enemy, or a witness who stands [unbiased] between the accuser and the accused—that is, one who is neither a friend of one nor an enemy of the other.

1.15.27. We shall speak of witnesses further in other sections where we discuss the general topics from which enthymemes are produced. And that will be in Book II of this treatise.

1.15.28. This has been an account of what [Aristotle] said on testimonies.

1.15.29. On Contracts

1.15.30. Contracts are the conditions on which some people agree with others. The conditions on which people agree are useful in only two ways. One of them consists in vilifying and blaming the man who recognizes these conditions but does not conform to them, while he is convinced they are true, and in praising him when he fulfills [the terms] of these conditions. The second one consists in believing the plaintiff and discrediting the defendant when he denies the conditions. In this situation, there is no difference between conditions and witnesses. In effect, the conditions, when they are written or witnesses have testified about them, assume the role of witnesses in establishing evidence on the matter about which there is a dispute and also in establishing evidence on the condition of the opponents. I mean how their conditions are with respect to virtue and vice, since abiding by the terms of the condition is a sign of virtue, whereas violating them is a sign of vice.

1.15.31. When the opponent acknowledges the condition and claims that it is not binding for him, the speaker needs to argue for the necessity of making the condition binding by saying, "The condition is a proper and particular law; therefore, it must be obeyed the way the laws must be obeyed."

1.15.32. When the law conflicts with the condition, the opponent says, "The law does not govern the condition and rule it, since the law necessarily implies the general interest, whereas the condition implies a particular interest, and the particular governs the general; therefore, it is the condition that rules the law. The law does not rule the condition."

1.15.33. If the law does not conflict with it—I mean with the condition—the opponent says, "The condition is a kind of law," if the law is instituted for those people by convention. Or he says, "The law makes it obligatory to abide by the condition," if the law has been instituted for those people by revelation from Allah, the Most High.

1.15.34. Another situation is that we say, "The conditions are the ones that necessarily imply the particular interests that are proper to each particular person and at each particular time. If the conditions are not observed, the interests are annulled, for it is to the condition that a person engages by choice and through deliberate reflection; and nobody is excused for not obeying what is defined in this way." And we can go on, with respect to situations similar to this one, which will make the discussion longer if we seek to examine them thoroughly in this part.

1.15.35. This has been an account of what [Aristotle] said about the things by which conditions are established.

1.15.36. As to the things from which conditions are adulterated, when the speaker considers that it is more correct and more appropriate to adulterate conditions, they are the written laws and the general laws, as when he says, "Written laws are more akin and more appropriate to interests, for the written law is common to all, and what is common to all is more akin to the general interest than what is particular, which is the condition, and the general interest is more important than the particular interest."

1.15.37. Another situation is that it is possible for a man to engage in observing the conditions because of fraud and trickery being practiced on him. But it is not possible to practice trickery on what the law requires. Therefore, the laws are worth more than the conditions.

1.15.38. Another situation is that the speaker says, "It is the judge who searches for justice and reveals it. I mean the justice that is proper to the city. This is why the judge must search for the justice that the two contractors have stipulated on themselves, so that if it is there in the city, he leaves them bound by the condition, and if it is not there, he declares the condition null and void."

1.15.39. Also, the laws are instituted neither by force nor by mistake, whereas in the case of conditions, it is possible to have force and error in them.

1.15.40. In general, we must trace the opposites of the condition in the laws. If we do not find the condition in the written law, we may find it in the universal law, and in this way we may adulterate the condition. If we find it in the written law, we use this law to argue for the elimination of the condition, whether the law is the law of that city or the law of another city ruling this city.

1.15.41. Of the things that make contracts null and void is the existence of contradictory contracts, whether previous or subsequent. Subsequent contracts in most cases always destroy the previous ones. Previous contracts may destroy subsequent contracts when they are correct and when the subsequent contracts are fraudulent and deceiving.

1.15.42. Again, the man who adulterates the condition must carefully consider its terms. If he finds something that can possibly be distorted, he distorts it and takes it out of the meaning that requires the cause of the legal qualification. This can be done only by someone who has insight into common terms and nuances of meaning.

1.15.43. This is the end of what [Aristotle] said about contracts.

1.15.44. On Torture

1.15.45. [Aristotle] said: As to confessing under torture, it is a testimony given by the man being tortured. In the confession, there is some conviction because the man being tortured fears that if he tells lies, he may be tortured again, and he also imagines that by telling the truth, he will be saved from the evil that falls upon him, except that the truth he is telling is extracted from him by force. This is why it is difficult to understand the things by which it is possible to establish confession under torture [as a form of evidence] when it agrees with the speaker and to adulterate it when it agrees with the opponent. However, to adulterate the confession and destroy it is in itself based on the truth, since due to coercion, confessing to what is not true, under torture, does not happen less frequently than confessing the truth. People confessing under torture say what they are told to say so that they escape from torture even if what they say is not the truth. Also, when they have endured the torture and have not told the truth, they often rush to tell untruths to give the impression that they have told the truth and this way to escape quickly from torture. This is why the judges must not use this kind of inference; they must go back and use other proofs, since many people, because they have healthy bodies and pride, very much endure the pain and do not confess to what is true. As to cowards and feeble people, they confess to what is not true even before they see the hardships. This is why there is nothing to be trusted in torture. For this reason, the law in our tradition has rejected the legal sanctions related to confessions given under torture.

1.15.46. On Oaths

1.15.47. [Aristotle] said: As to oaths, they are used for four reasons. In effect, a man swears an oath either to give something and to take something, like what happens in sales; or to give nothing and to take nothing; or to give and not to take; or to take and not to give. The oath a man swears in order to give something happens only because of other things that are harmful to him—that is, when he abstains and does not give.

1.15.48. An oath comes either from the plaintiff or from the defendant.

1.15.49. There is nothing convincing in an oath if the man who swears the oath is known to be a rascal.

1.15.50. When one of the two opponents must swear an oath [to the truth of his statement] and he refuses to do so, he must provide the evidence. In effect, to demand an oath [from the adversary] is a challenge to the truth [he claims], and when he fails to swear [to the truth of his statement], he must provide the evidence.

1.15.51. [Aristotle] said: Since the man from whose part an oath is demanded hesitates between two detestable things, one of which [is] concerning what will happen to him from swearing a false oath—which is contempt of Allah and of His sacred orders—and the second concerning what happens to him if one takes something from him or if he gives something, he will only do the detestable thing that is less harmful to him. This is why some people tell the truth when they swear an oath, while others tell lies. This is one of the means by which recourse to proof by oaths is adulterated.

1.15.52. [Aristotle] said: An excellent man sometimes convinces the judges and is considered to tell the truth even if he does not swear an oath. But the fact that the judges believe he tells the truth is not because he has sworn an oath but because of his moral excellence, and also because he is not one of those people who commit perjury and he does not lie when he does not swear an oath, let alone when he swears an oath.

1.15.53. [Aristotle] said: As to the challenge posed by the oath, it often comes from the part of the morally depraved man and is addressed toward the trustworthy man, since the fact that the trustworthy man abstains from swearing an oath is what leads one to be convinced that the morally depraved man is telling the truth.

1.15.54. [Aristotle] said: This is like when the impetuous man defeats the man who is prudent or invites the latter to defeat him and challenges him, and in this way the prudent man avoids him.

1.15.55. [Aristotle] said: However, even if the matter is like this, the trustworthy man is not permitted to take [an oath] without swearing it when his opponent does not think that he is trustworthy, but he does not take [an oath] unless he swears it.

1.15.56. [Aristotle] said: This is what so and so judged—by so and so, he thinks of a man who, as judge, was famous among the Greeks. And this is what the law is like in our tradition.

1.15.57. [Aristotle] said: When it is hard for the trustworthy man to swear an oath as the charge is pressed against him, if he would rather give, honor Allah, and not swear an oath, he must not deny the false charge when he gives what has been demanded of him. If he denies the false charge and offers [an oath], he gives the false impression that the plaintiff speaks the truth and that he, the trustworthy man, has given only because of the false oath that rests with him. This is why he must not put himself in a situation where he is called upon to swear an oath, since when he is called upon to swear an oath and he does not do so, they will think he is not telling the truth.

1.15.58. [Aristotle] said: We know how a man, at the time of a court ruling in the case of a particular or general dispute, defends himself, or is defended, when he breaks the oath he has sworn and how the man who breaks an oath is reprimanded and blamed. In effect, the things in which an oath is broken are those four on which an oath is sworn, and they are the things that every particular man desires, and that is, either he takes and gives; or he does not take and he does not give; or he gives and he does not take; or he takes and he does not give. When a man swears an oath on one of these four things, the words he uses to establish that thing do not fail to be either consistent with the thing on which he swears an oath or inconsistent with it. And that happens when the man denies the oath.

1.15.59. If the man breaks the oath, one of the ways he is reprimanded is that one says, "An oath is a law among the laws, so that when a man breaks it willingly and denies it, he has done wrong, and to do wrong is to break the law voluntarily." As to the man defending himself for having broken an oath, he defends himself by saying that he swore the oath under constraint, or by mistake, or through negligence; that when he swore the oath, he did not intend to swear the one that he broke, and he intended to swear an oath other than the one he had broken; that the thing that led him to swear the oath was stubbornness, opposition to the adversary, anger, anguish, and, in general, the disposition to be the first one to rush and swear the oath and to deny it and forswear it.

1.15.60. Of the things used to maintain consistency in the laws and oaths, as well as commitment to them, is that we say, "You must firmly keep your oaths and not break them, for an oath is a legal order to which a man commits himself voluntarily and knowingly, and that, therefore, he must not break it. As to those who swear an oath because of trickery or negligence, or the disposition to deny an oath and rush to swear an oath, they do not keep their oaths. And so with things similar to what has been said here and by which an oath is exalted and magnified.

1.15.61. This has been an account of the means of persuasion that take place without syllogism and the ways they are used in this art.

1.15.62. And here we come to the end of the discussion of the meanings [of persuasion] in this book, which is the first one. Praise be to Allah, for He is sufficient for us.

Conclusion

The unifying thread throughout the three Arabic treatises on Aristotle's *Rhetoric* that I have rendered in English has some important characteristics. We can recognize traces of Islamic discourse in the commentaries, for the commentators open their commentaries with the formulaic expression "In the name of Allah, the Merciful, the Compassionate" and close with words of praise addressed to Allah, with some variations: "Praise be to Allah, truly" (al-Fārābī); "Praise be to Allah, the guardian of praise" (Avicenna); and "Praise be to Allah, for He is sufficient for us" (Averroes). The formulaic expression "In the name of Allah, the Merciful, the Compassionate," known as *al-basmalah* in Islamic discourse, is the invocation uttered at the beginning of the 111 chapters in the Qur'an. It is traditionally spoken or written before the undertaking of any type of task, physical or intellectual, so that the person performing the task will earn assistance from Allah. The expression opens a space of mercy and compassion from the divine and puts the speaker or writer and the audience in the presence of the divine because the name of the divine has been appropriately invoked.

The closing with words of praise addressed to Allah, known as *al-ḥamdalah*, marks the completion of the task. *Al-ḥamdalah*, which we read in the first chapter of the Qur'an, is the invocation uttered after the completion of any type of task, physical or intellectual. The expression allows the commentator to show humility before the task to be completed and before the power of Allah, and it also allows him to recognize assistance from Allah. In *al-ḥamdalah*, we recognize the word *al-ḥamd* (praise). We also recognize the names or attributes given to the Prophet of Islam, Aḥmad, Muḥammad, or Maḥmūd, all of which literally mean "the praiseworthy."

In sum, the two invocations, *al-basmalah* and *al-ḥamdalah*, do two things here: First, they serve the purpose of completion of a task from the beginning to the end, which is the task of interpretation of a text. Second, and most important, they both constitute a new frame of reference for the treatise of a pagan philosopher to be introduced into Islamic discourse and the land of Islam.

Additionally, in the three commentaries, logic is placed at the head of rhetorical discourse. Despite the resistance to the study of logic in various stages of Islamic philosophy, the usefulness of the discipline was hard to ignore.[1] For example, al-Ghazālī, well known for his polemical attack on the philosophers,[2] makes this concession to the role of logic in his *Al-Munqidh min al-Ḍalāl*: "Logic is merely the study of the methods of proof and reasoning, the requirements for premises in a demonstration and the manner in which they are to be combined, or the requirements for a sound definition, and the manner in which it is ordered."[3] By emphasizing the instrumental character of logic, and also by defining knowledge as "either a conception, which is known through a definition, or a judgment, which is known by demonstration," al-Ghazālī removes any possible concern that theologians might have about the use of this "alien" science as an instrument of reasoning about theological matters. Unlike Ibn Taymiyya, who launches a fierce attack on logic and logicians, al-Ghazālī reassures theologians that "nothing in logic touches religion one way or another."[4] In fact, it was Avicenna who, as L. E. Goodman explains, "emancipated logic, transforming it into a non-Greek, non-foreign, widely accepted, and widely used organon that no longer made any necessary reference to the ideas or works of Aristotle."[5]

Further, the task carried out by the three commentators is commonly known in Arabic as *al-sharḥ* (explanation or commentary). *Al-sharḥ* is indeed a significant metaphor in the philosophical projects of al-Fārābī, Avicenna, and Averroes. In his lexical work, *Lisān al-ᶜArab*, Ibn Manẓūr (d. 1311) devotes an

1. See the debate on the place of logic between grammarian Saᶜīd al-Sirāfī and logician Mattā ibn Yūnus in Abū Hayyān al-Tawḥīdī's *Al-Imtāᶜ wa al-Mu'ānasa* [Enjoyment and conviviality], ed. A. Amin and A. Al-Zayn (Cairo, 1953). Also see Al-Suyūṭī, Jalāl al-Dīn. *Jahd al-qarīḥah fī tajrīd al-Naṣīḥah* [Against the Greek logicians]. Edited by ᶜAli Sāmī al-Nashshār. Cairo: Maṭbᶜat al-Saᶜāda, 1947.

2. Abū Ḥāmid al-Ghazālī, *Tahāfut al-Falāsifa* [The destruction of philosophers], ed. M. Bouyges, 2nd ed. (Beirut: Catholic Press, 1962).

3. Abū Ḥāmid al-Ghazālī, *Al-Munqidh min al-Ḍalāl* [Deliverance from error], ed. F. Jabre (Beirut: UNESCO, 1959), 22.

4. Ibid.

5. L. E. Goodman, *Avicenna* (New York: Routledge, 1992), 209.

entry to the various meanings of the word *sharḥ*. First, *al-sharḥ* and *al-tashrīḥ* carry the meaning of "dissection." Also, the verb form *sharaḥa* means, among other things, "to lay open, to display, to uncover, to expose to view."[6] One can conclude that the primary text was not available to al-Fārābī, Avicenna, and Averroes, given the fact that they did not read Greek or Syriac and could only work from an Arabic translation of a Syriac translation of a Greek text. The verb *sharaḥa* suggests in this sense that the role of the commentator was "to open" the primary text. This verb is used in a verse in the Qur'an that says, "Those whom Allah (in His plan) willeth to guide, He openeth their breast to Islam" (*faman yurīdu Allāhu 'an yahdiyahu yashraḥ ṣadrahu lil-islām*).[7] Openness of the heart of the text necessarily implies room to accommodate new ideas, new digressions, and new audiences. In this context, "to guide" the Greek text and introduce it to a Muslim Arabic-speaking audience, al-Fārābī, Avicenna, and Averroes "open its heart" in order to adapt it to the Arabic language and culture. This openness makes the Greek text even larger than it originally is. The commentary gives us a possibility of openness of the Greek text to a new linguistic and cultural space, which is very significant, especially when we are presented with two different languages, two different cultural spaces, and two different time frames.

Paying tribute to the Islamic philosophical tradition, Richard Walzer explains that Islamic philosophers, in addition to the fact that they have extended the Greek tradition through translations and commentaries, "can rightly claim to be understood and appreciated in their own setting and according to their own intentions which may be different from those of their Greek predecessors."[8] Today much of this philosophical tradition is available in English translations, and a careful reading of the commentaries of al-Fārābī, Avicenna, and Averroes should show strong links between the schools of Alexandria and Baghdad, to which al-Fārābī and Avicenna belong, on the one hand, and the Andalusian school of philosophy in Spain, to which Averroes belongs, on the other.

6. Ibn Manẓūr, *Lisān al-ʿArab* [The tongue of the Arabs], 15 vols. (Beirut: Dār Ṣādir, 1955–56), See Edward William Lane, *An Arabic-English Lexicon* (Beirut: Librairie du Liban, 1968), 1:1530.

7. Al-Anʿām 6:125.

8. Richard Walzer, *Greek into Arabic: Essays on Islamic Philosophy* (Cambridge, MA: Harvard University Press, 1962), 1.

Bibliography

Index

Bibliography

Afnan, Soheil M. *Avicenna: His Life and Works*. London: G. Allen & Unwin, 1958.

Al-Fārābī, Abū Naṣr. *Kitāb Fī al-Manṭiq: Al-Khaṭābah* [Book on logic: Oratory]. Edited by Muḥammad Salīm Sālim. Cairo: Dār al-Kitāb, 1976.

———. *Kitāb Iḥṣā' al-ᶜUlūm* [Book of the enumeration of sciences]. Beirut: Dār wa Maktabat al-Hilāl, 1996.

Al-Ghazālī, Abū Ḥāmid. *Al-Munqidh min al-Ḍalāl* [Deliverance from error]. Edited by F. Jabre. Beirut: UNESCO, 1959.

———. *Tahāfut al-Falāsifa* [The destruction of philosophers]. 2nd ed. Edited by M. Bouyges. Beirut: Catholic Press, 1962.

Al-Jābrī, Muḥammad ᶜĀbed. *Naḥnu wa al-Turāt* [We and the tradition]. Casablanca, Morocco: Al-Markaz al-Taqāfi al-ᶜArabī, 1993.

Al-Murrākushī, ᶜAbd al-Wāḥid. *Al-Muᶜjib fī Talkhīṣ Akhbāri al-Maghrib* [The admirable in an outline of the history of the Maghreb]. Casablanca, Morocco: Dār al-Kitāb, 1978.

Al-Qifṭī, Jamāl al-Dīn. *Ikhbār al-ᶜUlamā' bi-Akhbār al-Ḥukamā'* [History of philosophers]. Edited by Muḥammad Amīn al-Khā'ijī. Cairo, Egypt: Dār al-Kutub al-Khaddīwiyya, 1906.

———. *Tā'rīkh al-Ḥukamā'* [History of philosophers]. Edited by August Müller and Julius Lippert. Leipzig, Germany: Theodor Weicher, 1903.

Al-Suyūṭī, Jalāl al-Dīn. *Jahd al-qarīḥah fī tajrīd al-Naṣīḥah* [Against the Greek logicians]. Edited by ᶜAli Sāmī al-Nashshār. Cairo: Maṭbᶜat al-Saᶜāda, 1947.

Al-Tawḥīdī, Abū Ḥayyān. *Al-Imtāᶜ wa al-Mu'ānasa* [Enjoyment and conviviality]. Edited by A. Amin and A. Al-Zayn. Cairo, 1953.

Aristotle. *Rhetoric*. Translated by W. Rhys Roberts. New York: Modern Library, 1984.

Averroes. *Faṣl al-Maqāl* [On the harmony of religion and philosophy]. Translated by George F. Hourani. London: Gibb, 1961.

———. *Faṣl al-Maqāl Fī Taqrīri mā bayna al-Sharīᶜa wa al-Ḥikma min al-Ittiṣāl* [On the harmony of religion and philosophy]. Beirut: Markaz dirāsāt al-waḥda al-ᶜarabiyya, 1997.

Averroes (Ibn Rushd). *Commentaire moyen à la Rhétorique d'Aristote* [Middle commentary on Aristotle's *Rhetoric*]. Edited and translated by Maroun Aouad. 3 vols. Paris: Vrin, 2002.

Avicenna. *Kitāb al-Majmūᶜ aw al-Ḥikma al-ᶜarūḍiya fī maᶜānī kitāb rīṭūrīqā* [Al-ᶜArūḍī's philosophical treatise on the meanings of the Book of Rhetoric]. Edited by Muḥammad Salīm Sālim. Cairo: Maktabat al-Nahḍa al-Miṣrya, 1950.

Badawī, ᶜAbd al-Raḥmān, ed. *Al-Khaṭābah: Al-Tarjama al-ᶜarabiyya al-Qadīma* [Rhetoric: The ancient Arabic translation]. Vol. 23. Cairo: Dirāsāt 'Islāmīya, 1959.

———. "Averroes face au texte qu'il commente [Averroes faced with the text that he explains]." *Multiple Averroes: Actes du Colloque Internationale organisé à l'occasion du 850e anniversaire de la naissance d'Averroes. Paris 20–23 septembre 1976*. [Multiple Averroes: Proceedings of the international colloquium organized in commemoration of the 850th birthday of Averroes]. Ouvrage publié avec le concours du CNRS [Work published in collaboration with the National Center for Scientific Research]. Paris: Les Belles Lettres, 1978.

Balty-Guesdon, M.-G. "Le Bayt al-ḥikma de Baghdad [The house of wisdom of Baghdad]." *Arabica* 39 (1992): 131–50.

Black, Deborah L. "Knowledge ('ilm) and Certitude (yaqīn) in al-Fārābī's Epistemology." *Arabic Sciences and Philosophy* 16 (2006):11–45.

———. *Logic and Aristotle's "Rhetoric" and "Poetics" in Medieval Arabic Philosophy*. Leiden, Netherlands: E. J. Brill, 1990.

Boggess, William F. "Alfarabi and the 'Rhetoric': The Cave Revisited." *Phronesis* 15, no. 1 (1970): 86–90.

———. "Hermannus Alemannus and the Sandy Desert of Zarabi." *Journal of the American Oriental Society* 86, no. 4 (1966): 418–19.

———. "Hermannus Alemannus' Latin Anthology of Arabic Poetry." *Journal of the American Oriental Society* 88, no. 4 (1968): 657–70.

———. "Hermannus Alemannus's Rhetorical Translations." *Viator: Medieval and Renaissance Studies* 2 (1970): 227–50.

Borges, Jorge Luis. "Averroes' Search." In *Labyrinths: Selected Stories and Other Writings*, edited by Donald A. Yates and James E. Irby, 148–55. New York: New Directions, 1964.

Boudon, V., ed., *Galien, Tome II: Exhortation à l' Étude de la Médecine; Art Médical* [Galen, Volume II: Exhortation to the study of medicine; medical art]. Paris: Les Belles Lettres, 2000.

Bouyges, P. M. "Inventaire des textes arabes d'Averroès [Inventory of the Arabic texts of Averroes]." In *Mélanges de l'Université Saint-Joseph*, vol. 8, 1–54. Beirut: Imprimerie Catholique, 1922.

Bubenik, Vit. "Thematization and Passivization in Arabic." *Lingua* 49 (1979): 295–313.

Butterworth, Charles E. *Averroes' Three Short Commentaries on Aristotle's "Topics," "Rhetoric," and "Poetics."* Albany: State University of New York Press, 1977.

———. "Rhetoric and Islamic Political Philosophy." *International Journal of Middle Eastern Studies* 3 (1972): 186–98.

Cantarino, Vicente. *Syntax of Modern Arabic Prose*. Bloomington: Indiana University Press, 1975.

Conley, Thomas M. "Aristotle's *Rhetoric* in Byzantium." *Rhetorica* 8, no. 1 (1990): 29–44.

Copeland, Rita. *Rhetoric, Hermeneutics, and Translation in the Middle Ages*. Cambridge, UK: Cambridge University Press, 1991.

Copeland, Rita, and Ineke Sluiter, eds. *Medieval Grammar and Rhetoric: Language Arts and Literary Theory, A.D. 300–1475*. Oxford, UK: Oxford University Press, 2010.

Dodge, Bayard, ed. *The Fihrist of al-Nadīm: A Tenth-Century Survey of Muslim Culture*. 2 vols. New York: Columbia University Press, 1970.

Eche, Youssef. *Les bibliothèques publiques et semi-publiques en Mésopotamie, en Syrie et en Egypte au Moyen Age* [Public and semipublic libraries in Mesopotamia, Syria, and Egypt in the Middle Ages]. Damascus: Institut français de Damas, 1967.

Endress, Gerhard, and Dimitri Gutas, eds. *A Greek and Arabic Lexicon (GALex): Materials for a Dictionary of the Medieval Translations from Greek into Arabic*. Leiden, Netherlands: E. J. Brill, 1997.

Frank, Richard. *Classical Islamic Theology: The Ashʿarītes. Texts and Studies on the Development and History of Kalam*. Vol. 3. Edited by Dimitri Gutas. Variorum Collected Studies Series. Burlington, VT: Ashgate, 2008

Gabrieli, Giuseppe. "Ḥunayn Ibn Isḥāq." *Isis* 6 (1924): 282–92.

Georr, Khalil. *Les Catégories d'Aristote dans leurs versions syro-arabes* [The categories of Aristotle in their Syro-Arabic versions]. Beirut: Institut français de Damas, 1948.

Gohlman, William E. *The Life of Ibn Sina: A Critical Edition and Annotated Translation*. Albany: State University of New York Press, 1974.

Goodman, L. E. *Avicenna*. New York: Routledge, 1992.

Gracia, Jorge J. E., and Timothy B. Noone, eds. *A Companion to Philosophy in the Middle Ages*. Malden, MA: Blackwell, 2002.

Green, Lawrence D. "Aristotelian Rhetoric, Dialectic, and the Traditions of ἀντίστροφος." *Rhetorica* 8, no. 1 (1990): 5–27.

Hinkle, Roscoe. "Medieval Islamic Spain (al-Andalus) as a Civilizational Bridge between Later Antiquity and Early Modernity." *Comparative Civilizations Review* 61(2009): 87–104.

Ibn Abī Uṣaibiᶜa. *ᶜUyūn al-Anbā' fī Ṭabaqāt al-Aṭibbā'* [Essential information about the generations of physicians]. Edited by A. Müller. 5 vols. Cairo and Konigsberg, Germany, 1882–84.

Ibn al-Nadīm. *Kitāb al-Fihrist* [Book of the index]. Edited by Riḍā Taġaddud. Beirut: Dār al-Masīra, 1988.

Ibn Manẓūr. *Lisān al-ᶜArab* [The tongue of the Arabs]. 15 vols. Beirut: Dār Ṣādir, 1955–56.

Ibn Taymiyya, Taqī al-Dīn Abū al-*ᶜAbbas A*ḥmad. *Al-Radd ᶜalā al-Manṭiqiyyīn* [Against the Greek logicians]. Beirut: Dār al-Fikr al-Lubnānī, 1993.

Kennedy, George A. "The Composition and Influence of Aristotle's Rhetoric." In *Essays on Aristotle's Rhetoric*, edited by Amélie Oksenberg Rorty, 416–24. Berkeley: University of California Press, 1996.

Lane, Edward William. *An Arabic-English Lexicon*. 2 vols. Beirut: Librairie du Liban, 1968.

Langhade, J., and M. Grignaschi, eds. *Al-Fārābī: Deux ouvrages inédits sur la rhétorique* [Al-Fārābī: Two unpublished works on rhetoric]. Beirut: Dar el-Mashreq, 1971.

Langhade, J., and D. Mallet. "Droit et philosophie au XIIᵉ siecle dans al-Andalus [Law and philosophy in the twelfth century in Islamic Spain]: Averroes (Ibn Rušd)." *Revue de l'Occident musulman et de la Méditerranée* [Journal of the Muslim West and the Mediterranean] 40 (1985): 103–21.

Leaman, O. "Jewish Averroism." In *History of Islamic Philosophy*, edited by S. H. Nasr and O. Leaman, 768–80. London: Routledge, 1996.

Luquet, G. "Hermann l'Allemand." *Revue de l'histoire des religions* [Review of the history of religions] 44 (1901): 407–22.

Lyons, Malcolm C., ed. *Aristotle's Ars Rhetorica: The Arabic Version; A New Edition, with Commentary and Glossary*. Cambridge, UK: Pembroke Arabic Texts, 1982.

Mahdi, Muhsin, trans. *Alfarabi's Philosophy of Plato and Aristotle*. New York: Free Press of Glencoe, 1962.

Meyerhof, Max. "New Light on Ḥunain Ibn Isḥāq and His Period." *Isis* 8, no. 4 (1926): 685–724.

Murphy, James J. "The Historiography of Rhetoric: Challenges and Opportunities." *Rhetorica* 1 (1983): 1–8.

———. *Medieval Rhetoric: A Select Bibliography*. Toronto: University of Toronto Press, 1971.

———. *Renaissance Rhetoric: A Short-Title Catalogue*. New York: Garland, 1981.

———. *Rhetoric in the Middle Ages: A History of Rhetorical Theory from Saint Augustine to the Renaissance*. Berkeley: University of California Press, 1974.

Novikoff, Alex. *The Medieval Culture of Disputation: Pedagogy, Practice, and Performance*. Philadelphia: University of Pennsylvania Press, 2013.

Peters, F. E. *Aristotle and the Arabs: The Aristotelian Tradition in Islam*. New York: State University of New York Press, 1968.

The Qur'an. Translated by Abdullah Yusuf Ali. Elmhurst, NY: Tahrike Tarsile Qur'an, 2003.

Renan, Ernest. *Averroès et l'averroïsme* [Averroes and Averroism]. Paris: Maisonneuve & Larose, 1997.

Rescher, Nicholas. *The Development of Arabic Logic*. Pittsburgh: University of Pittsburgh Press, 1964.

———. *Studies in the History of Arabic Logic*. Pittsburgh: University of Pittsburgh Press, 1963.

Sorabji, Richard, ed. *Aristotle Transformed: The Ancient Commentators and Their Influence*. Ithaca, NY: Cornell University Press, 1990.

South, James. "John of Jandun." In *A Companion to Philosophy in the Middle Ages*, edited by J. J. E. Gracia and T. B. Noone, 372–73. Oxford: Blackwell, 2002.

Vagelpohl, Uwe. *Aristotle's Rhetoric in the East: The Syriac and Arabic Translation and Commentary Tradition*. Leiden, Netherlands: Brill, 2008.

Walzer, Richard. *Greek into Arabic: Essays on Islamic Philosophy*. Cambridge, MA: Harvard University Press, 1962.

Wolfson, Harry A. "The Twice-Revealed Averroes." *Speculum* 36, no. 3 (1961): 373–92.

Index

A native of Fes, Morocco, Lahcen Elyazghi Ezzaher is a professor in the Department of English at the University of Northern Colorado. He is the author of the book *Writing and Cultural Influence: Studies in Rhetorical History, Orientalist Discourse, and Post-colonial Criticism*, as well as articles and book chapters on issues of language and multiculturalism. His Arabic-English translation of al-Fārābī's commentary on Aristotle's *Rhetoric* won an award for the best essay published in *Rhetorica* (2008).

Landmarks in Rhetoric and Public Address

ALSO IN THIS SERIES

Lectures on Rhetoric and Belles Lettres. By Hugh Blair. Edited with an introduction by Linda Ferreira-Buckley and S. Michael Halloran

The Philosophy of Rhetoric. By George Campbell. Edited and with a new introduction by Lloyd F. Bitzer

Cicero on Oratory and Orators. Translated and edited by J. S. Watson

Selected Essays on Rhetoric. By Thomas De Quincey. Edited by Frederick Burwick

The Rhetoric of Blair, Campbell, and Whately. By James L. Golden and Edward P. J. Corbett

The Rhetorics of Thomas Hobbes and Bernard Lamy. Edited with an introduction and critical apparatus by John T. Harwood

Quintilian on the Teaching of Speaking and Writing: Translations from Books One, Two, and Ten of the Institutio Oratoria. Edited by James J. Murphy

Arguments in Rhetoric against Quintilian: Translation and Text of Peter Ramus's "Rhetoricae Distinctiones in Quintilianum" (1549). Translated by Carole Newlands. Edited by James J. Murphy

Elements of Rhetoric. By Richard Whateley

Puritan Rhetoric: The Issue of Emotion in Religion. By Eugene E. White

The Selected Writings of John Witherspoon. Edited by Thomas Miller